USING

microsoft®
windows 7

J. Peter Bruzzese
Nick Saccomanno

que®

800 East 96th Street, Indianapolis, Indiana 46240 USA

Using Microsoft Windows 7

Copyright © 2010 by Que Publishing

ISBN-13: 978-0-7897-4291-9

ISBN-10: 0-7897-4291-8

Library of Congress Cataloging-in-Publication data is on file.

Printed in the United States of America

First Printing: April 2010

Trademarks

Warning and Disclaimer

Bulk Sales

Que Publishing offers excellent discounts on this book when ordered in quantity for bulk purchases or special sales. For more information, please contact

U.S. Corporate and Government Sales
1-800-382-3419
corpsales@pearsontechgroup.com

For sales outside of the U.S., please contact
International Sales
international@pearson.com

Associate Publisher
Greg Wiegand

Acquisitions Editor
Loretta Yates

Development Editor
Kevin Howard

Managing Editor
Sandra Schroeder

Project Editor
Seth Kerney

Copy Editor
Box Twelve Communications, Inc.

Indexer
Tim Wright

Proofreader
Jennifer Gallant

Technical Editor
Todd Meister

Publishing Coordinator
Cindy Teeters

Book Designer
Anne Jones

Multimedia Developer
John Herrin

Compositor
Mark Shirar

Media Table of Contents

To register this product and gain access to the free Web Edition and the audio and video files, go to **quepublishing.com/using.**

Table of Contents

Dedication

We would like to dedicate this book to the Microsoft developers and others at Microsoft who put their hearts into their work each day to continue to develop the OS we've known and loved for years.

Acknowledgments

Although I've dedicated this book to Microsoft (something I do for all of my books that relate to the Windows operating system), my true thanks and dedication go toward my wife, Jennette, and our son, Lucas. My life as a husband and father brings me greater joys and blessings than one could imagine.

In addition, on a personal level, I have many others, family, and friends to thank for their support. Too many to number. On a professional level, the list is a bit shorter (but not much). I'd like to thank Nick Saccomanno for working with me on this book and keeping it moving forward. I'd like to thank others who have been supportive, including Greg Shields, Brien Posey, Wayne Dipchan, Alan Wright, Jack Blovits, and others both directly and indirectly who have contributed to my personal success and the success of this project.

I have many I work with that I would like to mention at this time, including Tim Duggan, my business partner with ClipTraining, as well as John Duggan and Ronald Barrett. I'd like to thank Joe Austin with Ventana PR. In addition, I'd like to mention those I work with at *InfoWorld*, including Galen Gruman, Ted Samson, Eric Knorr, Doug Dineley, and others. I'd like to also mention and thank Doug Barney and Lee Pender at *Redmond* magazine as well as Amy Eisenberg, Sheila Molnar, and Brian Winstead at *Windows IT Pro* magazine.

Last but certainly not least, I would like to thank Scott Skinger and all the folks at Train Signal. I'd especially like to thank Lisa Szpunar for helping keep my Exchange 2010 videos up to the highest possible quality, and thanks to both Matt Elias and Gary Eimerman for focusing all my efforts in the right direction. And to all my other friends at Train Signal— David Davis, Iman Jalali, Paul Gadbois, Eric Munn, Kasia Grabowska, Steven Maguire, Heather Ackmann, Kelly Atkinson, Brian Green, Ed Liberman, Bill Kulterman, Sandy Moran, Zach Monroe, Mel Godson, Gosia Grabowska, Rowdy Morrow, Eddie Barra and Zach Behrman—it is a pleasure working with all of you.

And I certainly want to thank my acquisitions editor, Loretta Yates, and everyone who assisted with the creation of this book, including Box Twelve Communications, Todd Meister, Kevin Howard, and Seth Kerney.

—*J. Peter Bruzzese*

I am grateful to the following for their unique contributions to this project: First, to Microsoft. We asked, you heard, and delivered Windows 7. Thanks to lead author and project manager, J. Peter Bruzzese, a true professional and guide throughout the entire collaboration process. Thanks to my family, who gave the love, support, motivation, and inspiration needed to endure the tough times. Thanks to my wife, Marie, who patiently endured and lovingly supported me every step of the way—a helper I couldn't be without. Thanks to all involved for making this a success!

—*Nick Saccomanno*

About the Authors

J. Peter Bruzzese (cofounder of ClipTraining) is an internationally published technical author and well-known tech speaker and journalist. Over the past 15 years, Peter has worked with Goldman Sachs, CommVault Systems, and Microsoft, to name a few. His focus has been, and continues to be, on enterprise environments with a special focus on Active Directory, Exchange, SharePoint, and desktop operating systems. He holds the following certifications:

- Microsoft: MCSA 2000/2003, MCSE NT/2000/2003, MCITP: Messaging with Exchange 2007, MCT

- Novell: CNA

- Cisco: CCNA

- CIW: CIW Master, CIW Certified Instructor

- CompTIA: A+, Network+, iNET+

J.P.B. recently joined forces with Train Signal to create powerful admin-oriented training videos that relate to a variety of subjects (starting with Exchange 2010).

Peter is also a contributor to *Redmond* magazine, *WindowsITPro* magazine, and several tech sites. He is a regular speaker for TechMentor Conferences and the FETC Conference. He has also spoken at Microsoft TechEd, the IT360 Tech Conference in Canada, the TEC Conference, and WinConnections. Last but certainly not least, he writes the Enterprise Windows column for *InfoWorld*.

Nick Saccomanno is a Microsoft Certified Professional (MCP) and has worked with various IT departments to provide technical support and network administration. As a screencast instructor and a technical author, he is on the forefront of the latest technologies, trying to help the everyday user get the most out of them. Nick has created screencasts for ClipTraining relating to Windows, Office 2007, and more. His unique style is due mostly in part to his love of technology and the gift of learning it quickly. When away from training, Nick enjoys playing guitar and speaking Bulgarian. Nick lives in Melbourne, Florida, with his wife, Marie, and their pets, Noah and JJ.

We Want to Hear from You!

As the reader of this book, *you* are our most important critic and commentator. We value your opinion and want to know what we're doing right, what we could do better, what areas you'd like to see us publish in, and any other words of wisdom you're willing to pass our way.

As an associate publisher for Que Publishing, I welcome your comments. You can email or write me directly to let me know what you did or didn't like about this book—as well as what we can do to make our books better.

Please note that I cannot help you with technical problems related to the topic of this book. We do have a User Services group, however, where I will forward specific technical questions related to the book.

When you write, please be sure to include this book's title and author as well as your name, email address, and phone number. I will carefully review your comments and share them with the author and editors who worked on the book.

Email: feedback@quepublishing.com

Mail: Greg Wiegand
Associate Publisher
Que Publishing
800 East 96th Street
Indianapolis, IN 46240 USA

Reader Services

Visit our website and register this book at quepublishing.com/register for convenient access to any updates, downloads, or errata that might be available for this book.

Introduction

The Purpose of This Book

Better performance, newer features, and an enhanced user experience. Microsoft has brought all this and more to its latest operating system, Windows 7. *Using Windows 7* provides an introduction to all the new features and shows you how to get the most out of them. For users coming from Windows XP, the transition will be smoother than ever. Vista users will be just as impressed with the ease of transition; they will also enjoy several new or improved features.

This book has been designed to give you, the reader, more than one method of learning. Some can read a book and look at a few screenshots and that is all they need. Others like a step-by-step approach to learning so they can follow along with the process laid out. Others like to see a task demonstrated because they are visual learners. We have taken all of this (and more) into account when preparing this book. *Using Windows 7* is not only a book, it's an adventure in learning.

Using This Book

This book allows you to customize your own learning experience. The step-by-step instructions in the book give you a solid foundation in using Windows 7, while rich and varied online content, including video tutorials and audio sidebars, provide the following:

- Demonstrations of step-by-step tasks covered in the book

- Additional tips or information on a topic

- Practical advice and suggestions

- Direction for more advanced tasks not covered in the book

- Each chapter includes some additional reading material in the form of online articles that take your learning to the next level by providing supplemental material, external resource information, and/or more detailed information about the chapter you are reading.

Here's a quick look at a few structural features designed to help you get the most out of this book.

Notes: Important tasks are offset to draw attention to them.

 Let Me Try It tasks are presented in a step-by-step sequence so you can easily follow along.

 Show Me video walks through tasks you've just got to see—including bonus advanced techniques.

 Tell Me More audio delivers practical insights straight from the experts.

We would like to encourage you to learn Windows 7 in the way you feel is most comfortable. Perhaps you might want to start with installing it and getting a feel for this new OS from Microsoft. Then you will want to explore the many features.

Special Features

More than just a book, your USING product integrates step-by-step video tutorials and valuable audio sidebars delivered through the **Free Web Edition** that comes with every USING book. For the price of the book, you get online access anywhere with a web connection—no books to carry, content is updated as the technology changes, and the benefit of video and audio learning.

About the USING Web Edition

The Web Edition of every USING book is powered by **Safari Books Online**, allowing you to access the video tutorials and valuable audio sidebars. Plus, you can search the contents of the book, highlight text and attach a note to that text, print your notes and highlights in a custom summary, and cut and paste directly from Safari Books Online.

To register this product and gain access to the Free Web Edition and the audio and video files, go to **quepublishing.com/using**.

This chapter will focus your attention primarily on the
new navigation enhancements within Windows 7.

1

Navigating Your Windows 7 Environment

The Windows 7 Desktop

Although initially Windows 7 may look like legacy systems you have worked on dating back to Windows 95, this new OS from Microsoft has a few new navigation features that are sure to make you more productive.

Some of the features you will really appreciate include jump lists, a more flexible Taskbar, new Aero features called AeroShake and AeroSnap and much more.

If you compare the desktop of Windows 7 with what you've become accustomed to in Windows XP (and especially with Windows Vista), you're going to be right at home (see Figure 1.1).

Figure 1.1   *The Windows 7 desktop.*

You have a desktop, you have a Recycle Bin, you have a Taskbar at the bottom, and you have a Notification Area on the right side of the Taskbar that shows the time and other notification items that can be hidden or displayed. In the bottom-left corner of your Windows 7 desktop, you have a Start orb (which is simply a modern version of the Start button).

Developers actually call the Start orb a jewel (or even a pearl), but it has become better known as the Start orb in the working world.

Although the desktop appears to be similar to older Windows versions (such as XP and Vista), you will learn some of the differences that make Windows 7 superior to its predecessors.

 LET ME TRY IT

Begin Learning How to Navigate Around Your Desktop

It's important for both newbies and experienced users to be completely comfortable with navigating around the desktop. That includes knowing the terminology for various aspects like the Taskbar, the Start Menu and so forth. As well as, knowing how to search for Help or applications and files within your system.

1. Click the Start orb, which is the circular button, or orb, in the lower-left corner of your desktop. Note the displayed menu of items. This is called your Start menu. Here you can find items like the Instant Search box directly above your orb, your programs, and your personal files and folders. And you can also see your administrative options, such as your Control Panel and your Shutdown options (located to the bottom-right of your Start menu).

2. Click the Help and Support option. From here you can search for help on using Windows 7.

3. Close the Help and Support dialog box by clicking the x in the top-right corner. You will return to your desktop.

The bar at the bottom of your desktop is called the Taskbar; it displays applications, folders and other items. You will note a few existing icons on the Taskbar that you can click to quickly access those applications or folders.

On the right side of your Taskbar is the Notification Area, which displays your date and time, your network connectivity, and other items that you can either continue to display or you can turn them off. To the far right of your Taskbar is a tiny sliver called Show Desktop, which you can use to make all your windows transparent.

Now that you have a basic grasp of the desktop and all of its elements, you'll learn how desktop Gadgets can enhance the look and usefulness of your desktop.

Desktop Gadgets

Gadgets were introduced to to the desktop with the release of Vista. The Windows team learned, however, that the use of the Sidebar made it too difficult for us to work easily with these Gadgets and the desktop itself. In Windows 7, the Sidebar has been removed but the Gadgets remain.

What are these Gadgets? They are a mini set of applications available to you quickly. You need the time, you need a calendar, you need a calculator, or maybe you need to know the weather. So how can you add Gadgets to your desktop?

 LET ME TRY IT

Let's Work with a Few Gadgets on Your Desktop

Before you can make adjustments to the location, look and even opacity of a gadget, you need to add them to your desktop. These instructions will show you how to do just that.

1. Right-click the desktop and select Gadgets. This displays the various Gadgets you can add (see Figure 1.2). You can add one or more Gadgets to your desktop.

2. Double-click the Gadget you would like to add and that Gadget will display on the right side of your desktop. As shown in Figure 1.3, we have added several Gadget to our desktop.

3. Close the Gadget window.

After the Gadget is on your desktop, you can customize it. If you place your cursor over the Gadget, some options will display:

- An x to close the Gadget.
- A wrench to make adjustments to the Gadget (options vary depending on the Gadget).
- A footpad to move the Gadget around the desktop.
- Some Gadgets include a box with an arrow so you can enlarge the Gadget.

Figure 1.2   *Optional Gadgets in Windows 7.*

Figure 1.3   *Window 7 Desktop with Gadgets.*

Right-click the Gadget to display options such as Opacity, which allows you to make the Gadget appear more transparent (you choose the percentage level of opacity you prefer).

Each Gadget has a different set of features and controllable options. Only by working with these can you get to know what your Gadgets are capable of.

 LET ME TRY IT

Locate and Download Additional Gadgets from the Internet

The initial number of gadgets you have within your onboard arsenal is a small subset of what is available online. In these instructions you will see how to locate and download additional gadgets for your system.

1. Right-click the desktop and select Gadgets.

2. In the Gadget Gallery, the bottom-right corner displays the option Get More Gadgets Online. Click this link, which will take you to the Microsoft personalization page.

3. From Microsoft's personalization page, you can download additional Gadgets. However, you can also search online for more Gadgets created by developers around the world.

Using Shortcut Keys

Most, if not all, of us have become so accustomed to using a mouse to accomplish our work in Windows. However, for just about every task you can accomplish with a mouse, you can also accomplish them by using a combination of keyboard strokes (or *shortcut keys*). Some love clicking their way around their Windows interfaces while others love pressing keys on their keyboards. A couple of quick keystrokes can accomplish quite a bit—but only if you know what buttons to push.

You probably already know that you push the Windows key on your keyboard to bring up the Start menu. But did you know that you also have several other standard Windows key shortcuts at your disposal?

We have listed many of the important ones here:

Windows + Up arrow—Maximizes window.

Windows + Left arrow—Uses a new feature called AeroSnap (described later in this chapter) to position the window quickly (or snap the window) to the left side of the screen covering half of desktop space. Repeat this shortcut to rotate the window between snap to left, snap to right, and restore to normal position.

Windows + Right arrow—Uses a new feature called AeroSnap (described later in this chapter) to position the window quickly (or snap the window) to the right side of the screen covering half of desktop space. Repeat this shortcut to rotate the window between snap to left, snap to right, and restore to normal position.

Windows + Down arrow—Minimizes the window. If the window is currently maximized, this shortcut restores the window to normal size and position.

Windows + Home—Clears all but the active window.

Windows + Space—All windows become transparent so you can see through to the desktop.

Windows + Shift + Left arrow—In a dual or multiple-monitor setup, this shortcut moves the active window to the adjacent monitor on the left.

Windows + Shift + Right arrow—In a dual or multiple-monitor setup, this shortcut moves the active window to the adjacent monitor on the right.

Windows + T—Shows a preview thumbnail of all running applications in the Taskbar. View each application by placing your mouse over each thumbnail.

Windows + P—Accesses the display options for your computer or projector.

Windows + + (Plus sign)—Zooms in.

Windows + -(Minus or dash)—Zooms out.

Shift + Click a Taskbar item—Opens a new instance of that particular item.

Other popular or common keyboard hotkeys which were available for use in legacy Windows systems:

Windows + d—Shows or restores desktop (minimizes or restores all windows).

Windows + M—Minimizes all windows.

Windows + U—Opens the Ease of Access Center.

Windows + F—Searches window.

Windows + G—Brings all Gadgets on top and foreground.

Windows + X—Runs the Windows Mobility Center.

Windows + R—Opens the Run command.

Windows + E—Runs Internet Explorer.

Windows + L—Locks the computer.

Windows + Pause/Break—Opens the System Properties window.

Windows + Tab—Activates the Windows Aero Task Switcher.

An interesting and helpful shortcut is Windows + [Number]: Press and hold the Windows key and then click a number. This number connects to an application located on the Taskbar. For example, if Internet Explorer is the fourth icon from the left, press and hold the Windows key and then press the 4 key. You will launch Internet Explorer. If Microsoft Word is the third application from the left, you would press 3 to launch Word.

If you want to increase or decrease the size of your desktop icons, an easy shortcut to do that is to press and hold your Ctrl key and then roll your mouse scroll wheel forward to increase the size or roll it backward to decrease the size.

 LET ME TRY IT

Let's Try a Few Shortcut Keys

Sometimes we might avoid shortcuts because we're comfortable with our mouse and don't see the need to use a new method. However, once you get comfortable with a few of these, you might find them much more productive to use than mouse clicks.

1. Open several windows—a mix of applications and folders.

2. Press and hold the Windows key and then press the letter m. You're returned to the desktop and your windows are minimized.

3. Choose an application on the Taskbar. Starting from the left, count the number places it sits on the Taskbar. Press and hold the Windows key and the number on your keyboard that matches that application's place on the Taskbar. The application opens.

4. Press and hold the Ctrl button and use your scroll button on your mouse to increase or decrease the size of your desktop icons.

An Enhanced Taskbar and Start Menu

Although the initial look of Windows 7 is similar to every OS produced by Microsoft since Windows 95 (which is a good thing in terms of familiarity), there are still some great changes in the details of how things work that you will appreciate.

For example, you will notice the Taskbar on the bottom of the desktop is a bit taller than in older versions of Windows. As previously mentioned, there is a Show Desktop glass sliver to the right that is new (and perhaps small enough to miss if it weren't pointed out). The Taskbar has always been a place where shortcut icons for open folders and/or files and applications are displayed and controlled. But with

Windows 7, you can now mix and match shortcuts for applications, folders, file objects, and so forth all on the same bar.

Windows 7 displays icons differently; open applications and windows include a visible border, but shortcuts for favorite programs and such don't display a border.

In Windows 7, the Taskbar gives you the ability to drag and drop shortcut icons wherever you like. Users have requested this functionality for years; finally, you can do this without needing a third-party solution.

As you move your mouse over shortcut icons on the Taskbar, previews of the underlying program or file appear above the icon. If you hover for any length of time it will make the preview full screen. There is also a new Jump List feature that you will learn about later in this chapter. These jump lists will offer a quick list of options for the application they are looking at.

In terms of Start menu changes, again, a first glance won't reveal all the new goodies in Windows 7. What you will find with Windows 7, however, is that there are Libraries (which are collections of one or more folders aggregated together) that will allow you to show as items in the Navigation Pane for your Start menu. In previous versions of Windows, your Start menu showed Documents (or in the case of XP, My Documents), Music, and so forth. But in your efforts to understand why those particular folders were included on your Start menu, you would not have much information to work with (other than an assumption that it was simply how Microsoft wanted to present it). With Windows 7, however, you now realize why Microsoft does it this way—because Libraries are allowed to be pushed to the navigation pane.

SHOW ME   Media 1.1—Working with the New Taskbar Features
*Access this video file through your registered Web Edition at **my.safaribooksonline. com/9780768695212/media.***

LET ME TRY IT

Working with the Taskbar

This set of steps is all about how to quickly identify an open application, folder, or file through a shortcut icon and then know if you have multiple instances of a particular item or if you need to move them around on the Taskbar.

1. Click the Start orb.

2. In the Instant Search box, type **Paint** and press Enter. The Paint application launches.

3. Click the Start orb and in the Instant Search box, type **Notepad** and press Enter. The Notepad application launches.

   On the Taskbar, note the difference between applications that are open and applications that are closed. The open applications are slightly brighter and display a box around them (see Figure 1.4).

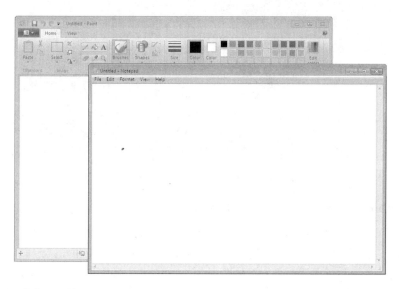

Figure 1.4 *Taskbar icons.*

4. To view the new functionality of the Windows 7 Taskbar, click the Notepad icon on the Taskbar.

5. Click and drag the Notepad icon to the left and watch how that icon moves the Paint icon to the right.

Jump Lists Help You Work Faster

One of the more exciting features of the Taskbar is the addition of Jump Lists. To see a Jump List, right-click an icon on the Taskbar (or you can left-click the icon and drag it toward the desktop to display the Jump List). Jump lists include lists of commonly used actions associated with the application you're selecting.

For example, Figure 1.5 shows that Internet Explorer includes pages that you can pin to the Jump List for quick access. By using the Internet Explorer Jump List, you can quickly access sites you frequently visit, launch InPrivate Browsing (for private viewing, which you will learn about in Chapter 6), and open new tab.

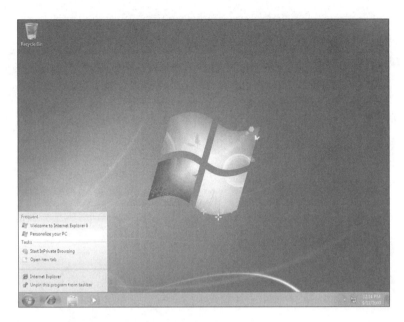

Figure 1.5   *Jump Lists in action with Internet Explorer 8.*

Obviously, applications that are Windows-savvy will be designed to work with Jump Lists a little better than legacy applications, but that doesn't mean Jump Lists won't be available for legacy apps. It means simply that legacy apps just will not be as populated with application-specific functionality.

Start menu items sometimes include right-pointing arrows; these arrows indicate a Jump List is available for programs listed on the menu (as shown with the Getting Started program displayed in Figure 1.6).

 **SHOW ME**   Media 1.2—Working with Jump Lists
Access this video file through your registered Web Edition at
my.safaribooksonline.com/9780768695212/media.

 **LET ME TRY IT**

Using the Windows Explorer Jump List

Each Jump List has its own set of features and functions and will require practice time with each to become comfortable with what they offer, however, in this set of steps we will focus on the Windows Explorer Jump List.

   1.   Right-click the Windows Explorer folder icon located on the Taskbar.

   2.   In the Jump List options, click one of your Frequent locations, such as Videos.

Figure 1.6   *Programs listed on the Start menu might include Jump Lists as well.*

Aero Shake and Aero Snap

Aero Shake and Aero Snap are a couple of very useful tools when it comes to working on your desktop, especially if you usually work with several windows open at
once. The goal here is to ease your working experience by allowing you to perform
certain functions with fewer clicks.

Aero Shake

This feature allows you to clean up the desktop. If you have multiple windows
open on the desktop and need to focus on just one, you might want to minimize
all the unused windows. With previous versions of Windows, you would need to
click the Minimize button in the top-right of each window (the left-most button).
With Aero Shake, you need only to grab the window (by left-clicking the top of the
window to grab it) that you would like to work in (the active window) and shake it
with the mouse. This minimizes all the other open windows. Once they're minimized, you can shake the active window again to restore all the other windows.

 **LET ME TRY IT**

Using AeroShake

The following steps show you how to use this new feature, which can help you
minimize windows quickly.

1. Use the Jump List option to open Windows Explorer on the Taskbar.

2. Click Music to open your Music library. Repeat Steps 1 and 2 to open your Videos library.

3. Take your cursor and grab the top of the Music window.

4. Shake the window back and forth (not slowly, somewhat furiously). Note that the Videos window minimizes automatically.

Aero Snap

This feature assists you when you need to work with more than one window at a time. For example, you might want to look at two open windows side by side. Usually, you would drag the windows to where you want them and then resize them so that they don't overlap. With Aero Snap, you need only to grab the window you would like to quickly resize and drag it to either the left or right side of the desktop.

As the desktop shade changes (see Figure 1.7), release the mouse. The window automatically locks to the side of the screen and resizes. You can then pull the window away from the side to restore it to its original size. If you drag the window to the top of the desktop, you will maximize the window.

Figure 1.7   *Aero Snap helps to utilize screen real estate a bit better.*

🖱 LET ME TRY IT

Using AeroSnap

With screen real-estate changing between your desktop and laptop systems, you may find yourself having difficulty working with your windows in an organized way. AeroSnap helps you to quickly manipulate your windows, and this step-by-step shows you how.

1. Click the Start orb.

2. Type **Solitaire** into the Search Programs and Files box and press Enter.

3. Click the Solitaire window and drag it to the right until the desktop turns blue on the right side.

4. Release the window and it snaps to the right side.

5. Grab the window again and drag it to the top of the screen until the entire screen is blue.

6. Release the window and it snaps to full screen.

7. To see how this might work using shortcut keys, select the window again, press and hold the Windows key, and then press the Left arrow to snap the window to the left side of the screen.

Working with New Windows Explorer Features

You might have noticed Windows Explorer has changed slightly from Windows Vista (and it has certainly changed from XP). The address bar up at the top is not a static location showing you where you're at in the file system. Rather it provides you with drop-down arrows you can use to move forward in the structure (if there are more folders to delve into) or backward—all the way back to the drive letter source for the folder you're currently in. That is why the Windows Explorer address bar is also known as a *breadcrumb bar*.

The top of the Windows Explorer window displays an Organize menu if you click Organize and then choose Layout, several different panes are available to you. (This option also includes a Menu bar, which is familiar to Windows XP users.)

- The Details pane will appear at the bottom of the Windows Explorer window. It shows you the metadata behind a given selected document or folder. If you select an .avi file, you will be shown information such as the length of that file, the size, the title, and so forth.

- The Preview pane is disabled by default. When you choose Preview pane, you can select an item and see a preview of it in the right part of the window.

- The Navigation pane will appear on the right of the Windows Explorer window. It provides you with a list of drives and libraries to choose from in a hierarchical structure.

- The Library pane shows you the documents located within a library. A library is like a folder, but it doesn't officially hold content; rather it shows a view of content that has been aggregated within the library by pointing off to multiple sources.

Figure 1.8 shows Windows Explorer with all panes selected and the Menu bar activated. In the top-right corner, there are options to change how icons are displayed. Windows Vista featured a Views menu; in Windows 7, the viewing options are located within the Change Your View feature. Using this feature, you can either click the Change Your View icon to toggle through the different views or you can click the down-arrow to display the various viewing options.

Figure 1.8   *Windows Explorer with all panes selected.*

The Preview icon is now an on/off button to the right of the Change Your View icon. It is deactivated by default; simply click the button to turn on the Preview pane. The blue circle with the white question mark is your Get Help option. It looks like a blue panic button and can be located easily in every window.

You might also notice in the figure that, depending on the type of file you choose, you can play it (as in this case) by clicking the file and then clicking the Play icon on the toolbar (or you can select the down arrow next to the Play icon and play it with an application other than Windows Media Player if you have one installed). You can Play All, Share With, Burn, or create a New Folder. If you are choosing a document, you can click the Open icon or you can click the down arrow next to the Open icon to use a different application to open the file.

> Creating a New Folder with a single click in the Windows Explorer window might seem like a simple time saver, and it is. But it's also a detail that was badly need-ed. We don't consider it a *feature*, per se, but a detail. In Windows Vista, you had to first click Organize, thenchoose New Folder (or right-click in the working pane and click New Folder).

Searching

Windows Vista provided some tremendous search features—so impressive, in fact, that Search was actually removed from the Start menu because you no longer needed to 'ask' for it. Vista pinned Search to practically every window. Windows Search 4.0 enhanced the search features even more, but Windows 7, along with desktop search, introduces Federated Search as well.

Click the Start orb to display the Search Programs and Files box at the bottom of the menu for instant search of programs, files, email and so forth. Open any folder or library and the upper-right corner displays a Search box. This is true even when working with elements such as Administrative Tools or Control Panel.

When working within a standard folder, you can select your starting location from the navigation pane to the right (or you can use the address, or breadcrumb, bar near the top of the window) to locate your starting folder or drive. Then, in the Search box, type the name of the file you're looking for.

> The more commonly trafficked document repositories (such as Documents, Pic-tures and so forth) are indexed by default. Other areas are not. If you search an area that isn't indexed, a dialog will alert you to the fact Searches Might be Slow in Non-Indexed Locations... and you can add the non-indexed location to the index if you choose.

If you click inside the Search box, you can Add a Search Filter that searches accord-ing to whatever filter you apply to the search. For example, a video file search pro-vides a length filter.

LET ME TRY IT

Performing a Search Using the Filter Features

Being able to search is extremely important as our documents begin to sprawl in all directions on our systems. In addition to searching for a document by name, you can search using filter features such as a file type or a file size, or perhaps even filtering by length of the song or video. The following steps will help you get started in doing just that.

1. Typically your initial Libraries (Documents, Music, Pictures and Videos) will have content included. Click the Start orb.

2. Click Music from the Start menu.

3. In the Search Music box at the top-right of the Windows Explorer window, type **mp3** and press Enter.

4. Several results should display. Typically you can find what you need at this point. However, if the number of results is excessive, you can click the Search box again to filter the contents further. Figure 1.9 shows the filters you can choose for searching music files, including Album, Artists, Genre, and Length.

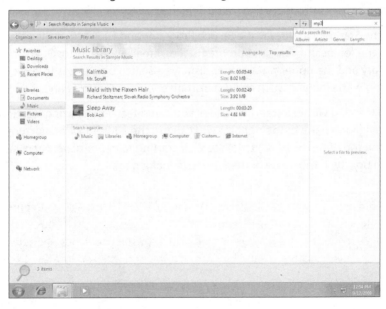

Figure 1.9   *Searching with a filter.*

Filter options will vary depending on the type of folder you're looking at and/or the type of content you're searching for.

5. Select a filter and follow the prompts to narrow down your search results.

Federated Search

We mentioned at the start of this section that Search has been enhanced by Federated Search. This extends the scope of your Windows Explorer search capabilities beyond the desktop; your searches now reach out to remote repositories through *search connectors*. Search connectors allow your Windows search to reach out to the Internet for social media sites, various photo sites, and so forth.

Federated Search is based on OpenSearch (an open-source standard) and the RSS format. So you can download search connectors for Twitter, YouTube, Flickr, and other applications, and then you can search for items in those applications through Windows Explorer.

Keep in mind that this isn't entirely new as a feature. Internet Explorer and SharePoint Search both have these features. It is, however, a new search feature to Windows Explorer.

 LET ME TRY IT

Using Federated Search

Although you might not have a problem reaching out to the Internet from a browser to search for items you need, having that ability directly within your Windows Search is a neat new feature worth investigating. The following steps will help you get started.

1. You need to locate a search connector you like, so open Internet Explorer.

2. Go to your favorite search engine. We will use www.bing.com but you can go with www.google.com or another.

The default search engine for Internet Explorer is Bing. In the top-right corner of your browser, you can also just type your search request.

3. Search for Windows 7 Search Connector.

4. Navigate to a site among the search results and download a search connector to your liking. In our case, we clicked http://chris.pirillo.com/windows-7-search-connectors-twitter-youtube-amazon-ebay/ and located a download that provides search connectors for Amazon, eBay, PriceGrabber and much more. We downloaded and opened the zip file, which contained different connectors to choose from.

5. To add any of the search connectors, just double click the file and a dialog that asks for permission to install the Search Connector to Windows.

6. Click Add to continue. Once you have installed your connectors, you can use Windows Explorer to search for items in those locations. As shown in Figure 1.10, your connectors are placed inyour Favorites folder.

Figure 1.10   *Using Federated Search.*

7. Select a connector. In the Search box in the top-right, simply type what you're searching for.

For example, Figure 1.10 shows that we typed **vado** (a high-definition camera from Creative) in the Search box of our Pirillo YouTube connector, which promptly searches through the website of Chris Pirillo (noted tech geek and technovangelist) and lists relevant YouTube videos. When you click on a result, the Preview Pane shows more details to the right.

Libraries

Libraries do not replace folders per se. Rather, while you still have folders that hold documents on the traditional side of your system, some of your main locations (like your Documents folder) have been changed into Libraries. A Library provides you with the ability to see more than one folder's worth of content in one location. So, for example, the Documents Library contains two locations (by default). Click the 2 Locations link to see the Documents Library Locations dialog, which shows you your two default locations (see Figure 1.11):

Figure 1.11   *The Documents Library Locations dialog.*

My Documents: C:\Users\<*username*>\Documents

Public Documents: C:\Users\Public\Documents

There are default Libraries created for Contacts, Documents, Downloads, Music, Pictures and Videos. With libraries that are created by the operating system, there are content styles programmed in. What that means is that the library is designed to provide you with a style that is appropriate to the chosen content.

On the one hand, this feature isn't entirely new to Windows. With Vista, you can perform saved searches and create virtual folders in Windows Explorer. However, Libraries offer you the ability to write to these 'saved searches', something you couldn't do before Windows 7. Each Library has a save location specified that allows you to save a file to the library and it will be placed in that saved location. (If you needed a file to go elsewhere, you have to save it to the specific folder you choose.)

 **LET ME TRY IT**

Create a New Library and Add Folders

Once you come to appreciate the power behind using Libraries to aggreate a view of content from multiple folder locations, you may want to start creating your own Libraries and adding folders to them, as the following steps show you.

To create a new library in Windows Explorer:

1.   Open Windows Explorer.

2. Click the Libraries link in the Navigation Pane.

3. Click New Library on the tool bar. This creates the new Library and gives
    you the option to name it. After you name it, you will have a Library with
    no folder connecting points.

4. Double-click the Library you just created and you will notice the Library is
    empty.

5. Click the Include a Folder button to navigate to your folder structure and add
    the folders you want for this Library.

> You can delete a Library you have created without any fear of deleting the fold-
> ers that make up that Library. The Library is more of a view of aggregated data
> from multiple locations. It is not the folder itself; it's a view of the content within
> that folder aggregated with data contained in other folders as well.

 SHOW ME   Media 1.3—Utilizing Libraries
Access this video file through your registered Web Edition at
my.safaribooksonline.com/9780768695212/media.

 LET ME TRY IT

Showing Libraries on the Start Menu Navigation Pane

1. Click the Start orb.

2. Right-click Documents and note the option Don't Show in Navigation Pane.

3. With the dialog still open, click Properties and notice the Documents fold-
    er is actually a Library that can be made up of folders located in multiple
    locations (see Figure 1.12). Also take note of the Attributes section, which
    displays the Shown in Navigation Pane checkbox.

4. To add another location, click the Include a Folder button. You will now be
    able to navigate to the folder you would like to add.

5. After you locate the folder, select it and then click the Include a Folder button
    You will see this folder added to the list of Library locations.

Shutting Down Your System

In XP, when you want to turn off your computer, you get three options: Stand By,
Turn Off, and Restart. If you know how—and if you've been working with XP for
more than a day, you likely know how already—you can press and hold Shift to get

Figure 1.12 *Documents Properties dialog box.*

the Hibernate option. You probably understand that Stand By is the fastest to recover from but still requires power from your battery (if you're using a laptop) or your power supply. If you Hibernate, you freeze your system and you can leave all your applications up, but it takes longer to come back to life from hibernation than it does to recover from Stand By mode. The benefit of using Hibernate is that it doesn't use battery life.

Sleep mode was introduced in Windows Vista and it gives you the best of both worlds. It is actually the default way to shut down your system, regardless of whether it's a desktop or a laptop. When you click the Start orb, there is a button at the bottom-right of the Start menu that reads Sleep by default. You can change this default setting by right-clicking your Taskbar and choosing Properties. In the Taskbar and Start Menu Properties dialog box, click on the Start Menu tab. In the Power Button Action setting, click the down arrow and choose your preferred setting.

When you're using a desktop, Sleep means your system state will be written from RAM to Hiberil.sys and then your system will go into Stand By. This provides a quick return from Sleep mode when you sit back down at your computer, but it also ensures recovery in cases of emergency (in the event the power goes out). The system is actually still drawing power for things like the CPU, RAM, and a few chipset features.

Desktops will, by default, also go into Sleep Mode if you leave your system for an extended period of time. Microsoft says this will save huge amounts of energy, thus assisting the environment with global warming issues.

Laptops work a bit differently. Initially, when the system is put in Sleep mode (by closing the lid, leaving the system idle for any extended period of time, or telling it to sleep), your system state is put only in Stand By mode without writing to the hard disk and Windows 7 uses a really low power mode (lower than in XP or Vista) to keep the state alive. Power is drawn from the battery like it is in Stand By mode, but not as much power is drawn. If left in this state long enough, you will still run low on power. But before your battery runs out, your system wakes up, puts itself in Hibernate mode, and then shuts off.

When a system returns from Sleep mode (whether it's a laptop or a desktop), if it hasn't hibernated then it should return quickly and restore your system and applications instantaneously (just like Stand By mode). If your system has hibernated, it will pretty much come back to life the same way an XP system comes out of hibernation.

 LET ME TRY IT

Putting Your System To Sleep

1. Click the Start orb.

2. Look to the bottom-right of your Start menu. Note the button, which might display Shut Down or Sleep at this time.

3. If it displays Sleep, click the button to put your system in a suspended state.

4. If it displays Shut Down, click the arrow to the right of the button and choose Sleep.

Note the other options you can choose, including Hibernate, Log Off, Lock, Restart and Switch User.

 TELL ME MORE   Media 1.4—A Discussion of Windows 7 Navigation Features
Access this audio recording through your registered Web Edition at
my.safaribooksonline.com/9780768695212/media.

This chapter will help you make your system an extension of your personality.

2

Personalizing Your System

Changing Display Settings

Your Display settings can be located through Control Panel. You can also get to them quickly by working off the Screen Resolution settings, accessed off the desktop through a new shortcut you can access by right-clicking the desktop and choosing Screen Resolution.

The new Screen Resolution settings (see Figure 2.1) are very easy to work with. You can choose your display and resolution. You can click the Detect button to locate attached monitors/projectors. Click the Identify button to display a number for the display you are looking at. Using that information, you can choose the monitor and the display and resolution settings for that particular monitor (which is especially helpful in a multi-monitor situation).

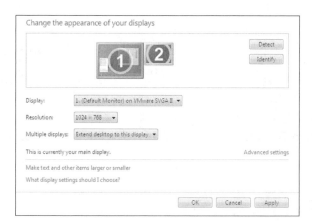

Figure 2.1   *Screen Resolution settings.*

If you click the link Make Text and Other Items Larger or Smaller, you return to the Display settings (see Figure 2.2). (Or you can click the Display option in the address bar.) The Display screen is where you can choose Smaller, Medium or Larger; each option provides a Preview of what that particular display looks like. You can also quickly select one of the links to the left to make other changes. For example, you can click the Set custom text size (DPI) option change your text size to a size that suits your needs. The default, or normal, scale is set at 96 pixels per inch. If that size is too small for you, the second option of 125% is 120 pixels per inch (which might be too large).

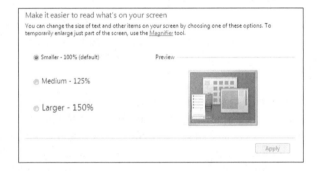

Figure 2.2   *Display settings.*

One of the quirky aspects to the Display panel is that the Adjust Resolution link and the Change Display Settings link each returns you to the Screen Resolution options.

Clicking the Adjust ClearType Text link displays the ClearType Text Tuner, which you can use to turn ClearType on or off and then click through various steps of a Wizard to refine your ClearText.

SHOW ME   **Media 2.1—Display Configuration**
Access this video file through your registered Web Edition at
my.safaribooksonline.com/9780768695212/media.

 **LET ME TRY IT**

Adjusting Your System to Work With Multiple Monitors

At times, you might have more than one monitor to manage. You might need a little more screen real-estate with your particular type of job or to operate more smoothly in your work or hobby.

1. Connect both monitors to the computer and ensure your system can 'see' them both.

2. Right-click the desktop and choose Screen Resolution.

3. Both monitors should displays in the preview window (see Figure 2.3). Click Monitor 1.

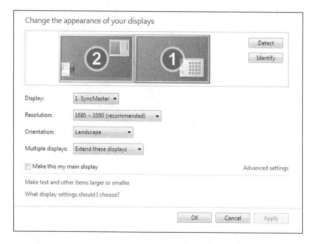

Figure 2.3   *Adjusting screen resolution on multiple monitors.*

4. Below the preview image, note the Display, Resolution, Orientation and Multiple Displays settings.

5. Click Monitor 2. Note its settings as well.

6. Click the monitor you want to use as your main display. Make sure the Make This My Main Display checkbox is checked for this monitor.

7. If you want to duplicate the screen from your primary display onto your secondary display, .select the Multiple Displays drop-down arrow and choose Duplicate Displays (which makes the second monitor a duplicate of the primary monitor). Otherwise, you will probably want to leave the default Extend These displays option selected (which provides the extension of screen real-estate you may be looking for).

8. If it's difficult for you to determine which monitor represents which number in the preview window, click the Identify button. Large numbers will display on your monitors so that you can more easily discern which monitor is which.

Altering Personalization Settings

As for Personalization settings (see Figure 2.4), Windows 7 supports different Styles which combine a background color or image, a glass or window theme, a sound scheme, and a screensaver to form a unique style. Styles are packaged as themes so you can share them with others as a whole—not just in individual settings.

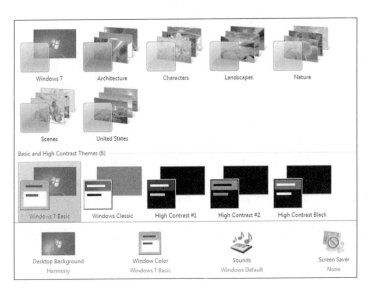

Figure 2.4   *Personalization settings.*

You can configure any Style (or Theme). You can choose preconfigured ones or click the Get More Themes Online link. You can alter desktop icons, mouse pointers, and so forth.

Some Themes are determined by the language of your operating system. So, you might have a Theme specific to the United States or you might have a Theme specific to Germany, depending on the language of your OS.

 LET ME TRY IT

Adjusting Your Background

When you are ready to add a little personality to your system, you typically want to start with the background.

1. Right-click your desktop and then select Personalize.

   You can now change the visuals and sounds of your operating system. You will also notice under the My Themes section that you can click Get More Themes Online to access more Themes.

2. Browse and select one of the seven default Aero themes:

   Windows 7 (the default setting)
   Architecture
   Characters
   Landscapes
   Nature
   Scenes
   United States (depending on the language of the operating system)

3. If you click each Theme, the Desktop Background, Window Color, and Sounds settings (all listed below the list of Themes) change to reflect your selection. When you click each setting, you can customize each Theme.

4. Click your preferred Theme and then close the Personalization box. You have now changed your desktop Theme.

You might have noticed the Screen Saver link and that, by default, no Screen Saver is selected. You'll learn how to customize a Screen Saver next.

 SHOW ME   Media 2.2—**Personalization Settings**
Access this video file through your registered Web Edition at
my.safaribooksonline.com/9780768695212/media.

 LET ME TRY IT

Customizing Your Screen Saver

There are a variety of different screen savers to choose from and the following steps show you how you can adjust the one you are using.

1. Right-click your desktop and select Personalize.

2. At the bottom-right of the Personalization window, click the Screen Saver link to display the Screen Saver Settings dialog box (see Figure 2.5).

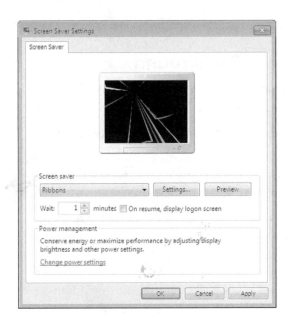

Figure 2.5 *Screen Saver settings.*

3. In the Screen Saver area, click the down arrow display the list of available screen savers.

4. For this example, choose Photos.

5. Click the Settings button to display the Photos Screen Saver Settings dialog box.

6. In this dialog box, click Browse to select a folder that contains the photos you would like to use for your Screen Saver. You can also adjust the Slide Show Speed at which the photos change—Fast, Medium (the default), or Slow. Click the Shuffle Pictures box if you want to shuffle the photos.

7. After you choose your settings, click Save to save your changes and return to the Screen Saver Settings dialog box.

8. In the Screen Saver Settings dialog box, click Preview to see your Screen Saver in action. In the Wait box, you can set how many minutes to wait before your Screen Saver turns on. If you check the On Resume, Display Log on Screen box, you will be prompted for username and password when Windows 7 comes out of the Screen Saver mode.

9. After you choose your settings, click OK to save the settings and close the dialog box.

> The Screen Saver Settings dialog box also provides you with Power Management options via the Change Power Settings link. Click this link to see your options.

Configuring the Taskbar and Start Menu Properties

To access the Taskbar and Start menu properties in Windows 7, simply right-click the Taskbar and choose Properties. You can also locate the Taskbar and Start Menu Properties item from within Control Panel. Additionally there is a new Notification Area Icons item that you can select from within Control Panel if you are looking at large or small icons rather than a category view.

Whatever manner you choose to access these properties for your Start menu and Taskbar, you will note three tabs (there were four in Vista and only two in XP): Taskbar, Start Menu, and Toolbars.

Taskbar Tab

On the Taskbar tab (see Figure 2.6), you can select or deselect the following Taskbar appearance options:

- Lock the Taskbar
- Auto-Hide the Taskbar
- Use Small Icons

You can also determine the Taskbar Location On Screen (Bottom, Left, Right, or Top). In most cases, users choose Bottom (the default setting).

The Taskbar Buttons option is a new feature in Windows 7. A Taskbar button is an icon that represents a program or document that you have opened. As you open more programs and documents, you create clutter on your Taskbar. By using the Taskbar Buttons feature, you can choose to Always Combine, Hide Labels, Combine When Taskbar Is Full, or Never Combine.

The Taskbar tab also includes a Notification Area section. Simply click the Customize button to display the Notification Area Icons window, where you can select which icons and notifications appear in the Notification Area (which is also known as the Notification Tray or System Tray; see Figure 2.7). Basically, you can tell Windows 7 to hide certain icons and notifications from your notification tray. Sometimes you have icons or notifications that you just don't want or need.

Figure 2.6   *The Taskbar tab of the Taskbar and Start Menu Properties dialog.*

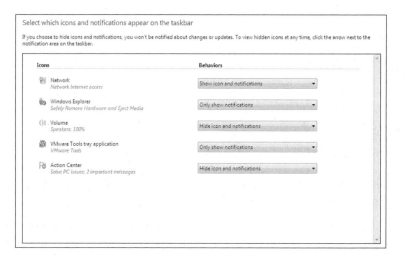

Figure 2.7   *The Notification Area Icons settings.*

If you would like to set the behaviors of system icons, click the Turn System Icons On or Off link near the bottom of the window. The Systems Icons page displays, whereby the Clock, Volume, Network, Power and Action Center icons can be turned On or Off.

 **LET ME TRY IT**

Adjusting the Notification Area

The following steps show you how to remove the Action Center icon from the Notification Area while still allowing notifications to continue to be shown from the Action Center.

1. Right-click the Taskbar and select Properties to bring up the Taskbar and Start Menu Properties dialog box. The Taskbar tab displays by default.

2. On the Taskbar tab, in the Notification Area section, click the Customize button. A list of Icons and their respective Behaviors displays.

3. For the Action Center icon, click the Behaviors drop-down and choose Only show Notifications.

4. Click OK.

With XP and Vista, the default behavior of the notification area (also known as the system tray) is for application icons to just jump into the tray until the point at which the icons grew to annoying proportions. Windows 7 prevents this by allowing only five standard items (Action Center, Power, Network, Volume and Clock), all of which can be seen by clicking the Turn System Icons On Or Off link from the Notification Area settings. As you add new applications to the Taskbar, their icons and notifications are hidden by default. If you want to show them, you have to adjust their respective notifications.

The Taskbar tab also includes the Use Aero Peek to Preview the Desktop checkbox. If you want to temporarily view the desktop when you move your mouse to the Show desktop button at end of the Taskbar, make sure this checkbox is selected. If you look closely at the far-right of your Taskbar, you will see a small box that is a shade of blue that is darker than the rest of your Taskbar. Click this square to launch the Show Desktop feature.

The new Show Desktop feature wasn't available in Windows XP and Vista; those systems featured a Show Desktop icon that could be accessed from the Quick Launch toolbar (off the Taskbar). With the new Show Desktop feature, you can peek at your desktop by hovering your mouse over the Show Desktop square, which makes other windows transparent.

Start Menu Tab

On the Start menu tab (see Figure 2.8), you can click the Customize button to access a variety of ways links, icons, and menus look and behave on the Start menu. For example, they can display as a link, as a menu, or not at all in some cases. Drag the scroll bar to see the many ways you can adjust the Start menu to your liking.

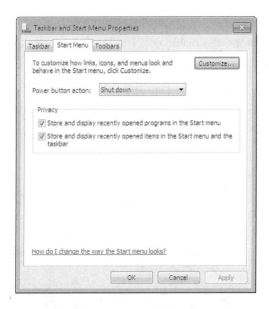

Figure 2.8   *The Start Menu tab of the Taskbar and Start Menu Properties dialog.*

The various customization options give you more control of Windows 7. Two Start menu items that I like to personally see expanded out off my Start menu are Administrative Tools and Control Panel; this is accomplished through the customization options.

The Start Menu tab also provides quick access to Power Button Action, from which you can choose to Switch User, Log Off, Lock, Restart, Sleep, Hibernate, or Shut Down when press the Power button to end a session. In the Privacy area, you can select (or deselect) checkboxes that store and display recently opened items in the Start menu and/or the Taskbar.

Toolbars Tab

The Toolbars tab allows you to add one or more toolbars to the Taskbar for frequently used features, such as an Address toolbar or a Links toolbar. If you select the Desktop toolbar and click Apply or OK, a Desktop toolbar appears on your Taskbar. Now you can click the upper-right arrows next to Desktop on your Taskbar to display a menu from which you can access whatever might be stored on your Desktop.

SHOW ME   Media 2.3—Making Taskbar and Start Menu Changes
Access this video file through your registered Web Edition at
my.safaribooksonline.com/9780768695212/media.

 LET ME TRY IT

Adding the Address Bar to the Taskbar

There are toolbars you can add to your Taskbar to help you personalize the bar.

1. Right-click the Taskbar and select Properties to bring up the Taskbar and Start Menu Properties dialog box.

2. Click the Toolbars tab.

3. Select the Address checkbox and click OK. You will now see an Address bar located on the Taskbar.

There is a shorter way to get this done. Right-click the Taskbar, go to Toolbars, and then click Address. You can use this same approach to add any toolbar you would like to see on your Taskbar.

Configuring Time Options

Typically, the Date and Time options are part of a discussion of the Control Panel because you find those setting there. However, your clock is part of your initial Desktop settings. And in Windows 7, there are some cool options you can take advantage of.

For example, you can actually set up multiple time zone clocks to be displayed for your personal or business needs.

To see the time and current calendar month, you can click the Time/Date option in your notification area. Click the Change Date and Time Settings link to display the Date and Time dialog (see Figure 2.9).

This dialog box features the following tabs:

*   **Date and Time:** Configure your Date, Time and Time Zone settings, and more.

*   **Additional Clocks:** Select the Show this Clock checkbox to display up to two additional time zones.

Figure 2.9   *Date and Time dialog box.*

- **Internet Time:** Synchronize your system time with an Internet-based time server (typically already determined). You can click the Change Settings button to choose a different Internet time server.

 LET ME TRY IT

Adding an Additional Clock to the Notification Area

You may have a need or simply a desire to know what the time is in other parts of the world at a glance. Windows 7 allows you to add two additional clocks to your Notification Area.

1. Click the time and date on your Taskbar to display a larger view of the calendar and clock.

2. Click the Change Date and Time Settings link. The Date and Time dialog box displays.

3. Click the Additional Clocks tab.

4. Select the first Show this Clock checkbox so you can choose a time zone and a display name.

5. Click the Select Time Zone drop-down arrow and choose a time zone different than the one you already use.

   6. In the Enter Display Name box, type a display name for the additional clock. Click OK.

   7. Hover your mouse over the date and time on your Taskbar and you will see the other time zones you have configured (see Figure 2.10).

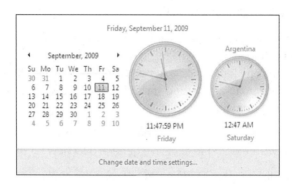

Figure 2.10   *Multiple time zones.*

This is a great tool for travelers who like to call home or for business employees who have offices and clients in other time zones. Of course, you could also setup Gadgets to show you multiple times.

Installing Applications

You have configured the operating system to reflect your personal settings and to enhance the way you work (or play), but you're not quite finished personalizing Windows 7. The operating system is just the foundation for your applications. You still must install the applications you need to perform your tasks and to protect your desktop/laptop. This is where you will need to answer the question, "Why did I buy this computer?" There are so many available applications to install, and some of the more common apps are:

- Microsoft Office (Word, Excel, Access, Power Point, and so on)
- Antivirus (Norton, McAffee, and so on)
- Photo/Picture Editors (Live Essentials Photo Gallery, Picasa, Photo Shop, and so on)
- Utilities (Winzip, MagicIso, File Transfer Protocol, and so on)
- Gaming (Madden NFL, Descent, and so on)
- Email (Outlook, Lotus Notes, and so on)
- Internet Browsers (Firefox, Chrome, Safari, and so on)

This by no means is an exhaustive list of all the applications available. Also, most applications will incur some cost for licensing.

 LET ME TRY IT

Installing an Application

There are many approaches to installing an application, and they vary according to the type of application you're installing. If it is a downloaded file, or a file on a USB device, or perhaps one located on a network drive or CD/DVD, there are minor differences in your approach to getting started. In the following steps, you will learn how to install from from a CD or DVD.

Keep in mind that there will be some variation on the install process for different applications, so we are going to explain a general overview for the install procedure:

1. Insert the diskisk into CD-ROM/DVD drive. If the application was downloaded from the Internet, then navigate to your Downloads folder (or the location to where you choose to download your files).

2. The CD-ROM/DVD disk might have an auto-start feature that automatically presents you with options; one option would be to install the application. If there isn't an auto-start feature, navigate to the CD-ROM/DVD drive or to the location to which you downloaded the application and click on the setup.exe file (this is usually the name of the install file).

3. Follow the screen prompts, which request you to answer some questions and provide license keys.

4. Once the installation finishes, you might be instructed to reboot the computer.

There are many configuration changes we can make to Windows 7 to allow it to fit our personal needs and wants. However, personalization does not end with just the operating system. You need to install applications before you can use the computer for work and/or play.

 TELL ME MORE   Media 2.4—A Discussion About Personalizing Your System

Access this audio recording through your registered Web Edition at my.safaribooksonline.com/9780768695212/media.

Windows 7 comes with a variety of onboard applications that, in some cases, have evolved from previous versions; in other cases, they are brand new.

3

Working with Onboard Applications

In this chapter, you will learn about the various applications that have been Windows staples over the years (such as WordPad) and have perhaps been given a bit of an overhaul. We will also consider newer applications (as in the case of the Snipping Tool, released in Windows Vista) and see how all of these tools work together.

Using WordPad and Paint

It might not seem like a big deal, but after years of an application looking a certain way, it's nice to see a dramatic interface change to match what we have seen in Office 2007 with the Ribbon interface. That is the case with WordPad and Paint. Keep in mind, however, for the most part, the actual feature set is the same with these applications.

WordPad

WordPad (see Figure 3.1) now features a Home Ribbon and a View Ribbon. Just like in Office 2007, you can double-click a Ribbon tab heading to shrink the Ribbon from view altogether and regain some working real estate.

Note that above Ribbon is the Quick Access toolbar that you can customize by clicking the down arrow to the right of the Quick Access toolbar and then choosing to add any features you want. Make sure you customize this drop-down menu with your most commonly used functions. By default, the Quick Access toolbar contains the Save, Undo, and Redo buttons. You can also move theQuick Access toolbar below the Ribbon if you like.

 LET ME TRY IT

Adjusting the Quick Access Toolbar

The Quick Access toolbar can be adjusted toward the top of the ribbon or the bottom. Placing it at the bottom provides a little more room for additional commands.

1. Open WordPad by clicking the Start orb, clicking All Programs, clicking Accessories, and then clicking WordPad.

2. On the Quick Access toolbar, click the down arrow to gain access to the customizable options for the toolbar (see Figure 3.2). Check marks indicate that those options are already displayed as buttons on the Quick Access toolbar.

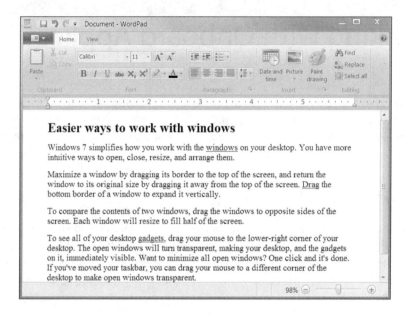

Figure 3.1   *The new Ribbon interface of WordPad.*

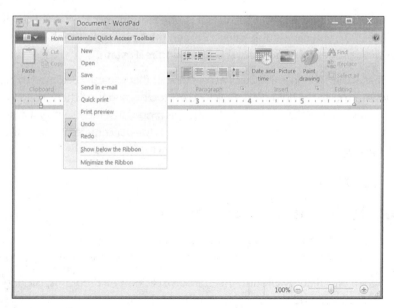

Figure 3.2   *Customizing the Quick Access toolbar.*

3. Choose Show Below the Ribbon to move the Quick Access toolbar below the Ribbon.

The View tab displays to the right of the Home tab. Use the View tab to place items on the Ribbon (like Word Wrap settings, Zoom In and Zoom Out icons, and more); these settings were located on the Options menu with previous versions of Windows.

One of WordPad's best features is that it gives you the ability to preview changes before you make them to your document. You can see a live preview of font, font size, font color and highlight color before you change it. This live preview is activated by selecting the text you plan to change and then, rather than changing the font color (as an example), selecting the drop-down arrow off the Ribbon under the Font group and hovering your mouse pointer over different colors to see a preview of what that color looks like.

 LET ME TRY IT

Preview a Change in Font Style

The ability to preview changes before making them was introduced (along with the new Ribbon interface) in Office 2007. These features have been added to WordPad and we will explore their use through the following steps.

1. In your WordPad document, select a portion of text.
2. On the Home tab, in the Font group, click the down-arrow for the font type.
3. Move your mouse pointer up and down the list of font types. As you point to a font style, look at your selected text in your document. The font of that selected text changes to the font style you're pointing at.
4. To change your font style, left-click your preferred font.

Also located on the Home tab is the Insert group, which provides you with the option to insert four types of objects: Date and Time, Picture, Paint Drawing, or Insert Object (which might include an Adobe Acrobat document, an Excel worksheet, and a host of other items).

 LET ME TRY IT

Insert and Resize a Picture in WordPad

Inserting graphic elements into a document helps enhance the presentation at times. Let's examine how you insert and resize a picture in WordPad.

1. On the Home tab, in the Insert group, click the Picture icon. The Pictures Library displays.
2. Browse through your files and folders to select a picture by either double-clicking it or by clicking it and then clicking the Open button. The picture is inserted in your document.

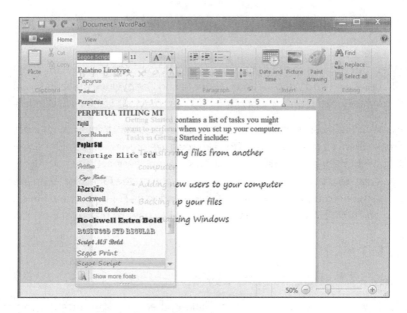

Figure 3.3   *Previewing a change in font style.*

3. Click the picture once to select it, go to the Insert group, click the drop-down arrow immediately below the Picture button, and then click Resize Picture.

4. In the Resize dialog box, type (or click the arrows to choose) new Horizontal and/or Vertical percentage sizes that change the picture size.

You can also change the size of document view. That feature isn't new to WordPad, but manner in which you change the view size has changed. There are two different ways to do this:

- Click the View tab and use the tools in the Zoom group.

- Click and drag the magnification slider located at the bottom-right of WordPad. You can also click the + or - buttons to adjust the magnification percentage.

   LET ME TRY IT

Using the Zoom Feature on the View Ribbon in WordPad

Zoom is a simple feature in WordPad but an important one to work with at times.

1. Click the View tab.

2. Note the 100% icon to zoom in the document to 100% of the normal size, which is the default setting.

3. Click the Zoom In icon to increase viewing size or click the Zoom Out icon to decrease the viewing size.

To the left of the Home tab you will see a blue WordPad button. Click this button to view several standard WordPad commands: New, Open, Save, Save As, Print, Page Setup, Send in E-mail, About WordPad, and Exit. The Save As command allows you to save documents as Rich Text Format (RTF), OpenOffice XML Document (OOXML), Open Document Text, Text Document, Text Document - MS-DOS Format and Unicode Text Document.

Document incompatibility can create a little problem for those reading of your documents. If you are not sure what type of viewer will be used to read your WordPad documents, you should save your document as a Rich Text Document. A Rich Text Document can be viewed by most operating systems. If you know your readers use Word 2007, save your document as an Office Open XML Document, which saves your file with the .docx extension necessary to be read in Word 2007. This is a great format if you have pictures included in your document because you get excellent quality with compression that reduces the size of the document.

The Print option includes a right-pointing arrow. Hovering over the Print option displays a menu that presents you with three choices:

Print allows you to select the printer, choose the number of copies to print, and other printing options before printing. These options will vary depending on the printer and printer drivers you have installed.

Quick Print sends the document directly to the default printer without making changes. Be sure you have all your print options configured before choosing this.

Print Preview allows you to preview and make changes to document pages before printing.

A fast way to access your print options is by placing them on the Quick Access toolbar. Remember, we explained earlier how to add these you can customize by clicking the down arrow to the right of the Quick Access Toolbar and then choosing to add any features you want. From the drop-down you can select the Quick Print option and Print Preview option.

The Page Setup command allows you to configure options such as the paper Size, Orientation (Portrait or Landscape), and Margins, among other options.

LET ME TRY IT

Using Page Setup to Change the Orientation

Being able to adjust your page orientation between landscape and portait will help you ensure your documents are formatted the way you need.

1. Click the WordPad button to the left of the Home tab.

2. Choose Page Setup. The Page Setup dialog box displays.

3. In the Orientation area, click the Landscape radio button.

4. Click OK. Your document is now rotated horizontally in the WordPad viewing window.

 **LET ME TRY IT**

Using Page Setup to Modify the Document Margins

Adjusting a document's margins may allow you to fit more text on a single page or may allow you to place other elements in the margin (like a graphic element) that you prefer. The following steps show you how to adjust margin settings.

1. Click the WordPad button to the left of the Home tab.

2. Choose Page Setup. The Page Setup dialog box displays.

3. In the Margins (Inches) area, replace 1.25 by typing **0.75** in the Left box.

4. Replace 1.25 by typing **0.75** in the Right box.

5. Click OK. Your document margins have changed in the WordPad viewing window.

Paint

Paint (see Figure 3.4) has the new Ribbon interface as well. The Home tab and View tab provide a more modern look to a program that has been around for many years.

The Home tab provides five groups: Clipboard, Image, Tools, Shapes, and Colors. One of the things you might notice with Paint is the easy access to each feature. When you can see your options graphically, you're more likely to find more easily. For example, clicking the Paint button (to the left of the Home tab) and seeing the Properties command made me think these options were new. They aren't new, however. In previous versions of Paint, these options were located by clicking Image and then choosing Attributes.

Thanks to the Ribbon layout, working with menu items becomes much more intuitive. The Home tab, under Brushes, displays watercolor brush or oil brush, which helps in the creative process. Also, more shapes are available now than ever before.

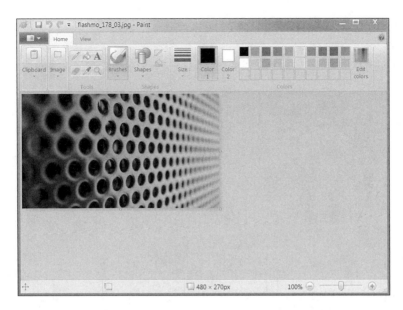

Figure 3.4 *The new Ribbon interface of Paint.*

If you have a tablet to work with, you can get the most out of Paint. With prices for tablets dropping in recent years, you might find that a small investment in a tablet can help you either with Paint or, in truth, any digital painting application.

Another nice feature of the Ribbon is that it provides access to contextual tabs. When you are working with a specific feature, such as inserting text onto a picture, Paint automatically opens a new Text tab (see Figure 3.5).

The benefit of this contextual tab is that it shows you virtually every text option you have to work with. Contextual tabs were introduced in the Office 2007 suite and they have proven to be an incredibly useful feature.

Don't forget to take advantage of Paint's ability to save your photos in a variety of file types. You can select from PNG, JPEG, BMP, GIF and more. At the end of this chapter will see how to take a screenshot of something on your computer, save it in Paint, and then insert it into WordPad.

SHOW ME Media 3.1—Notepad, WordPad, and Paint
Access this video file through your registered Web Edition at
my.safaribooksonline.com/9780768695212/media.

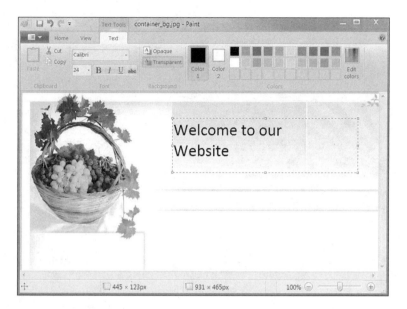

Figure 3.5   *A contextual tab in Paint.*

Using the Calculator

What could be so interesting about a calculator that it warrants being mentioned? Well, when you first open the Calculator, you will note that it looks like the standard Windows Calculator we know and love (with perhaps a few buttons moved around). In XP and Vista versions of the Calculator, only Standard and Scientific modes were available. In the Windows 7 version, however, Programmer and Statistics modes have been added. Simply click on the View menu to access the mode that suits your needs. You will quickly see that some work has been put toward creating a Calculator for everyone.

The View menu also features the following options:

- **Basic:** Provides the typical calculator with the ability to perform calculations using the number keypad along with some additional options for basic math.

- **Unit Conversion:** Allows you to convert one unit type (Area, Energy, Length, Power, and so forth) to another unit type.

- **Date Calculation:** Allows you to calculate the duration between two dates in Years, Months, Weeks, and Days.

- **Worksheets:** Allows you to determine calculations for Mortgage, Vehicle Lease, Fuel Economy (MPG) and Fuel Economy (L/100 km).

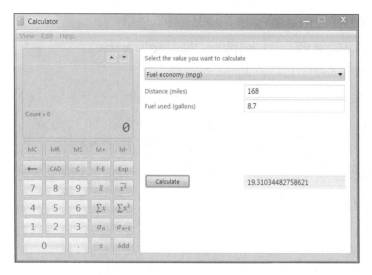

Figure 3.6   *The new Fuel Economy (MPG) worksheet available in Calculator.*

These new templates are incredibly helpful. Before the Windows 7 version of Calculator came along, you likely had to search online for these worksheets. Most folks wouldn't even know to look here for something new.

You might not have thought the good, old-fashioned Calculator could be improved, but like most applications in Windows 7, Microsoft has given it a new look and new functionality as well.

SHOW ME   Media 3.2—Working with the Calculator
*Access this video file through your registered Web Edition at
my.safaribooksonline.com/9780768695212/media.*

Using the Snipping Tool

In the past (and present), we used the Print Screen method of obtaining screen-shots. Otherwise, we used to have to find and download tools that allowed us to take a screenshot of certain parts of our systems (especially those of you who put together presentations). Vista included a tool that continues to be helpful in Windows 7 and allows you to do a few different types of screen snips.

You can find the Snipping Tool either via Start, All Programs, Accessories, Snipping Tool or by simply typing **Snip** into the Instant Search box. You can capture the entire screen, the active windows, a rectangular location of your choosing, or (our favorite) a freestyle selection. You can then save the capture as:

- **HTML:** Viewable through a web browser.

- **JPG:** Great for email because of their small file size.

- **GIF:** Good for low-resolution files.

- **PNG:** A format compatible with most computers.

- And you can even email the file.

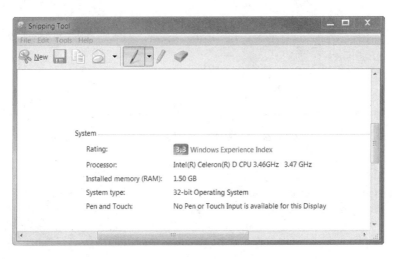

Figure 3.7   *The Snipping Tool is more than just an updated Print Screen method.*

Beyond just capturing and saving part of your screen, you can annotate or highlight parts of the capture with the pen and highlighting tools. The following steps show you how to use the Snipping Tool to capture a part of your desktop.

 **LET ME TRY IT**

Taking a Freeform Snip with the Snipping Tool

Capturing your entire screen or rectangular windows of your screen is an important aspect of work for many. The Snipping Tool provides even greater flexibility by providing a freeform snip feature that allows you to capture what you want, in the way you want it.

1. While on your desktop, open the Snipping Tool by clicking the Start orb, typing **snip** in the search field, and then pressing Enter. You will notice the background change to a shaded color when the Snipping Tool opens.

2. Click the down arrow next to the New button and select Freeform Snip. You will notice that your mouse icon changes to a pair of scissors.

3. Holding down your mouse button, draw a line around the portion of the desktop you would like to snip.

4. When you release the mouse button, your selection appears in the Snipping Tool window.

5. Now you have the option to use the tools to:

    *   Save the snip

    *   Copy the snip

    *   Email the snip (also as an attachment)

    *   Annotations with a pen (choose the color)

    *   Highlight

    *   Erase (erases items you add to the snip—not the snip itself).

All in all, the snipping tool offers a pretty hefty feature set for such a small package. It even outperforms several expensive third-party options. This is a very valuable addition to Windows 7 standard features.

> The Snipping Tool version for Windows 7 is 6.1 (Snipping Tool 6.0 was in Vista SP1), but I'm hard-pressed to find what the difference is between the two versions other than an option missing from Snipping Tool Options to display an icon in the Quick Launch toolbar for the tool (because Windows 7 doesn't have a Quick Launch toolbar).

SHOW ME   Media 3.3—The Snipping Tool
Access this video file through your registered Web Edition at
my.safaribooksonline.com/9780768695212/media.

Using DVD Maker

Windows DVD Maker helps you create DVD movies playable in a standard DVD player or on a computer using DVD playback software. The interface of Windows DVD maker is simple yet effective. You can access DVD Maker through All Programs, through Windows Live Movie Maker, or through Windows Live Photo Gallery (which are both downloadable applications discussed further in Chapter 4). Accessing it from Movie Maker or Photo Gallery is as simple way to select the videos and photos to burn.

A nice feature of DVD Maker is that it automatically creates video thumbnails of separate chapters. It does this whether you are making a video or whether you are making a photo slideshow. When viewing a DVD created by DVD Maker on a standalone DVD player, it's easy to navigate between chapters using your remote control. And since DVD Maker has an interactive preview that you can access before you create your DVD, you can say goodbye to *frisbees* (mistake-filled DVDs). The professional menu choices that you can customize are sure to make you the expert among your peers as the ultimate DVD creator!

Another helpful feature is the ability to take videos directly from your video camera to burn. This makes for a fast transition from camera to DVD. While business users or professionals might require a more robust feature set, home users will find that DVD Maker can handle virtually all of their DVD movie-making needs. Once again, Microsoft has included in Windows 7 a very powerful application that rivals third-party creations. When it comes to making videos, it doesn't get any easier than this.

 LET ME TRY IT

Creating a Custom DVD from Stored Video

You might have videos you have personally taken or video you have downloaded from the Internet that you would like to burn onto a single DVD that includes menus and navigation. The following steps show you how to do this.

1. Verify that you have at least five gigabytes of free space on your hard drive. Most modern computers have more than enough space, so this should be no problem. To view your hard-drive space, click the Start orb and then select Computer. Right-click the C drive and select Properties. Verify that you have at least 5 GB of free hard-drive space. If you don't, delete or move some files off your hard drive.

2. Insert a blank DVD into your DVD drive. If nothing happens, it might turn out that your drive is either a CD-based drive or DVD read-only drive. In that case, DVD Maker will not run successfully.

3. Click the Start orb, select All Programs, and then choose Windows DVD Maker. The Windows DVD Maker intro screen appears (see Figure 3.8).

4. Click Choose Photos and Videos. To select files to add to the DVD, click Add Items and locate the files you would like to add to the DVD (see Figure 3.9). (You can navigate to the public folder and open the Public Videos folder for a sample video to use in this exercise.)

When you first look through your computer to add files to your DVD, you might see only a limited number of files. To see all possible files to add to your DVD, select the drop-down box in the lower-right corner of the screen and select All Files. Now you can see all available files to add to your DVD.

5. At the bottom of the DVD screen is a box called DVD Title that inserts today's date by default. You can change this to any title you want.

Figure 3.8   *The Windows DVD Maker introduction screen.*

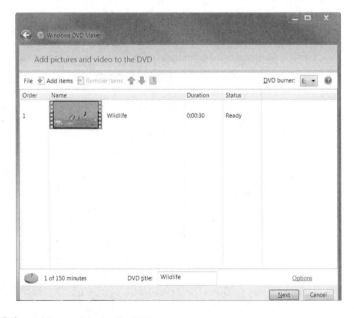

Figure 3.9   *Adding a video to the DVD.*

6. In the upper-right corner of the screen, verify that the DVD burner selected contains your blank DVD. In most cases, this will be the drive lettered E.

Understanding DVD Maker Options

For the most part, the settings on DVD Maker are ready to burn a DVD right from the get-go. It is a good idea to understand what options you have, especially if you want to customize the DVD. Access this advanced menu by selecting Options in the lower-right of the screen.

The first choice you have is Choose DVD Playback Settings. From here you can choose from one of three options:

- Start with DVD Menu gives you the option to select Play or choose which scene you want view from choices on-screen.

- Play Video and End with DVD Menu means that the movie will start the moment the DVD is inserted into the player and will return to the home screen at the end of the movie.

- Play Video in a Continuous Loop means that the movie will repeat when completed.

DVD Aspect Ratio refers to the output screen size the movie will play in. 4:3 is the standard video screen for the United States, while 16:9 is the international standard.

Video Format determines which kind of DVD player your disc can play on. NTSC is a format that generally plays on American DVD players. PAL refers to a format that can be viewed on DVD players abroad.

DVD Burner Speed determines the burner speed of the DVD. By default, this is set to fastest. Depending on your disc and the speed of your burner, you might find it helpful to select a slower speed, especially if you have a failed DVD burn.

Temporary File Location determines the location from which your computer will create a temporary copy of your new disc and burns a copy when you burn a DVD. If you have multiple hard drives, choose your fastest one.

---

7. Click Next. The Ready to Burn DVD dialog box appears. On this screen, you can customize the look of your DVD's home screen.

8. The top menu on this screen contains these choices (see Figure 3.10):

- Preview allows you to see how your DVD will behave in a player once it is completed.

Figure 3.10   *Windows DVD Maker offers several choices to customize your menu.*

- Menu Text allows you to set the fonts for your menu.

- Customize Menu lets you add foreground and background video to your menu. It even lets you add an audio track to the menu. If you want to use this customized menu again, select Save as New Style.

- Slide Show permits you to create a slideshow to appear when your DVD is inserted into a player.

9. On the right side of the Ready to Burn DVD dialog box is a Menu Styles drop-down you can use to choose from attractive pre-made menu styles.

10. You are now ready to create the DVD. Click Burn to start the DVD burning process. You will see a dialog box that states Creating DVD Please Wait. First the video is encoded (see Figure 3.11) and then it's burned to the CD.

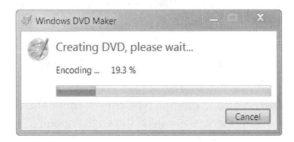

Figure 3.11   *Windows DVD Maker automatically encodes your video.*

The time it takes to the finish this depends on the size of the video, the burn rate (Fast, Medium, or Slow), and the speed of your computer. Although you can keep working on your computer while it's burning a DVD, you might want to let the computer finish this task before using other applications.

11. Once it's burned, the disc automatically ejects. You're then presented the option to make another copy of the DVD. If you select OK, insert a new DVD; DVD Maker burns another copy identical to the one just created.

12. Try out your DVD in a traditional DVD player to make sure it's just what you wanted.

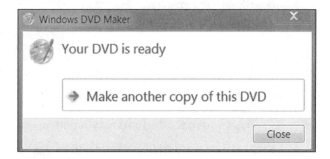

Figure 3.12   *Windows DVD Maker has successfully created your DVD.*

Using the Command Prompt (For Users and Admins)

If you open a command prompt in Windows XP, you might never have noticed that it says Version 5.1.2600 at the top with a 1985-2001 copyright attached. (This information might change according to whatever upgrades you might have installed.) Vista showed a version change to 6.0.6001. Windows 7 reads 6.1.7600, respectively. One interesting aspect about the Windows 7 command-line application (which was first introduced in Vista) is the fact that there is a standard user mode and an administrator mode.

The reason for this distinction is that there are powerful items you can perform through the command line and this could be dangerous to a system, especially if the system is connected to a network.

To open a standard command prompt, type **cmd** or **command** at the Instant Search box off the Start menu; you will be shown the option to select.

You can also select Start, All Programs, Accessories to locate the standard command prompt. To open it as an Administrative command prompt, you can do one of the following:

1. Right-click the Command Prompt option from the Start menu and choose Run as Administrator. When the Windows Security dialog appears, enter credentials (or just say OK) to bring up the Administrator's command prompt (if, indeed, you have permission to open it on your system, which might not be the case).

2. Another method is to type **cmd** in the Instant Search box and then press and hold Ctrl+Shift+Enter. The security dialog appears.

How do you know you are working with one command prompt over another? Microsoft has cleverly positioned the word Administrator in the Window bar at the top.

One thing you can do to make it clear that you are in the Administrator's command prompt is type **color 4f** to change the background color to red. You can type **color /?** to learn of other colors you might wish to choose.

Most users do little or nothing with the command prompt on a daily basis. They rely on Microsoft's graphical interface to complete tasks that used to require a command prompt. However, advanced users continue to use this tool to quickly troubleshoot and execute computer commands.

Combining Tools Project

 LET ME TRY IT

Putting All Our Onboard Tools Into One Task

Let's put a few of the applications we learned about in this chapter to work. We'll create a screenshot using the Snipping Tool, edit it with Paint, and then insert the finished product in a WordPad document.

1. Navigate to the Start orb, click All Programs, and then click Accessories. Locate the sound recorder and click on it to open the program.

2. Move the sound recorder dialog box to a place where you can easily snip it.

3. While on your Desktop, open the Snipping Tool by clicking the Start orb, typing **Snip** in the search field, and then pressing Enter.

4. Click on the down arrow next to the New button and select Rectangular Snip. You will notice that your mouse icon changes to cross-hairs.

5. Now using your cross-hairs, select the sound recorder application. If you make a mistake, simply click New again on the Snipping Tool and try again.

6. After you have the snip that you like, in the Snipping Tool, choose File and then select Save As. Browse to a location where you will easily be able to find the picture, name it sound recorder photo and save it as a JPG.

7. Close the Snipping Tool application.

8. Now, navigate to the Start orb, type **Paint** in the search, and then press Enter.

9. In your open Paint application, click the drop-down arrow on the blue tab located to the left of the Home tab.

10. Select Open (the second button on the menu).

11. Browse to the location where you saved the picture named sound recorder photo.jpg. Click on this JPEG image and click Open.

12. You will notice a small white box in the lower-right corner of the picture. Left-click this box and drag the corner of this box to expand it approximately half way down the screen and three-quarters across the screen.

13. On the Home tab, locate the Tools group and then click on the paint can.

14. Now locate the colors on the right side and choose a color to replace the white background.

15. Move your mouse anywhere over the right background and then left-click it. This changes the color of the white background.

16. In the upper-left corner of the Paint application, click the Save button.

17. Close the Paint application.

18. Click the Start orb and in the Search, type **WordPad** and press Enter.

19. In the open WordPad document, type the following sentence: This is the Windows Seven Sound Recorder.

20. Highlight the entire sentence and on the Home tab in the Font group, click the Font drop-down box and choose Freestyle Script.

21. Change the font size to 36.

22. Make sure the cursor is now blinking at the end of the period following the word *Recorder*.

23. Find the picture icon in the Insert group and click it.

24. Browse and find the file sound recorder photo.jpg and then click Open.

25. Click the drop-down arrow from the document menu, choose Save As, and then choose Office Open XML Document.

Congratulations! You have successfully taken a snapshot of your Desktop with the Snipping Tool, edited it in Paint, and then imported that picture in WordPad. We've only scratched the surface of the possibilities available with these tools.

 TELL ME MORE   Media 3.4—A Discussion About the Onboard **Applications in Windows 7**
Access this audio recording through your registered Web Edition at ***my.safaribooksonline.com/9780768695212/media***.

In this chapter, we will review the use of the Windows
Live Essentials tool suite.

4

Windows Live Essentials

Download Windows Live Essentials

If you have worked with Windows 7 for more than five minutes, you might have noticed something missing. Applications! Where is your Windows Mail, Calendar and so forth? If you are a Windows XP user, you might have noticed only a few missing pieces, but Vista users expect a bit more to start with—such as Movie Maker and Windows Mail. In Windows 7, those have been moved off the OS and made available for download.

 LET ME TRY IT

Downloading and Installing the Windows Live Essentials Tools

Because the Live Essentials tools are not automatically installed on your system, you need to download them from the Internet.

1. Click the Start orb and type **Live Essentials** in the Instant Search box. A link appears; click it to visit the Live Download site (http://download.live. com), where a single Windows Live Essentials download installs applications for Instant Messaging, email, blogging, photos, movies, and more.

2. Click the Download button and then download (the file should be wlset-up-web) and run the application. The User Account Control dialog might ask for permission to continue. Click Yes.

The bottom of the Download screen includes a comment that reads SmartScreen Filter Checked This Download and Did Not Report Any Threats. In a future chapter, you will learn about IE8 security options, but just to let you know, this is a new feature in IE8 to help protect you from unsecure downloads.

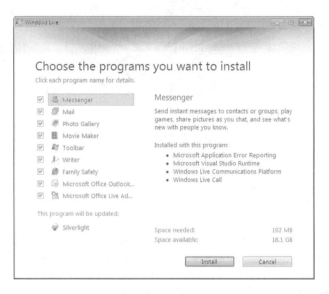

Figure 4.1 *The main Windows Live installation setup screen.*

3. Choose the applications you want to install (see Figure 4.1). Applications include the following:

   • **Messenger:** Send instant messages to contacts or groups, play games, share pictures as you chat, and see what's new with people you know.

   • **Mail:** With Windows Live Mail on your desktop, you can access multiple email accounts, your calendar, newsgroups, and feeds in one program. And it's part of Windows Live Essentials, so you can view your calendar online and see when Instant Messenger contacts are available to chat.

   • **Photo Gallery:** Easily edit, view, organize, and share your favorite photos. You can also tag people in photos, stitch photos together into panoramas, and more.

   • **Movie Maker:** Add and arrange video clips and photos, add a soundtrack, preview your movie, and then publish your movie to one of several popular videos sites.

   • **Toolbar:** Add Windows Live Toolbar to Internet Explorer and get quick, at-a-glance access to your Windows Live Hotmail, calendar, photos, and more.

   • **Writer:** Create great-looking blog posts, including photos, videos, maps, events, and tags. Publish them to almost any blog service—Windows Live, WordPress, Blogger, Live Journal, TypePad, and many more.

   • **Family Safety:** Helps keep your kids safer online. With Family Safety, you decide how your kids experience the Internet. You can block or allow certain websites and contacts and monitor where your kids are going online.

- **Silverlight:** This is Microsoft's response to Flash and can be used to enhance your experience with photos and videos on Windows Live and MSN, including rich slide shows and high-definition video. In addition, enjoy a superior browsing experience across many popular news, sports, and entertainment sites powered by Microsoft Silverlight technology.

4. Choose the applications you want to install and click Install to begin enhancing your Windows experience (see Figure 4.2).

Figure 4.2   *Installation in progress.*

5. Finally, answer a few questions regarding the setting of your search provider (the hope is to let Live Search handle your search needs), setting your home page (the hope is for MSN to be your browser home page), and being a part of the process by allowing Microsoft to collect information on how your system performs and how you use their software, including the web sites you visit. Choose what you agree with and click Continue. You can then sign up for a Windows Live ID if you don't already have one and/or click Close to finish.

You do not have to be running Windows 7 to enjoy the Windows Live applications we just discussed. You can download them to a system running Windows XP SP2 (32-bit only) and Windows Vista (32- or 64-bit). With the exception of Movie Maker, which will not run on XP, the applications work the same. You might need to install additional components in some cases, so be sure to review the System Requirements off the Live Download site.

After the process is complete, you can locate your new applications under the Windows Live folder off the Start menu, All Programs options. You will see they are named Windows Live Call, Windows Live Mail, and so forth.

Windows Live Messenger

This is the latest version of MSN Messenger that you might have used in the past (or are using in the present). Live Messenger includes some great features (beyond the obvious IM functionality), including the following:

- **.tif-to-Phone Calling:** This is a feature supported through Windows Live Call.

- **Interoperability:** Live Messenger works with several difficult types of clients, including Yahoo, Google Talk, AOL, ICQ, and XMPP.

- **Games:** You can play free games or games you subscribe to with people you have in your contacts list.

- **Exchange Pictures:** You can drag photos into the conversation window to show others while you are chatting. They can save those photos on their systems.

- **Contact Updates:** When a contact of yours does something new, like post to their blogs or add photos, you can see it through the Live Messenger window under a What's New dialog.

- **Send Mobile Text Messages:** You can text a phone from Live Messenger to keep your conversation going even if a person has to leave his computer.

 LET ME TRY IT

Altering the Live Messenger Background

At times, especially with tools that are personal to us (like Messenger), we want to customize it and personalize it according to our tastes. The following steps show you how to alter the background you see within Live Messenger.

1. Start Windows Live Messenger.

2. Click the Tools menu and choose Backgrounds, which opens the Background.

3. Choose from one of the available backgrounds by clicking on it.

4. To use a picture saved on your computer, click Browse, select the picture, and then click Open.

5. Click Set Default and then click Close to make the change.

That's it. You have changed your background and made this the default setting.

We often use messaging to send information that really should stay private. Identity theft is an issue that is not going away and will only continue to grow larger. To help offset this problem, Windows Live Messenger has an important feature you need to use when working in a shared environment (such as using public library computers or working in an Internet café). To help with security, you can choose to *not* save your contacts on the machine when you are done with messaging.

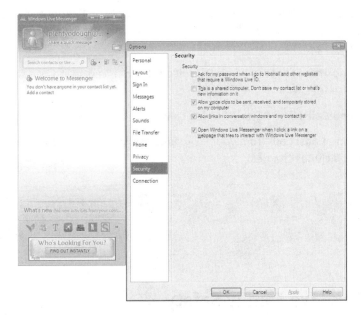

Figure 4.3 *The Security tab in Live Messenger.*

 **LET ME TRY IT**

Configure Live Messenger to Not Save Your Contact List in a Shared Environment

If security is a priority, as it should be, and you want to prevent your contact list from being saved for others to see, choose the following settings.

1. Start Windows Live Messenger.

2. Click the Tools menu and choose Options, which opens the Options dialog box.

3. Click Security on the left pane.

4.   Select the checkbox that reads This is a Shared Computer. Don't Save My Contact List or What's New Information on it.

Now when you log off your computer session, your contacts won't appear on that computer.

Windows Live Call

You must be logged into Windows Live Messenger to use Windows Live Call. It is basically the Microsoft version of Skype and it allows you to make calls in one of three ways.

- **Computer Call:** Free PC-to-PC voice calls to others using Windows Live Messenger.

- **Video Calls:** Free PC-to-PC video calls.

- **Phone Calls:** Calls from your PC to landlines and wireless (however, this feature includes charges).

If you like the Windows Live Call application, you might like the Windows Live Messenger Phone. This phone allows you to make calls through the local telephone service or through your Windows Live Messenger.

Windows Live Family Safety

When you first open Windows Live Family Safety, you're asked to provide a Live ID to get started. This is your primary account for the settings you choose.

Once you log in (after determining which accounts you want to monitor), you can turn the Family Safety Filter on or off with a simple slider. When you log into the Windows Live Family Safety site, you can do the following:

- Categorize and block unwanted web content for yourself and your family.

- Create your own list of allowed or blocked sites.

- Monitor Family Safety users' Internet activity.

To start protecting your family with Family Safety, you are instructed to do the following:

1.   Install Family Safety on all computers your children use in your home (however, if you have only one computer, you need only to install the Live

Essentials tools one time). Install Family Safety from the Windows Live Family Safety website. (http://download.live.com/familysafety).

2. **Create user settings and set up reporting.** Configure custom user settings for each family member at the Windows Live Family Safety website by designating which content types and sites users can access. Customize reports to keep an eye on what your children are viewing online.

3. **Respond to requests.** When your children want to see blocked content, they will send you a request and you can decide if you want them to see it or if you want to keep it on their blocked list.

SHOW ME   Media 4.1—Windows Live Family Safety
Access this video file through your registered Web Edition at
my.safaribooksonline.com/9780768695212/media.

LET ME TRY IT

Setting Up the Family Safety Filter

It takes a few extra steps to make sure your family is protected, but these steps are necessary to ensure the filter is blocking what you feel in inappropriate for certain family members.

1. Start Windows Live Family Safety.

2. Login with your Windows Live ID. If you don't have one, simply click Sign Up.

3. Visit the Family Safety website (http://fss.live.com).

4. On the Family Summary page, click Add Child.

5. Log-in with your Windows Live ID.

6. The Web Filtering page provides you with options of what you want to allow your child to view on the Internet. Choose which sites to block or allow.

7. Monitor their online chat capabilities by clicking Contact Management.

With these basic steps completed, you have set up the Family Safety Filter. You can verify that it's running by looking for the family safety icon in the notification area of Windows 7. Check the Family Safety site to generate full reports about your child's Internet activities.

One of the things I really like about the new Family Safety site is that you can handle requests remotely. If you are at work and your child makes a request from home, you can address that request without being home with them. You can also remotely monitor where they are going and what they are doing in the activity log. My only criticism on this is that it requires so much attachment to the Live accounts, which are free to create but still a bit too much of a tie.

Windows Live Mail

From Outlook Express in XP to Windows Mail in Vista, we have now graduated to Windows Live Mail. When comparing the three applications, you will find Windows Live Mail has a very polished look to it. It's as smooth and soothing as an application can be.

Windows Live Mail makes it easy to route multiple email accounts for Gmail, Hotmail, and Yahoo into a single location. You also have a much better security setup, including improved spam filters that better help you to decide if something is truly dangerous, for you to delete a message, and/or for you to block a sender easily.

 LET ME TRY IT

Create and Configure a New Email Account

Before you can begin sending and receiving email with Windows Live Mail, you need to ensure all your email account settings are in place.

1. Before starting Windows Live Mail, make sure you have the following:
    - Email Username and Password (your email provider has all this information).
    - Incoming email server address (for example, pop.emailhost.com).
    - Outgoing email server address (for example, smtp.emailhost.com).
    - Server authentication information of required.

2. After you have collected your information, start Windows Live Mail.

3. In the left pane, click Add E-Mail Account (although you might be prompted the first time you start Live Mail if you don't have an account configured).

4. Enter your email address and password. Click the check box Remember Password.

5. Enter your display name. This is the name that appears in all your outgoing emails.

6. Click Next.

7. In the Add an E-mail Account dialog box. Insert the data you collected in Step 1 (the POP or IMAP and SMTPinformation; see Figure 4.4).

8. Click Next and you will receive a message stating You Have Successfully Entered the Information Required to Setup Your Account.

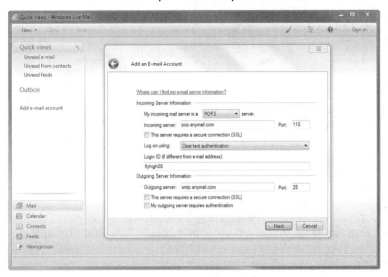

Figure 4.4   *Adding an email account to Live Mail.*

9. If this is your default mail account, check the box in the lower right.

10. Click Finish.

11. To modify the email account after it has been created, right-click the account name in the pane on the left and choose Properties.

Keep in mind that every time you set up a new email account in Live mail, five new folders are created: Inbox, Drafts, Sent Items, Junk E-mail and Deleted Items. Things can get pretty confusing when you add several accounts. Try to understand the folder structure of each account as it's created. That will go a long way in helping you keep your email organized right from the start.

Wondering when you have new email? Just look for the Windows Live Mail icon to notify you when you have a new email message. Simply click it to open up your email interface.

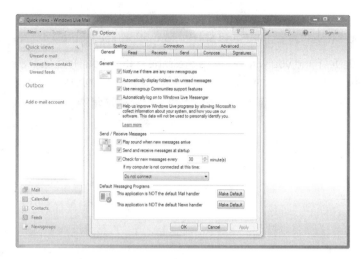

Figure 4.5   *The Options dialog box for Mail.*

Configuring Mail Options

Before going further with Live Mail, let's take a look at the laundry list of options you have available in the application. Start by going over to the top menu in Mail and clicking the Menus drop-down. Then select Options to see your tabs (see Figure 4.5).

General: From here you can configure the interval to check for new messages, display options for unread messages, and set up your alert for when new messages arrive. If you mistakenly install another email application, that application might try to wrestle control of email away from Live Mail. At the bottom of the General tab, you can set matters straight by selecting your default mail handler.

Read: You might want to visit this tab first so you can change the fonts and default encoding style used when reading messages. Alternatively, in the Reading Messages part of the Read tab, you can set all your messages to display in plain text.

Receipts: A nice feature to turn on is Request a Read Receipt for All Sent Messages. In truth, read receipts don't always work and it is up to the recipient to allow it to send a receipt back your way in many cases. Many recipients choose not to allow this, but it is still an interesting option to consider using.

Send: Verify here that you approve of the default send options. Then select how you want your mail to look when sent: HTML (the default) or plain text.

Compose: Set up your compose font for mail and news here. You can also create a digital business card that you can attach to Mail and News from here.

Signatures: It seems like no email is complete without a custom signature. Perfect yours from this tab.

Spelling: If you are like me, you'll quickly want to come here and select Always Check Spelling Before Sending.

Connection: Windows Live Mail shares your Internet connection settings with Internet Explorer. Click this tab to modify these settings and also configure your Windows Live ID Sign-in credentials.

Advanced: Options for IMAP, Message Threads, and Reply/Forward are here along with a Maintenance and Troubleshooting section. Clicking Maintenance brings up a new dialog box that provides you with options for cleaning up messages and creating troubleshooting logs.

 LET ME TRY IT

Customizing Your Interface Colors

At times you might want to personalize your email client by altering the color scheme. The following steps show you how to replace the interface colors with custom ones of your choosing.

1. Find the brush icon on the top menu towards the right and click it.

2. If you like one of the 12 colors shown, you can choose one of them.

3. If you don't like one of the 12 colors shown, click More Colors to choose from a wider range of interface colors.

4. After you make your selection, click OK and start enjoying your new colors.

To the right of the brush is the Menus button. From here you can customize the layout, options, and toolbars. It's really surprising to see so many available choices on the Options menu. That's a good thing. Clearly, this is more than just a stripped-down email application.

Make sure you take advantage of the available quick links buttons. These are found towards the bottom-left corner of the Windows Mail application. The buttons are: Mail, Calendar, Contacts, Feeds, and Newsgroups. Click each link to see the corresponding section that opens.

You might remember working with Windows Mail in Vista and using the calendar/contact features. Embedded within Windows 7's Live Mail application are two other programs that are tightly interwoven with it. They are called (not surprisingly) Calendar and Contacts (see Figure 4.6). Like Microsoft Outlook, Windows Live Mail integrates these separate features into one application. With basic calendar and contact options, many users find this is all they need to work with. Especially when considering they are free!

One of the interesting features of Windows Live Mail is that you not only have a personal calendar on your system, you can use the Windows Live account to sync with your Windows Live Calendar. So if you are working offline, the edits you make to your calendar will synch with Windows Live (at calendar.live.com) when you come back online. The great part about this feature is that you can check, edit, and update your Windows Live Calendar from any browser.

Figure 4.6 *Windows Live Calendar—ready for your schedule!*

Don't forget about the different calendar views you have. After you click on Calendar, you can select Day, Week, or Month at the top of the screen.

 **LET ME TRY IT**

Add and Save an Appointment with Your Calendar

Calendars are all about appointments, so the following steps show you how to add and save an appointment.

1. Open Windows Live Mail.

2. In the lower-left pane, click Calendar.

3. Using the mini-calendar in the upper left, navigate to the month in which you want to schedule your appointment.

4. On the main calendar, double-click the date. This opens the New Event dialog box.

5. In the Subject line, type the title of your appointment.

6. In the Location box, type the location of the appointment (if necessary).

7. By default, the checkbox All Day is selected. Uncheck this box to select specific times during the day. To the bottom of the New Event dialog box is a large white area where you can preview and add extra data regarding your appointment.

8. What you have completed your appointment, click Save and Close.

When you're ready to print your calendar, click the Print button located in the top menu of Calendar. As in Outlook, you can print a single day of the week or you can print an entire month. Don't forget to set your date range at the bottom before clicking OK. Leaving the print range on one day fills the entire page with the current month and part of the next month. A very discreet water mark of your current month shows up at the bottom of the page. This adds a professional look and feel to your calendar without going overboard.

SHOW ME Media 4.2—A Look at Windows Live Mail
Access this video file through your registered Web Edition at
my.safaribooksonline.com/9780768695212/media.

LET ME TRY IT

Adding Calendars

Different types of calendars can be used for different reasons. You might have a work calendar that you maintain separately from a family or personal calendar. The following steps show you how to add an additional calendar.

1. Start Windows Live Mail.

2. Click Calendar in the lower-left pane.

3. Under the Calendars heading in the left pane, click Add Calendar.

4. In the Calendar Name field, type the name of your calendar.

5. Select a color for the title of this calendar that appears in the left-middle pane.

6. In the Description field, type a short description for this calendar.

7. If this will be your primary calendar, check the box Make This My Primary Calendar.

8. Click Save.

Your new calendar now appears under the Calendars heading in the left-middle pane.

You can edit your calendar options by clicking on the calendar name in the left-middle pane. From this mini-menu you can add a new event, set the properties of the calendar, or delete it. If you have multiple calendars, you also have the additional choices of setting a calendar as your primary calendar or hiding the calendar from the list. Tell me, do you really need a hidden calendar?

I was just starting to enjoy the Calendar feature of Windows Live Mail when I discovered something unpleasant. Although I can add up all sorts of data in the notes area of an appointment, I was sorely disappointed that I was unable to add .BMP or .JPG files. I've come to expect this type of functionality from applications like Outlook 2007.

Windows Live Movie Maker

Movie Maker was a quirky but fun tool to play with in Windows XP. It was enhanced in Vista before many users even began to notice it—mostly because there are just so many other tools on the market these days to merge photos, video, and sound and produce them into videos for instruction or sharing.

Live Movie Maker (see Figure 4.7) includes the new ribbon interface, which creates a more streamlined look. Contextual ribbons, such as video tools, enhance the workspace and focus your attention on essential work options.

You can publish your completed movies to the web through the Publish option.. You can quickly create a new video in WMV format for both high-quality or portable mobile players. Overall, Live Movie Maker has a long way to go before reaching the high standards of leading third-party tools, but it is free, easy to use, and it works well for what it does.

Figure 4.7   *Windows Live Movie Maker provides a simple approach to video editing.*

LET ME TRY IT

Create and Publish a Video

The following steps show you how to create a video and publish it to the Internet.

1. Open Windows Live Movie Maker.

2. On the right of the application, click Drag Videos and Photos Here or Click to Browse for Them.

3. Navigate to the location of the video, select it, and then click Open.

4. If you would like to add music to your file, click on the Home tab and in the Add group, click the Add Music button.

5. Once you have it put together, locate the Sharing group on the Home tab and click YouTube. This opens the Publish on YouTube dialog box (see Figure 4.8).

6. If you have an account, enter your Username and Password. If you do not have an account, click the hyperlink at the bottom of the dialog box to create one.

7. After you have logged in, follow the instructions to complete the uploading of your video.

Figure 4.8 *Windows Live Movie Maker lets you easily share your video on YouTube.*

Do you have a lot of pictures and your computer? What do you do if you want to show them to people? What if you want to distribute them? You can solve these issues by creating a photo slide show through Windows Live Movie Maker. Upon completion, you will have turned multiple photographs into a movie complete with visual effects and sound.

Build an Impressive Photo Slide Show

The following steps show you how to create a photo slide show that includes transitions and audio.

1. Open Windows Live Movie Maker.

2. On the right of the application, click Drag Videos and Photos Here or Click to Browse for Them.

3. Navigate to the location of the photo you want to add to the slide show and click Open.

4. Repeat Step 3 until you have acquired all the photos for the slide show.

5. In the right pane, left-click and drag each photo to the position you want it.

6. In the bottom of the left pane, click the blue play triangle to watch your slide show without any transitions or visual effects.

7. To add a transition, click the Animations tab.

8. Make sure your slide show is at the very beginning. You'll see a limited selection of transitions on the left part of the ribbon.

9. Click the Crossfade transition.

10. Click Play to advance the slide show to a position where you would like to add another transition.

11. The selection of transitions expands. Click the drop-down arrow in the transitions box on the right to see the full selection of transitions.

12. Scroll down to any transition you like and place your mouse over it to preview it.

13. Left-click to add a transition.

14. Repeat this process until you have added all desired transitions.

15. Click on the Home tab.

16. In the Add group, click the Add Music button.

17. Navigate to the location of the audio you want to add to the slide show and click Open.

18. The green Music Tools contextual ribbon opens above the options tab. On this ribbon, locate the Audio group.

19. Change the Fade In drop-down box from None to Slow.

20. Click the Home tab.

21. Click the drop-down button in the sharing group.

22. Click the third icon under the heading Other Settings to Save a Movie on Your Computer.

23. Browse to a location to save your slide show and click Save.

24. The slide show is saved as a .wmv file and can be played immediately when completed (see Figure 4.9).

Here's something to keep in mind: Transitions and effects are applied to each frame individually, so it's easy to remove or even change them. You can identify transitions by noting frames with effects on them. This indicates that an effect or transition has been inserted.

Figure 4.9 *Completed slide show shown playing in Windows Media Player 12.*

For an even faster creation build with special effects, choose AutoMovie. Just load up your videos, pictures, and audio and AutoMovie does the rest. It automatically adds effects, such as transitions and titles. Some find this feature more gimmicky than practical. Many times I didn't like the transition choices or placement within the slide show. I recommend trying it before you spend a lot of time creating a customized movie. Load all your media and click AutoMovie. You might actually like the result. If you don't, no harm done—like a recipe adjustment, just modify it to suit your taste!

Windows Live Photo Gallery

In the era of digital cameras, we are seeing how quickly the number of photos we have can grow into the thousands. It's so different from the days of the traditional camera, when you had to go down to the developer to see the pictures you took months ago. Now you simply push those pictures to your desktop and start making them into memories with video and sound included. Amazing. And disorganized, typically.

Live Photo Gallery (see Figure 4.10) is the next version of the Photo Gallery tool that was released in Vista. Just like its predecessor, Live Photo Gallery allows you to organize your photos by providing tagging ability (so you can add metadata to those photos one at a time or in bulk) and also providing searching abilities.

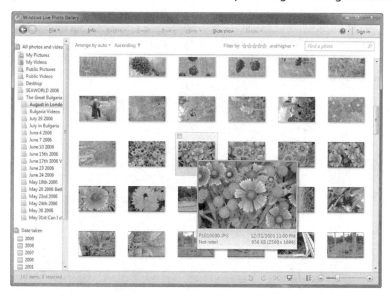

Figure 4.10   *View all your computer's pictures from the Windows Live Photo Gallery.*

Sharing is made easier because you can upload photos to Live Spaces or Flickr (perhaps others in the future) directly from the Photo Gallery. Videos can be published to YouTube (as mentioned previously for Live Movie Maker).

The following features are included in Live Photo Gallery:

- Improved import tool for tagging photos.

- Tools to adjust a photo's color histogram with shadow and highlight adjustment or sharpness.

- Panoramic stitching to put multiple pictures together into a panorama.

- Batch resize of photos and rotation of videos.

- QuickTime 7 support for playing videos.

- Support for Live Sync, where you can synchronize your photo library between two systems with Photo Gallery that use the same Live ID.

As its name suggests, in Windows Live Photo Gallery is a place to view photos from your computer. What you might not have known is that you can also view your videos from this application. However, when you first start Windows Live Photo Gallery, only a limited number of photos/videos show. To add more photos, you'll need to click the File drop-down menu and choose Include a Folder in the Gallery. If you have an external hard drive or other location where you keep pictures and videos, you can add this to the gallery as well.

It wasn't too long ago that you needed a professional suite of photo-editing software to fix errant photos. Once again, Microsoft has addressed this with a nice set of photo-editing tools. You can access these by clicking the Fix button. You might still prefer to load other third-party software. But you might not be so quick to do so once you've given Windows Live Photo Gallery a try.

 SHOW ME   Media 4.3—Using the Windows Live Photo Gallery
Access this video file through your registered Web Edition at
my.safaribooksonline.com/9780768695212/media.

 LET ME TRY IT

Photo Straightening with Live Photo Gallery

Sometimes you need to fix a photo. That might involve a variety of different tweaks, including red-eye removal or cropping. The following steps show you how to straighten a photo in Photo Gallery.

1. Start Windows Live Photo Gallery.

2. Select a picture from the Gallery.

3. On the upper menu, to the right of File, click Fix.

4. Select straighten photo.

5. Your photo will instantly straighten, withLive Photo Gallery recommending its position.

6. You can accept this position by clicking on the blue Back arrow in the upper-left corner.

7. If you don't like this position, use the slider to position the photo where you feel it is straight.

8. Upon completion, click Back to Gallery in the upper-left corner.

Tags are a great way to easily identify a picture. The problem is, it can be pretty time consuming to enter tags for every picture. Windows Live Photo Gallery helps take some of the work out of this by letting you use information already entered on your contacts list. This is done through the People tag. Rather than re-enter the information, you get to reuse the data you have already typed. Of course, if you don't have the data in Contacts, you can always add it by hand. Take note, however, that these tags are part of the photo's metadata and thus stay with the photo as it travels through digital networks (such as the Internet or your network at work). After you post your relatives' pictures to your blog, don't be surprised if strangers start recognizing them...and calling them by their pet nickname!

There is no shortage of cool features in Windows Live Photo Gallery. One stunning feature mentioned before is stitching together your photos into a one panoramic view. The results are unbelievable. After you try it once, you'll never take photographs the same way again.

 LET ME TRY IT

Creating a Photo Panorama

Sometimes we might have more than one shot that we want to group together to form a panoramic scene. The following steps show you how to do this with Live Photo Gallery.

1. Take a series of photos on a digital camera that span from one end of a scene to another. Make sure each photo slightly overlaps the previous one.

2. Connect your digital camera to your computer. Windows Live Photo Gallery automatically imports these pictures to your computer.

3. Locate your photos for the panorama shot. To select all the photos, click on each photo while holding down the Control key (or click the checkbox associated with each image).

4. Release the Control key, right-click that group you have selected, and then choose Create Panoramic Photo. Live Photo Gallery then stitches these photos together (see Figure 4.11).

5. Upon completion, you'll be asked where to save the file.

6. Now apply any fixes to the photo, such as cropping it, auto adjusting it, or straightening it.

Figure 4.11 *Stitching together photos to create a single panoramic photo.*

Windows Live Writer

Windows Live Writer is a new tool that we haven't worked with before as part of an OS release, but it was released for download late 2007. There have obviously been some enhancements incorporated into this latest version. It's a blog-publishing application that allows you to blog (obviously), add photos and videos, and then publish to popular blogging services such as Windows Live Spaces, Blogger, WordPress, and TypePad.

After you configure your blog location, Live Writer opens and then provides you with a very simple WYSYWIG screen for blogging. It also provides a very simple set of Insert options so you can include pictures, videos, maps, hyperlinks, tables, and more.

Keep in mind that before you can use Live Writer, you need to have a blog URL that you can publish to. The account information is required in order to complete the setup. Of course, you're not limited to one account. Live Writer makes it easy to add another blog URL so you can keep on blogging.

 LET ME TRY IT

Opening an Additional Blog Account with Live Writer

The first time you start Live Writer you're asked to configure it. You can configure your blog at that time. However, if you want to add an additional blog, follow these steps.

1. Start Windows Live Writer.

2. Click Tools on the menu bar.

3. From the drop-down menu that appears, click Accounts. The Options dialog box appears.

4. In the left pane, highlight Accounts.

5. In the right pane, click the Add button.

6. Select the type of blog that you want to use (for example, Other Weblog Service) and click Next.

7. In the Add a Blog Account dialog box that appears, enter your blog information (such as the Web Address of Your Blog, Username, and Password fields).

8. Click Next.

9. Windows Live Writer automatically detects your blogging platform (in most cases) and asks for the name of your blog.

10. Click Finish. You're now ready to roll.

Experienced Bloggers Take Note

Windows Live Writer is set up very efficiently right out of the box. But for those who work with blogs on a regular basis, you might need just that little bit of extra configuration. Here are three points to remember:

1. Understand your Save Draft options. As you create your blog, where do you want it to save—locally or straight to the blog? Setting the Save Draft options puts you in control of where the data is saved. Choose from Save to Local Draft, Post Draft to Weblog (or) Post Draft, and Edit Online. A related option is saving your work at selected time intervals straight to your blog. Turn this on by going to Tools, clicking Options, and selecting 'Editing. Locate Editing and click the checkbox for Automatically Save Drafts Every and then determine the number of minutes.

2. Understand how to configure your spell check. There are two selections here that are mission critical to getting your blog spell-checked correctly before it publishes. Go to Tools and then click Options. Click the fifth button down, Spelling. Verify that both of the following boxes are checked: Under General Options, make sure you check the first box, Use Real-Time Spell Checking, and make sure the Check Spelling Before Publishing box is checked. Believe me, your readers will thank you for doing this.

3. Know the location of your Link Glossary. This is an easy one. You'll find it by going to Tools, clicking Options, and just below Spelling you will see Auto Linking. Maintain this list with the Add, Edit and Delete buttons. Pretty self-explanatory.

TELL ME MORE   Media 4.4—A Discussion of the New Enhancements Within These Various Applications
Access this audio recording through your registered Web Edition at my.safaribooksonline.com/9780768695212/media.

This chapter helps you in working with media applications in Windows 7 as well as sharing and streaming your media.

5

Viewing and Sharing Media

Using Windows Media Player 12

Regardless of the media player you use (Microsoft or a third-party), you will appreciate the changes made in Windows Media Player 12. These changes will especially impress you if you are coming from a Windows XP world where you might be using Media Player 9 (or 10, if you downloaded 10 to your system). However, if you are familiar with Media Player 11, you will still see some unique and surprising new features in 12.

For starters, you will quickly note that there are two modes now. There is a separation between the library management side of the player (the Library view) and the What's Currently Playing mode (the Now Playing view). See Figure 5.1.

Media information helps identify your library's data and allows you to sort it for easy viewing. Windows Media Player automatically checks an online database for data such as cover art or information about the tracks. A nice feature is that the player can scan the Internet from time to time to match items in your library to those in an online database and fill in your missing media information.

Figure 5.1   *Windows Media Player in the Now Playing view.*

LET ME TRY IT

Adding Media to your Windows Media Player 12 Library

The following steps show you how to add media to your Media Player Library. Media Player automatically locates and adds your media files for you, but you assist it by pointing it in the direction of files that might not be in the standard locations.

1. Start Windows Media Player 12.

2. If the player opens in Now Playing mode, click the Go to Library link the middle of the screen. Otherwise, you will be opening the player in Library mode.

3. Right-click the bottom-left of the application.

4. Select File-Manage Libraries- Music. This opens the Music Library Locations dialog box.

5. Click the Add button.

6. Navigate to a folder containing music. Left-click it and choose Include Folder.

7. Repeat this process to add more music to your library.

8. Click OK.

9. In the left pane, click Music to see the new music that you've added to your library.

 **LET ME TRY IT**

Edit Your Media Information Manually in Your Library

At times, the metadata (that is the data that describes your media) is automatically detected and included within the properties of the media file. However, you might want to edit or add to that information. The following steps show you how to do this.

1. Start Windows Media Player 12.

2. Navigate to Library mode (see Figure 5.2).

3. Right-click any item in the player library, such as an artist's name, a track number, a rating, or a title.

4. Choose Edit.

5. Type the media information.

6. Click Enter.

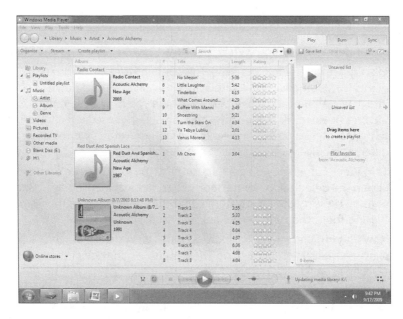

Figure 5.2   *Windows Media Player in Library view.*

After you have added files to your library, you might want to delete some. By default, Windows Media Player deletes the file in the library and on your hard drive. You can configure the option to remove the file from the library only and thus still keep the file on your hard drive.

 LET ME TRY IT

Deleting Files from the Library Only

There are times when you might want to remove a media file from the Library but not delete it from your computer. You might be prompted for your choice but the default setting is to delete from the computer when you delete from the library. The following steps show you how to change that.

1. Start Windows Media Player 12.

2. Navigate to Library mode.

3. On the top menu, click Organize and then choose Options. This opens the Options dialog box.

4. On the Library tab, uncheck the third check box, Delete Files from Computer when Deleted from Library.

5. Click Apply and then click OK (or simply click OK).

> **Comparing the Library View, the Now Playing View, and the Skin View**
>
> **Library View** (refer to Figure 5.2): This contains all the organizational elements to your media, like your playlists, as well as a breakdown of your music into Artist, Album, and Genre. Here is where you can set up ratings for music, pictures or videos as a one-stop-shop for all things media-related on the system. One interesting new aspect of the Library hierarchy is the ability to view different media types in the tree at the same time.
>
> **Skin View**: From here you get to customize the look of your Windows Media Player. The default skin has the look of a traditional media player. Get more skins by pressing the Alt key from either the Library view or the Player view, clicking Tools, choosing Download, and then clicking Skins.
>
> **Now Playing View** (refer to Figure 5.1): This view shows you the current playlist, visualizations, or videos. There is also a mini-viewer that goes on the Taskbar, as well as support for Jump Lists.

If you're wondering where all the familiar buttons and menus are, here's a tip to show the traditional menus. While in Library view, right-click anywhere in the bottom-left corner of Media Player and click Show Menu Bar. Now at the top of the application you have the traditional File, View, Play, Tools and Help menus. That looks better, doesn't it?

Windows Media Player 12 (WMP12) has a streamlined interface that fits in nicely with Windows 7. Also, in addition to adding Windows Media to the start menu, Windows 7 adds a list of recently opened audio files.

Here are some of the features:

- **Activity tabs:** Allow you to quickly select what you need:
  - The Play tab shows what loaded and playing. Doubleclicking any song skips right to it. The top shows the album title and gives you the opportunity to rate it as well.
  - From the Burn tab you can create audio CDs of your music that can be played in traditional CD players in your car or around the house. The instructions for this are in the middle-right pane where you have the choice of dragging items to create a burn list or import a play list. Once you have selected your music, click Start Burn at the top.
  - Go to the Sync tab after you have connected your computer to an MP3 player, jump drive, or other device with audio on it. Once again, you'll follow the instructions in the middle-right pane and then click Start Sync at the top.
- **Instant Search:** The search capabilities are once again an important aspect to Windows 7 features. As-you-type searching helps you quickly find your media.

- **Network Sharing:** HomeGroups simplify the sharing of your media with others in your group. In addition, WMP12 includes support for browsing iTune media libraries.

- **Stacking:** Albums that share the same characteristics (Artist, Album, Genre, Year, or Rating) are shown in "stacks," providing you with a visual reference that mimics a "stack" of CDs or records.

- **Preview:** This is a neat feature we haven't seen before. From within the Library view, you can hover your cursor over a song or video and select Preview to get a 15-second preview.

- **Codec Updates:** Support is now included for H.264 video, AAC audio, Xvid and DivX video, as well as all the supported codecs from Media Player 11 (which included MPEG2, WMV, MP3, and so forth).

- **Play To:** One of the interesting new features is the ability to Play To other computers in your HomeGroup. So music on one system can be played on another system that might have your super-cool sound system.

- **Remote Streaming to Digital Living Network Alliance v1.5 Devices:** You might have these networked devices with audio/video playback capabilities and will stream it to that device. From within the Library view, a Stream option is shown next to Organize. From here you can enable the ability to Allow Internet Access to Home Media and the ability to Allow Remote Control of My Player.

Windows Media Player 12 certainly has more than a few new features to keep you busy for a while. To take control of the application from the start, you might want to customize your navigation panes. Navigation options can be configured by clicking the Organize menu and selecting Customize Navigation Pane. This opens the Customize Navigation Pane dialog box. From here you can select the view shown for your libraries. Select the checkboxes to configure views for playlists, music, videos, pictures, recorded TV, and sync devices. If things get out of hand, simply click the Restore Defaults button at the bottom of the Customize Navigation Pane dialog box to restore the original settings and restore order back to your view.

Burning Versus Ripping: What's the Difference?

It's easy to get confused by the terms and *rip* and *burn* when talking about copying music. To clarify, we use the term *rip* when we copy music from a disk. We use *burn* when we write music to a disc. For example, you could rip a backup copy of a music CD to your My Music folder. Alternatively, if your friend emails you some music tracks that he wants you to listen to in the car, you would burn them to a CD.

To customize your rip and burn options, click the Tools menu and select Options. Let's look at some of those options now.

On the Rip Music tab (see Figure 5.3), you are first presented with the location where the music will be stored. Click the Change button to specify a new location. Keep in mind that if you rip music often, you might want to change this location often as well; otherwise all your music ends up in a big pile in one folder. Although typically you will go into this folder and begin organizing these files once they have been ripped.

Below this you can configure your Rip Settings. Choose from the style of format (such as Windows Media Audio, MP3 or WAV) and the audio quality (from 48 Kbps to 192 Kbps).

When you click the Burn tab, perhaps the most important setting to take note of is the burn speed. If you try to burn a CD and it fails, try lowering the burn speed to Medium. This often solves problems encountered when creating audio and data discs.

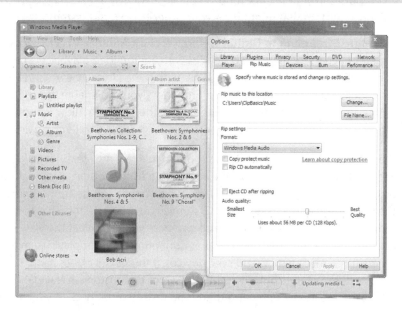

Figure 5.3   *The Rip Music tab.*

Using ratings are a nice way to help you organize your favorite media. For example, after creating ratings for some music, you can then sort your music by its rating. Windows Media Player 12 also allows you to create batch ratings of albums, songs, genres, and so forth. To do this, right-click a category, such as Artist, and then choose Rate All. Here you can choose 1 to 5 stars or you can choose Unrated. That should take the work out of rating multiple files. Once you have your songs rated, sort by your favorites to help you generate a playlist that compiles individual songs from across multiple albums, ready for your listening enjoyment.

 LET ME TRY IT

Creating a Personal Playlist

If you have a grouping of songs you want to play but these songs aren't necessarily all within the same folder, you can create playlists that help you pick and choose the music you want to play. The following steps show you how to do this.

1. Start Windows Media Player 12.

2. Navigate to Library mode.

3. If the Play tab is not selected, click it to select it.

4. Locate each song you want in your playlist and drag it to the right pane.

5. Once you have added all your songs to the playlist, click Save List on the top menu.

6. Type a descriptive name for this list.

7. To create another playlist, click Clear List on the top menu and repeat Steps 4–6.

Once you have your music selected and playing, you might be interested in adjusting the effects that are shown with the music. If you've never seen these, I recommend you get acquainted with them. To access them, start playing a music file and switch to Now Playing mode. Right-click in the center of the player. From the menu that appears, click Enhancements. With your music still playing, select Graphic Equalizer and move the controls. From the Custom drop-down, you can pick from various equalizer styles. There are plenty of other enhancements. My favorite? SRS WOW Effects. If you have a good set of speakers set far apart, crank 'em up. The result is, well...WOW.

 SHOW ME   Media 5.1—Using the Media Player
Access this video file through your registered Web Edition at
my.safaribooksonline.com/9780768695212/media.

 LET ME TRY IT

Altering the Video Border Color

There are a variety of settings that you might have never seen before or attempted to change within Windows Media Player. In the Options dialog box, there are a bevy of changes you can make that relate to performance and video playback. The following steps show you how to work within the Performance tab to alter the video border color. You should also note other settings you might want to change.

1. Start Windows Media Player 12.

2. Navigate to Library mode.

3. Click Organize and then choose Options. This opens the Options dialog box.

4. Select the Performance tab.

5. Find Video Border Color at the bottom and click the Change button.

6. In the Color box that appears, select a color and then click OK.

7. Click Apply and then click OK.

Videos that play that are not full screen now will have the border color of your choice.

In Vista and now in Windows 7, you might have noticed that video plays smoother than in XP. What accounts for the increased performance? For one thing, the Multimedia Class Scheduler boosts the priority of Media Player threads, which provides glitch-free audio and video. In addition, prioritized I/O and I/O bandwidth reservations keep the I/O pumping. The Multimedia Class Scheduler Service (MMCSS) is a new system service in Vista that runs in a svchost process through the Mmcss.dll used by Media Player. MMCSS enables multimedia applications to ensure that their time-sensitive processing receives prioritized access to CPU resources. The result? Video playback that is smoother than ever.

Windows Media Player 12 is a full-featured multimedia powerhouse with advanced audio and video playback and recording capabilities. Before installing other third-party applications to play your media, get familiar with this core feature of Windows 7.

Using Windows Media Center

Media Center was an available app for Windows XP Media Center Edition (which was only on OEM systems as a preinstalled OS). Vista users had the next version with their Home Premium and Ultimate editions. And Windows 7 includes the latest and greatest version of Media Center (see Figure 5.4).

One minor note on Windows 7 flavors and Media Center is that you must at least have Windows 7 Home Premium edition. (The Starter and Home Basic editions don't include the Media Center application or any other media capabilities (like DVD playback or DVD creation).

Figure 5.4   *Windows Media Center—The ultimate entertainment application.*

Some users like to use Media Center in lieu of Media Player on their system because they like the Media Center interface. But the true value of Media Center is that of a home-entertainment hub. It gives you the ability to leave the computer in the office and, over the network, view your media on multiple TVs using Media Center Extenders. Or you can even view your media on your Xbox 360, which features a built-in media extender. You can even search for and purchase an Media Center Extender (MCE) remote control that works with both your TV and your media options.

If you're new to Media Center, it might take a moment to get used to the navigation. It should take you two seconds to figure it out. All in all, it is very slick; it features a vertical rotating menu with arrows on the top and bottom and two buttons in the upper-left that go backto the Media Center main menu. Controls for the currently playing item are located in the lower-right of this menu and have a nice fade-away feature when they're not in use. A well-conceived, logical media environment, Media Center just gets better with each release.

For those of you wondering how to use your remote control to enter text, have no fear. Media Center provides you with an onscreen keyboard (see Figure 5.5). Onscreen instructions are provided (such as Press OK) on how to activate the keyboard. It's very simple and intuitive. A nice touch.

Figure 5.5 *Keyboard mode lets users with remote controls enter text.*

 LET ME TRY IT

Adding a Media Center Library

Newbies to Windows Media Center need to take some time configuring the Library and getting all your settings in place. The following steps show you how to do this.

1. Start Windows Media Center.

2. On the menu, navigate to Tasks and click Settings.

3. At the bottom of the list, click Media Libraries.

4. In the Select a Media Library window, choose Pictures and click Next.

5. In the Pictures window, click Add Folders to the Library and click Next.

6. Choose from one of the locations to add folders and click Next.

7. Using the checkboxes, select a location with pictures (use the plus signs to expand the folder trees).

8. Confirm changes by selecting Yes, Use These Locations and then click Finish. Media Center updates the library.

9. When completed, click the round green Windows orb in the upper-left corner.

10. On the menu, navigate to Pictures + Videos and then click Picture Library.

You can now see the folders you have added to the library.

Would you like to play games while still in Media Center? By default, seven games are enabled (these games are included within Windows 7 and can be played through Media Player but you don't have to use Media Center to play them). See Figure 5.6. These games are Chess Titans, Mahjong Titans, Spider Solitaire, Freecell, Purble Place, Hearts, and Solitaire. You will find them on the main menu under Extras-Extras Library.

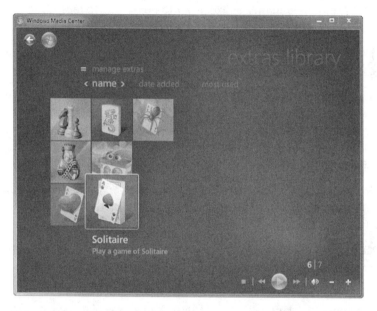

Figure 5.6 *Windows 7 Games can be played through Media Center.*

What better way to customize your Media Center than free, made-to-order downloads? Utilities such as mcePicasa (a free plug-in that lets you view Picasa and Flickr albums) let you custom fit MCE to your media. Are you a Netflix subscriber? You can use the MyNetflix add-on to view titles from the Watch Now instant library right in Media Center. Other downloads let you watch YouTube and other videos, download TV shows, record them, and encode them for playback on your iPod. Find all these and more at your favorite search engine with the search terms "Windows Media Center free plug-in" or "Windows Media Center free download."

For the most part, the interface might appear unchanged (which is nice because it makes it easier for us to feel comfortable with this new version). There are many great new features, however, including the following:

- **Dissolved Shows in Background:** When you are already watching something and you want to pull up a menu or browse the channel guide, the show you are watching dissolves into the background.

- **Thumbnail Forward/Rewind:** If you want to jump around when playing back HD video, you can move the time marker and see a thumbnail miniature of the show moving forward/backward at the same time.

- **TV Launch from Start Menu:** You can put your Media Center in the Start Menu and use a Jump List-like hover to go directly to recently recorded shows or other features you use frequently.

- **Turbo Scroll:** A chronological turbo scroll is great but now there is an alphabetical turbo scroll for media.

- **Drifting Cover Art:** This is not necessarily a functional improvement but when you are listening to a song, the album cover art appears, showing metadata included regarding that track. However, in the background, there is also cover art from other tracks in your library drifting around. Just a cool effect.

- **Scattered Photo Show:** While playing music, you can opt for a photo show of pictures in a folder of your choosing so that pictures are scattered around the screen and then Media Center will zoom in on them one at a time.

- **Copy Remote Content:** Allows you to quickly copy content when browsing other libraries or systems with Media Center.

- **Virtual Channels without TV Tuner:** With Internet video channels becoming very popular (like YouTube and Hulu), there is less of a need for a TV tuner to watch certain shows.

Customizing Media Center Settings

The MCE development team has worked hard on making Media Center a robust yet flexible application. If you don't believe it, take a peek under the hood by going to Tasks and clicking Settings.

General includes options for configuring Media Center's Startup and Window behavior, the application's Visual and Sound Effects, Parental Controls, Automatic Download Options, Optimization, and more. You can keep drilling down in each sub menu to get just the right blend for your setup.

Have you configured your display configuration in Media Center yet? A simple Wizard makes quick work of this. It's located under the next choice, TV, and the sub menu Configure Your TV or Monitor. Also from the TV menu you can set up your recording preferences, acquire your TV signal, and set up the usual language and closed captioning options.

Here's one trick to make ratings a little easier. Go to Pictures and choose Ratings. Here you can check a box that allows you to use shortcut keys to rate pictures and music as they play; the shortcut keys are the 0-5 keys on your keyboard or remote.

The Music menu features Visualizations that you can choose. However, they won't be shown until you activate them by checking the box for this on the Now Playing button (also located on the Music menu).

Other settings options include DVD, Start Menu and Extras, Extender, and Media Libraries.

There is no shortage of third-party applications you can use to burn CDs and DVDs. And some of them even do a good job. If you have the hardware that supports CD/DVD burning, you might want to check this out, especially if you're burning audio or video. Keep in mind this handles only very simple burn tasks, so don't get rid of Nero just yet.

 LET ME TRY IT

Burning a CD/DVD Using Windows Media Center

Although you might typically think of Windows Media Player when you want to burn a CD or DVD, the ability to do so is also present in Media Center. These steps will show you how.

1. Start Windows Media Center.

2. On the menu, navigate to Tasks and click Burn CD/DVD.

3. If you have not already done so, you will be prompted to insert a blank CD/DVD.

4. On the Select Disc Format screen, choose either Audio CD or Data CD and click Next.

5. Choose a name for the disc and click Next.

6. Navigate through the menu to select music for the disc. When complete, click Next.

7. You might be prompted for additional information, such as the track order. On completion, click Next.

8. Before burning the disc, you have the opportunity to review and edit the list.

9. When finished, click Burn CD to make your disc.

Just as with Media Player, Media Center (see Figure 5.7) gives you the option to sync data between your computer and a device (such as an MP3 player or jump drive). Start this option by choosing Tasks from the scrolling menu. Choices are provided for adding content according to how you have rated your media. To see more choices, an Add More option lets you choose from Music, Pictures, Videos, and Recorded TV. Although it's nice to have this feature available in Media Center, the Sync tab in Media Player just seems easier to work your way through.

Figure 5.7   *Viewing picture albums in Windows Media Center.*

Shortcut keys make quick work of common Media Center commands. Memorizing just a few will cut down on your hunting through menus to complete tasks.

Music & Radio shortcut keys (in alphabetical order)

Ctrl+A	Select radio
Ctrl I B	Replay previous song
Ctrl+F	Skip to the next song
Ctrl+Shift+F	Fast-forward through the audio
Ctrl+M	Go to music
Ctrl+P	Pause/Resume music
Ctrl+Shift+P	Pause music
Ctrl+Shift+S	Stop radio
Ctrl+R	Rip music to a CD

Video and DVD

Ctrl+Shift+A	Change the DVD audio
Ctrl+Shift+B	Rewind
Ctrl+B	Go one chapter behind
Ctrl+E	Go to videos
Ctrl+F	Go one chapter ahead
Ctrl+Shift+F	Fast-forward
Ctrl+Shift+M	Go to the DVD menu
Ctrl+Shift+P	Play current video or DVD
Ctrl+P	Pause video or DVD
Ctrl+Shift+S	Stop video or DVD
Ctrl+U	Change DVD subtitles
Arrow Keys	Change the DVD angle

Television

Ctrl+B	Skip back
Ctrl+Shift+B	Rewind
Ctrl+Shift+F	Fast-forward
Ctrl+F	Skip forward
Ctrl+G	Go to the Channel Guide
Ctrl+O	Go to Recorded TV
Ctrl+P	Pause/Resume TV show
Ctrl+Shift+P	Resume TV show
Ctrl+R	Record TV show
Ctrl+Shift+S	Stop recording or playing a TV show
Ctrl+T	Start live TV
Page Up	Go to next channel
Page Down	Go to previous channel

Pictures

Ctrl+I	Go to Pictures
Ctrl+Shift+P	Start a slideshow
Ctrl+P	Pause a slideshow
Ctrl+Shift+S	Stop a slideshow

Other

Ctrl+Shift+C	Toggle closed captioning on/off
Ctrl+D	Display the content menu
F8	Mute volume
F9	Volume down
F10	Volume up

Perhaps one of the most compelling reasons to use Media Center can be summed up in two letters: TV. Add HD to the equation and now you have my attention. In fact, you can watch programming from several different inputs. For example, setting up a TV Tuner is easier than ever with Windows Media Center. By taking advantage of Windows 7 increased hardware driver libraries, most tuners work out of the box with no additional configuration required (see Figure 5.8).

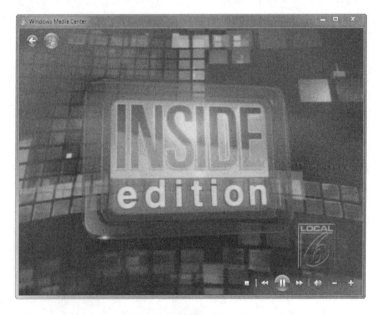

Figure 5.8 *Watching and recording HD programming.*

SHOW ME   Media 5.2—Using Media Center
Access this video file through your registered Web Edition at
my.safaribooksonline.com/9780768695212/media.

 LET ME TRY IT

Setting Up and Configuring a TV Tuner for Playback in Windows 7

To allow for incoming TV viewing, you need to setup a tuner. The following steps show you how to do this.

1. Plug in your hardware TV tuner. Windows 7 should automatically install drivers for it. If not, a Wizard prompts you with instructions to complete the installation.

2. Once the TV tuner is installed, start Windows Media Center.

3. Navigate to Tasks on the vertical ribbon menu.

4. Click Settings.

5. Click TV.

6. Choose TV Signal.

7. Click Set Up TV Signal.

8. You might receive a warning that reads Changing These Settings Will Affect TV Recording and might Interrupt TV or Radio on an Extender. Do You Want to Continue?

9. Click Yes to proceed.

10. Follow the Wizard for setting up your Internet connection. When this is complete, select your region and click Next.

11. If you agree to the Terms of Service, select I Agree and then click Next.

12. If you agree to the Microsoft PlayReady License terms, select I Agree and then click Next.

13. The Update TV Setup Data window appears, asking if you want to download new data. Click No.

14. When asked if you want to continue, click Yes. Once the installation finishes, you can return to Settings to download the guide listings.

15. At this point, Windows Media Center examines your TV signals. On successful completion, you are asked if the configuration is correct and complete. (If it was unable to detect your tuner, see the box entitled Troubleshooting your TV Connection.) If the tuner was detected, click Yes, Configure TV with These Results and then click Next.

16. A window to confirm the TV signal configuration appears. Click Next.

17. A TV channel scan begins, with updated results shown in a window below. Any over-the-air HD channels are now located by the tuner.

18. When completed, click Next.

19. On the TV Signal Setup Finished screen, click Finish.

You are returned to the TV Signal screen. Click the round green Windows logo in the upper-left corner to return to the vertical scroll menu. Scroll to and click TV and then click Live TV. That's it, your first channel loads and you're ready to watch it.

For those of you who really want to design and build the ultimate Media Center environment, you'll need all the approved dfMCE (Designed for Media Center Edition) equipment. The link http://tinyurl.com/guceo) takes you to the Microsoft site where you can download a list of components that are dfMCE-compliant. This includes DVD decoders, graphics cards, TV tuners, remote controls, and wireless routers. The document from Microsoft is "Designed for Media Center Edition Master List."

Troubleshooting Your TV Connection

UHF/VHF over-the-air television broadcasting is a thing of the past. Now that the digital transition is complete, we're all compelled to upgrade (if we haven't done so already) to watch TV. This brings its own set of problems. For those who purchase a TV tuner to receive HDTV over the air through a Windows 7 machine, you will likely be pleasantly surprised with the experience. The following are some reminders to help you ease into the process.

- Make sure your TV tuner is installed correctly before starting Windows Media Center. If it's not installed, you won't be watching TV—it's as simple as that. An easy way to verify it's working correctly is to right-click the Sound icon in the Windows 7 notification area and select Recording Devices. If you see your device in the list, all is good. If you don't see it, you need to check that it's been installed correctly. If need be, consult the hardware manufacturer's website for technical support.

- Does your antenna need power to it? Some antennas require an external power supply and won't receive a signal without it. Be sure the antenna is plugged in and also turned on if necessary.

- Speaking of antennas, make sure you have them in a position where they will receive a signal. I have had the experience of having everything working correctly but because of a bad position for my antenna, I was unable to pick up any TV signal. After setting up the tuner three times, I finally moved it in front of a window. This fourth time, the antenna picked up 18 channels. Lesson learned.

No section on Windows Media Center is complete without going over the Music Library features. Sorting through music is done by main categories: Album, Artists, Songs, Playlists, Years, and so forth. The search feature located at the top of the Music Library screen once again utilizes the on-screen keyboard for remote-control users. If you get tired of your collection, you can always listen to the radio— through Media Center, that is. Plug in your FM tuner to pick up local FM broadcasts (see Figure 5.9). There is simply no shortage of ways for you to connect to your choice of entertainment through WMC.

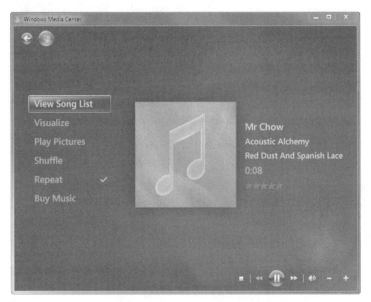

Figure 5.9 *Playing music is a breeze for Media Center.*

Volume Mixer Improvements

Don't you hate it when you are listening to a great song and you get an IM at the same time with that stupid ding sound? Well, a feature you might have missed in Vista that is still with us (thankfully) in Windows 7 is per-application volume control.

Click the audio icon in the Notification tray and open the mixer. You will see sound adjustments for several devices. You can use a volume control slider to alter the sound for every running program that produces audio output. When the program is closed, its slider is removed from the mixer options. Even though you might close a program, the volume control remembers what settings you had for that application (see Figure 5.10). So the next time you open the same app, it has the same volume settings—which is great because it means you don't have to configure sound each time. After you get the hang of it, Windows 7 will never sound the same again.

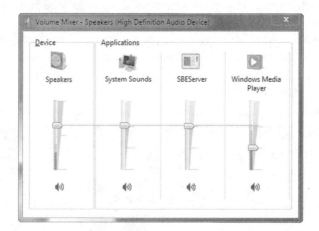

Figure 5.10 *Per-application volume control gives you more audio control.*

 **LET ME TRY IT**

Lowering Specific Application Audio

At times, you might want certain applications to be louder than others. Perhaps you have an application that provides warning or update information and you want the volume to remain pretty high. Yet with another application, you would like to reduce the volume to the bare minimum. The following steps show you how to do this.

1. Open Windows Media Player and play an audio file.

2. Right-click the Sound icon in the Windows 7 Notification area.

3. Choose Open Volume Mixer. You will see the green meter moving for both your speakers and Windows Media Player.

4. Bring the Windows Media Player down to 25.

5. Close the Volume Mixer.

Troubleshooting your audio can be done with this tool, too, because you have a green meter that shows you the sound for each device. So if you see a program is producing audio output and the green meter is responding, but you still don't hear any actual sound, it indicates that the problem is not with the application. Your speakers might be turned down or unplugged.

Turning Features On and Off

According to Microsoft, one of the ways Windows 7 applies the theme of "choice and control" is in allowing you to determine what features you want to have included. Windows 7 includes a comprehensive list that you can use to alter the features included with your Operating System. Keeping in mind that there are different definitions of what a feature is within an OS, the Windows development team listened to users who requested the ability to pull out certain pieces, such as:

- Windows Media Player
- Windows Media Center
- Windows DVD Maker
- Internet Explorer 8
- Windows Search
- Handwriting Recognition
- Windows Gadget Platform
- Fax and Scan
- XPS Viewer and Services

To turn features on or off, go to the Control Panel, open the Programs and Features applet, and click Turn Windows Features On or Off (see Figure 5.11). Here you will see all of the features you have control over, including the media features we have discussed in this chapter.

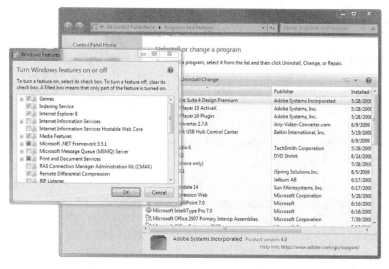

Figure 5.11   *Adding features to Windows 7.*

 **LET ME TRY IT**

Turning the Index Service

We didn't want you to turn a feature on or off accidentally, so we picked the Index Service for this exercise because it isn't your Windows 7 index for search (which is handled a little further down on the list under Windows Search, which is on by default) but your legacy index service that is off by default. The following steps show you how to turn it on and then turn it off again (just as how you might do it with another option).

1. Click the Start orb.

2. Open the Control Panel.

3. Click Programs and Features.

4. In the upper-left pane, click Turn Windows Features On or Off.

5. Select the Indexing Service checkbox and click OK. This opens a window stating Please Wait While Windows Makes Changes to Features. This Might Take Several Minutes.

6. After it is complete, click Turn Windows Features On or Off.

7. You will see the second checkbox has a check mark in it, indicating the program is already installed. If you prefer, you can uncheck the box to remove it. Then click OK.

Media Streaming

Sharing has become much easier to implement and configure, two enhancements that certainly were needed in the area of media sharing. The features introduced in Vista were appreciated but somewhat difficult to work with at times. Now, from within the HomeGroup, you can click a checkbox that reads Stream My Pictures, Music and Videos to All Devices on My Home Network. If you want to change your media streaming options, click the link and you will be taken to the first options screen for media sharing.

The Choose Media Streaming Options for Computers and Devices dialog box (see Figure 5.12) allows you to configure some basic settings.

Figure 5.12   *Choosing media streaming options.*

One thing you will note is that you can choose to allow or block certain media on the PC. You can quickly click the Allow All or Block All buttons or you can select the device and click the Allow or Block option.

In addition, you can filter the items that are shared either by establishing default settings or by customizing it on an individual settings basis by selecting the Customize option (see Figure 5.13). Note that you can use Choose Star Ratings to determine what is streamed (and you can even decide if you want to share unrated files). You can also use the Choose Parental Ratings option.

SHOW ME   Media 5.3—Sharing Media
Access this video file through your registered Web Edition at
my.safaribooksonline.com/9780768695212/media.

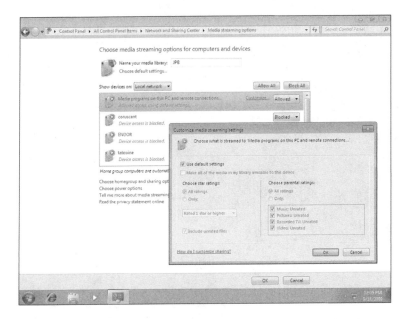

Figure 5.13   *Customizing media streaming options.*

 LET ME TRY IT

Using Media Streaming

1. Assuming you already have a HomeGroup established (if you do not, please see Chapter 8, "Networking with Windows 7"), you can locate your Media Sharing options by going to your Control Panel and choosing the HomeGroup applet (or by choosing your Network and Sharing Center and then clicking the Choose HomeGroup and Sharing Options link).

2. From within the HomeGroup settings you have two different concepts to consider. A top section (see Figure 5.14) allows you to click checkboxes to share your libraries. Some of your libraries include media elements, but this is not the same as media sharing or streaming; it is simply sharing of folders (or libraries) with others on your network. To enable media streaming, select Stream My Pictures, Music, and Videos to All Devices on my Home Network.

3. Click Choose Media Streaming Options.

4. At this point, you can name your media library.

5. If you click Choose Default Settings, you can determine the star rating.

6. Under the Star Rating section, click the Only radio button.

7. Choose the number of stars you want displayed as part of your media streaming options.

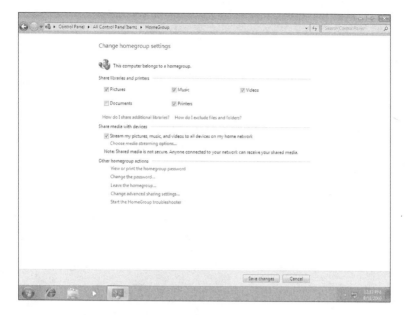

Figure 5.14   *Homegroup settings.*

8.   Click OK.

You can also determine who is allowed or blocked from accessing your streaming media library. You have complete control over who has access to you.

Media Sharing might evoke different sentiments in different people. Parents working on two different systems in the home might see it as an opportunity for each of them to access the family photo album of their kids. However, the fear that certain media on your system might be inappropriate for the 'whole family' to view (for example, perhaps you don't want your kids listening to Pearl Jam just yet, but it is part of your Music settings) might make you wince at the idea of being so open. Using star ratings or parental settings can help you keep some of those things in check. Share what you want without moving Pearl Jam to another folder that isn't in the Music library (although that is another option if you do not want to work with star or parental settings).

 TELL ME MORE   Media 5.4—A Discussion with a Well-Known **Media Center Guru About the Changes in Windows 7**
Access this audio recording through your registered Web Edition at
my.safaribooksonline.com/9780768695212/media.

This chapter provides an in-depth look at Internet
Explorer 8.0.

6

Internet Explorer 8.0

The Evolution of IE8

Microsoft has been losing market share to Mozilla's Firefox browser over the past few years. Many would admit that Firefox is the first thing they installed after installing their OS. IE7 was Microsoft's first shot at redeeming itself and it did a pretty decent job of that. IE8 hopes to continue to push through the battle with Firefox, Safari, and newcomer Google Chrome. It's doubtful any one will be proclaimed the victor. Sometimes it is just a matter of what you are used to.

Even if you are not using Windows 7, you can download IE8 from the Microsoft site. There is, however, a distinction between IE8 solo and IE8 with Windows 7. Windows 7 allows for certain unique features and functionality, like Windows Touch and Jump Lists, which you won't have if you install IE8 on XP or Vista.

Would you like to take a visual tour through the features of IE8? Then watch the following video.

 SHOW ME   Media 6.1—A Tour of Internet Explorer 8.0
Access this video file through your registered Web Edition at
my.safaribooksonline.com/9780768695212/media.

There are features in IE7 that have continued in moving forward with IE8. For example, one thing IE7 finally included was tabbed browsing. But the feature we really like is that there is always a tab waiting for us (it's always slightly annoying that Firefox doesn't have that; Google Chrome does have that feature, however). You can press Ctrl+T in both Firefox and IE7 to bring up a new tab; it's nice that IE8 has a new tab sitting on the tab bar whenever we need it.

 LET ME TRY IT

Using Tabbed Browsing in IE8

The following steps show you how to open new tabs in the browser. This allows you to quickly switch between several websites. While this is very simple to execute, it can be a very powerful technique for viewing multiple Web pages.

1. Click your Internet Explorer icon on the Taskbar.

2. Note your initial tab automatically loads IE. This is your home page (or pages—if you have multiple home pages already configured).

3. Click the little tab outcropping located to the right of your existing tab (see Figure 6.1). This opens a new tab.

4. Press and hold the Ctrl button and then press the letter T to open another new tab.

Some additional features that carry over from IE7 are covered in the following sections.

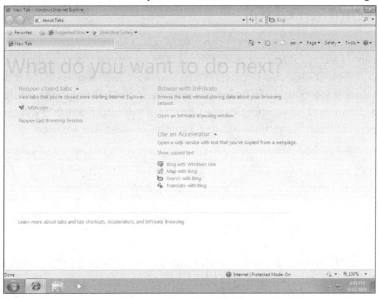

Figure 6.1   *Internet Explorer with a New Tab showing.*

Quick Tabs

This allows you to see all your open tabs in mini windows (see Figure 6.2). Quick Tabs provides a thumbnail view of your tabs so you can visually identify the pages you are working with, which is something that becomes more difficult as you open more tabs.

 LET ME TRY IT

Using Quick Tabs

1. Open your IE browser from the Start menu by clicking Internet Explorer. Or you can open IE8 from a shortcut on your desktop if you happen to have one.

2. Open three or four Web pages on different tabs by clicking on the available tab or by keying Ctrl+T and typing a new Web address in the Address Bar.

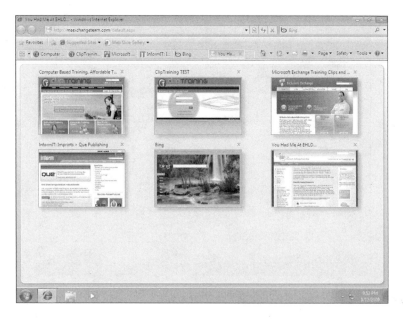

Figure 6.2   *Quick Tabs can be accessed using the Quick Tabs button or by pressing Ctrl+Q.*

3. There a few ways to view thumbnails of all tabs:
   - Go to the Menu bar, click View, and then select Quick Tabs.
   - Click the Quick Tabs button to the left of all the tabs (it looks like four little boxes together).
   - Press Ctrl+Q on your keyboard.

There is also a drop-down button (right next to the Quick Tabs icon) that lists all the tabs you have open. This is a quick way to see which pages are open (which becomes more difficult when you have more tabs open because you cannot see all the tabs).

Tab Settings

You can adjust many of the settings for your tabs. To accomplish this, click the Tools drop-down arrow, select Internet Options, and then on the General tab, click Settings next to the Tabs category (see Figure 6.3). Some of the items you can change include the following:

- Enable Tabbed Browsing
- Warn Me When Closing Multiple Tabs
- Always Switch to New Tabs When They are Created
- Show Previews for Individual Tabs in the Taskbar
- Enable Quick Tabs
- Enable Tab Groups
- Open Only the First Home Page When Internet Explorer Starts

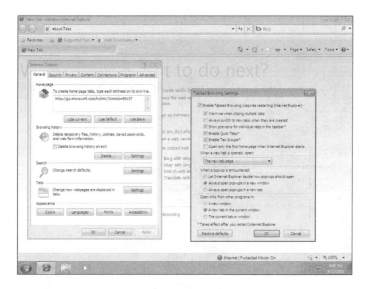

Figure 6.3   *The Tabbed Browsing Settings dialog box.*

You can also determine how you want a new tab to be opened and how you want a link opened, so that when you click a hyperlink on a Web page, it opens in a new window, opens a new tab of the current window, or the current tab of the current window—lots of options to work with.

 LET ME TRY IT

Modifying your Tabbed Browsing Settings

The following steps show you how to change how tabs open after you click hyperlinks on Web pages. Use this feature to customize your view of opening Web pages. Pay attention to the variety of choices and return to these steps to try out different options.

1. From within Internet Explorer, click the Tools drop-down arrow and select Internet Options.

2. On the General tab, look for the Tabs category and click Settings.

3. Ensure that all of the current settings are those you prefer for your tabs. (Typically, you want links to open as new tabs in the current window.)

Tab Groups: Grouped Favorites and Multiple Home Pages

Carried forward from IE7, you can open up a collection of tabs and then select an option to Add Current Tabs to Favorites. This allows you to select that group with one click and open it all at once.

LET ME TRY IT

Saving a Collection of Tabs to Favorites

Follow these steps to discover a fast way to store multiple Web pages to your favorites. Then, return later to open them all instantly.

1. Open all the desired Web pages in separate tabs.
2. Go to the Menu bar and click Favorites.
3. Select the drop-down arrow next to Add to Favorites.
4. Select Add Current Tabs to Favorites.

You are presented with an option to name the folder for this group and, if needed, you can create the folder within another Favorites folder.

 **LET ME TRY IT**

Setting Up More Than One Home Page to Open

After completing the following steps, you can have several different home pages open at the same time when you start your browser. In addition to saving time, it also ensures you are opening the correct URL every time.

1. Go to the Menu bar, click Tools, and then choose Internet Options.
2. On the General tab, in the Home Page box, type more than one Web address. Each address should be on a separate line.

Alternatively, you can do the following:

1. Open the Web pages you would like to have as home pages in separate tabs.
2. Select the drop-down option next to the House icon in the Command Bar and select Add or Change Homepage.
3. You are presented with three options:
   • Use This Webpage as Your Only Home Page
   • Add This Webpage to Your Home Page Tabs
   • Use the Current Tab Set as Your Home Page
4. Select Use the Current Tab Set as Your Home Page.

I know for myself personally, when I open my browser, I like to see my email accounts (Yahoo, Gmail, and so forth), the news, and a fresh Google site for me to begin my work. In previous versions of IE, this wasn't possible to create. But with IE7 and continuing in IE8, it is a staple feature.

In the Tabbed Browsing Settings dialog box, you can select the option to only Open Only the First Home Page When IE Starts. This is a nice feature if you're distracted by too many pages showing at once. You can still open all the home pages by selecting the Home button on the toolbar.

Additional IE7 Features Carried Over to IE8

Some of the additional improvements carried over from IE7 include the following:

- **Printing Settings:** It was frustrating in the past to print certain Web pages because the right side of the page was cut off so often. Many users would copy what they wanted to print into a Word document and then print the Word document. You could also change the mode to Landscape and print this way so that it printed the whole page; however, this approach used more paper. Now there is a Shrink to Fit setting that ensures the page prints on paper of any size. You also now have a Print Preview window that allows you to manipulate your print settings.

- **Search Toolbar:** To the right of the Address Bar is the Search bar. There are search providers you can choose from, plus you can actually add extra ones if you like. There is an arrow to the right of the Search bar that allows you to add additional search providers (for example, you can add a YouTube search).

 LET ME TRY IT

Adding Search Providers

The following steps show you how to choose from a variety of search providers and select your default provider when performing a search from within the browser. Also, after completing these steps, you can add search providers that you can quickly switch to just before perfroming a search.

1. Click the Down arrow to the right of the Search bar and select Find More Providers. This will bring you to a gallery of search providers (see Figure 6.4).

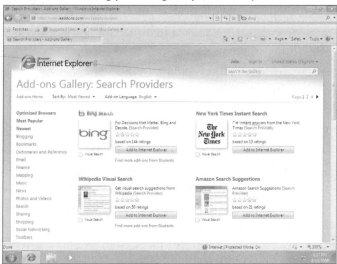

Figure 6.4   *The Add-ons Gallery: Search Providers page.*

2. When you find a search provider that you would like to add, just click the Add to Internet Explorer button.

3. You will then be able to select if you want this search provider to be the default search engine and if you would like to use search suggestions from this provider. Make your selections and click Add.

- **Zoom:** Another great feature, it allows you to increase the size of both text and graphics of a page. You can increase (Ctrl +), decrease (Ctrl -), or return to 100% (Ctrl+0).

- **Supports RSS Feeds:** RSS Feeds are supported and located under the Favorites settings under Feeds. You can find settings for Feeds under the Tools, Internet Options, Content under the Feeds and Web Slices section, Settings button. You can easily see if a site has an RSS feed because the orange square on the Command Bar lights up when you are on a site with a feed.

Using New Features in IE8

IE8 is not a minor upgrade from 7—it doesn't havejust a few new bells and whistles. It actually has a bevy of important features that make your browsing experience more enjoyable and safer.

The following section details some features that are new to IE8.

Suggested Sites

This is an online service that uses your browsing history to make personalized website suggestions. It can be turned on or off at any time (it is turned off by default). To turn it on or off, click the Tools button and then choose Suggested Sites (from where you can choose to turn it on or off).

It might take a little bit of time for the browser to collect information regarding your patterns, but once it has enough information, you can go to the Favorites menu and choose Suggested Sites Web Slice to locate suggestions.

 LET ME TRY IT

Using Suggested Sites

The following steps show you how to turn on the Suggested Sites feature. Use this feature to be automatically provided with simliar websites based on your browsing history.

1. Click the Suggested Sites button that is next to your Favorites options. Note you have to Turn On Subscribing to Web Slices first. Click that link.

2. You are asked to confirm that you want To Turn On Automatic Feed Updates. Click Yes.

3. Now that Web Slices is turned on, when you click the Suggested Sites button again, you are provided with a Turn On Suggested Sites link. Click the link.

4. You are asked Do You Want to Discover Websites You Might Like Based On Websites You've Visited? Click Yes to turn on the feature.

Before it makes any suggestions, it sees what sites you visit. In this demonstration, we visited technology oriented sites. Then we clicked Suggested Sites and, as shown in Figure 6.5, we were given additional sites we haven't visited before.

Figure 6.5   *Suggested Sites.*

You can also turn on Suggested Sites by clicking the Favorites button and, at the bottom of the dialog, selecting the Turn On Suggested Sites link. Click Yes to use the service.

One thing to keep in mind is that Suggested Sites will not work if you have turned on InPrivate Browsing (discussed in the next section) because that would be a conflict of the concept of 'private' browsing. It is also disabled if you visit a SSL-secured site. You see, the way Suggested Sites works is by sending your browsing history to Microsoft, where it is compared to related websites.

This feature is something that most users are not pleased about. Microsoft has said they will not store this information, but at the same time, the Windows Help and Support information says that even items deleted from your browsing history "will be retained by Microsoft for a period of time to help improve our products and services." So, it's your choice as to whether you want to enable this new feature.

Accelerators

The idea behind accelerators (see Figure 6.6) is to allow you to do in one (or a few) clicks what used to take you more; you can use cutting and pasting, among other editing tools, to accomplish various tasks. The tasks include mapping locations, translation of words, and more.

Figure 6.6   *Accelerators in action.*

You select the text you need and then you will see a little blue square accelerator icon that you can click to obtain directions, see a definition, get a translation, email content, search for information—all with a click or two.

You can also select More Accelerators to go to the Add-ons Gallery so that you can select other items that might be more in line with what you typically do on the Web.

LET ME TRY IT

Using the IMDB Accelerator

At times you might be reading an article in the news and you want more information about the person within the article. That person might be a political figure, a sports figure, or a member of the entertainment world. If the latter, the Internet Movie Database (IMDB) accelerator can prove to be very helpful. Follow these steps to access this feature.

1. Locate a news article with a famous movie person in the text. (In our example, we went to www.cnn.com/SHOWBIZ to find an entertainment personality.)

2. Find the name of an actor or actress and select the text on the screen.

3. When the blue box appears, you will see that there is no IMDB accelerator shown. Click the All Accelerators link.

4. Click Find More Accelerators.

5. Search within the Gallery for the IMDB accelerator and add it to Internet Explorer.

6. You are asked, Do You Want to Add This Accelerator? (see Figure 6.7). Click Add.

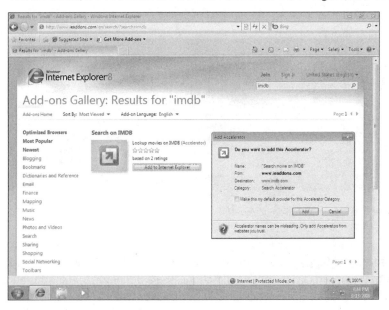

Figure 6.7   *Adding the IMDB accelerator.*

Now when you select the name of this actor or actress, you will see an option in accelerators to Search IMDB. Click that link to have the name automatically researched on the movie database site.

Web Slices

Web Slices are also known as "automatic feed updates" and they have to be turned on to work. The concept is that your system periodically checks online for updates to specific feeds, much in the same way you might check for RSS feeds for blog posts and other RSS-enabled sites. But this is a "slice" of that and the checks will be made even if IE isn't on.

eBay is a great example. You find an item you've been looking for and you want to bid on it. You want to be notified how the bidding is going but you don't want to keep the whole eBay site up. If you have enabled Web Slices for eBay, you will see the RSS feed button light up green (rather than orange).

You can do one of two things to subscribe to a Web Slice. You can locate the item on the page that has the slice established and hover your mouse over it to display a green square. You can click the square, which displays the Add a Web Slice dialog box, where you can click Add to Favorites Bar or click Cancel. The other way you can subscribe it is to select the Down arrow next to the green square on the Command Bar (see Figure 6.8) and select the slice you want. Sometimes this might be easier on an eBay site, where there are many slices to choose from.

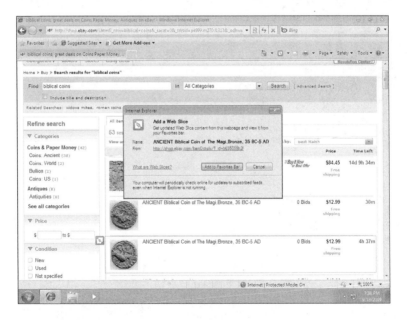

Figure 6.8   *Web Slices in action.*

One you have added a slice, it will display in your Favorites Bar. You will know when the item has changed because it will go from standard text to bolded text. You can see information about that item by selecting the Web Slice from the Favorites Bar.

SHOW ME Media 6.2—Accelerators and Web Slices
Access this video file through your registered Web Edition at
my.safaribooksonline.com/9780768695212/media.

LET ME TRY IT

Adding a Web Slice

The following steps show you how to set up a Web Slice for a stock market quote. After completing these steps, results will automatically update without having to open IE.

Although eBay is an excellent example of working with a Web Slice, a stock site might be a better example. Rather than having to return to a site and constant look for updates, you can Web slice the stock and be updated more regularly directly within the browser without going to the site.

1. Go to Bing (www.bing.com) and search for a stock quote you want to follow or one that you are already invested in.

2. Hover your mouse above the quote and look for the green Web Slick button to appear (see Figure 6.9).

Figure 6.9 *Web Slices in action.*

3. Click the Web Slice button. The Add a Web Slice dialog appears.

4. Click Add to Favorites Bar.

Now you can see the stock quote as it changes (see Figure 6.10), including the P/E Ratio, 52 Week Range, Market Cap, and more.

Figure 6.10   *Web Slices in action.*

Microsoft makes it clear that Web Slices "may not update in real-time and cannot be relied upon for obtaining up-to-the-second stock quotes. Also note that quote values may differ between services, even between Bing and MSN Money."

If you right-click the Web Slice for any given link and choose Properties, the Web Slice Properties dialog appears (see Figure 6.11). If needed, you can set a User Name and Password. You can also adjust the schedule to use either the default schedule or a custom schedule.

Want to see the Accelerators and Web Slices features in action? Then watch the following video.

Compatibility View

Sometimes Web developers need to redesign a site (in some cases requiring some necessary compatibility alterations for new browsers), but they haven't done it before a new browser is released. In those cases, you might go to a site and it won't look right or display data correctly. IE8 provides a Compatibility View feature, which is located to the right of the Address Bar. The button for Compatibility View automatically appears when you reach a page that is not compatible. Simply click this

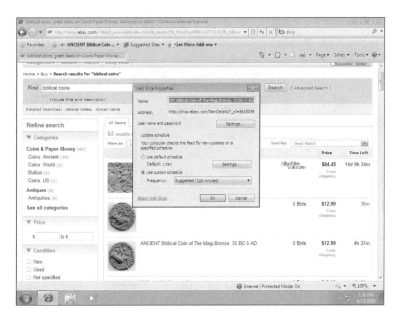

Figure 6.11 *Altering the Web Slices schedule.*

button to request IE8 to fix the page to display it in a way that works with the former coding. IE8 remembers your request the next time you visit the page, too.

Go to the Tools menu and choose Compatibility View Settings to add sites that should always be viewed in Compatibility View or to remove sites that have been added to the list.

There are several checkboxes you can choose, too, including:

- Include Updated Website Lists from Microsoft
- Display Intranet Sites in Compatibility View
- Display all Websites in Compatibility View

Working with Security Enhancements

Internet Explorer has been around for a little over a decade and has been riddled with so many security holes that over the past few years it has been losing ground to other browsers. With the release of IE7, Microsoft recaptured some of the market by matching the feature sets of newer browsers and also plugging the security holes. Internet Explorer certainly turned the security corner with IE7 and this continued commitment to security is shown clearly in IE8.

One point to mention with IE7 (and now IE8) is that IE is no longer integrated with Windows Explorer. Now when you perform an operation such as opening a file, or trying to view a Web page, each process takes over and performs its own task; they are not joined, and this is a major security enhancement.

You will find your security options in two locations. There is now an entire Safety drop-down button located on the IE8 toolbar (see Figure 6.12). You can also locate additional security settings by going to Tools and choosing Internet Options, where you can locate items on the Security, Privacy, and Advanced tabs.

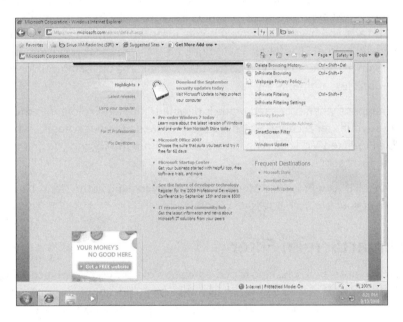

Figure 6.12   *Safety options.*

Protected Mode

On the anti-spyware/malware front, IE8 (like IE7) helps to protect us with a new Protected Mode. This works off of User Account Control features which will be discussed in a later chapter. Essentially, Protected Mode has IE working under restricted settings so that a standard user cannot do much more than simply search the Web. No software installation (or worse, malware sneakily installing itself), no file changes without you being aware, no changing your home page or search engine settings—in short, none of the things that make you want to scream. This is because IE8 is allowed to play only in its own sandbox, isolated from all the other applications or processes. Data can be written only to the Temporary Internet Files folder and this folder also has restrictions, so a fence is put around it as well.

> As great as Protected Mode is, you can turn it off. Go to your IE settings by clicking Tools, choosing Internet Options, and then selecting the Security tab. Uncheck the Enable Protected Mode (Requires Restarting Internet Explorer) check box.

Now what happens when a program wants to get out from under this protection? Let's say you download something and you really do want it to run. There is a broker process that asks for your permission so that you absolutely know what is going on and you have to approve it before it can write anywhere other than the Temporary Internet Files folder. That's right, no malware sneaking in without your permission (so make sure you read the boxes that come up asking you for permission—don't just arbitrarily say yes).

What happens when Protected Mode is disabled? Internet Explorer has the same ability as your user account, which is a much more dangerous scenario. When you disable Protected Mode, IE is no longer isolated from the OS and you aremore vulnerable to attack.

You can tell if your Protected Mode is on or off by looking at the status bar at the bottom of your browser. It tells you very clearly.

The SmartScreen Filter

Protecting users from phishing is part education of your users, part technology. The scenario is simple. A user gets an email from a bank (possibly even what appears to be their bank) or another merchant that is familiar to them (like Amazon, eBay or PayPal), asking for some information. If the user thinks the site is valid and doesn't know how to determine otherwise, he is at risk of providing information that might breach his financial or personal identity. The user provides his information and then the site redirects him to the real company site so that the user doesn't even know that they've been tricked.

These sites look so real sometimes that it can be very difficult for users to know otherwise. In IE7, Microsoft introduced a Phishing Filter into the browser to help protect users. The Phishing Filter helps by notifying your users if a site is suspicious. It can do this by comparing the site address that you type into your Address window to a list of known phishing sites already on your computer. If you type a site that isn't on that list, but seems suspicious, it checks that site automatically, too. Sites are sent to a Microsoft server for confirmation. This provides up-to-the-minute security for users because these servers are updated constantly with new phishing sites. This global database is maintained by a list of providers as well as by user reports that come in from users who stumble upon sites that appear "phishy."

In IE8, Microsoft has built upon the feature set of the Phishing Filter and provided a SmartScreen Filter. According to the IE Team at Microsoft, this new filter improves upon the Phishing Filter in the following ways:

- An enhanced user interface
- Increased performance
- Advanced heuristics and telemetry
- Support for anti-malware
- Better support for Group Policy

 LET ME TRY IT

Turning On the Smart Screen Filter

The following steps show you how to turn on this new feature of IE8. Once you complete the steps, advanced security features will be enabled. You will be notified while browsing the Internet if the software detects a known threatening website.

1. Open Internet Explorer and click the Safety button located on the top-right of the browser.

2. Select SmartScreen Filter and then click Turn on SmartScreen Filter.

3. A dialog appears, asking you if you want to turn on the SmartScreen Filter. Select that option and click OK.

What Happens When You Go to a Suspicious or Bad Site?

When you come upon a site that the SmartScreen Filter knows is a scam, the Address Bar turns red and the message This Website Has Been Reported as Unsafe appears with a startling red background (see Figure 6.13).

Figure 6.13 shows a response from a true malware site that was reported. There are many sites that offer you a full, day-to-day rundown of new phishing sites.

You'll notice that it recommends you don't proceed and offers for you to Go to My Home Page Instead. Typically, depending on the site, you can continue to the bad site if you really want to.

If you happen to come upon a site that isn't clearly a phishing site but IE is suspicious for some reason, the Address Bar background turns yellow and a Suspicious Website message appears in the Security Report section.

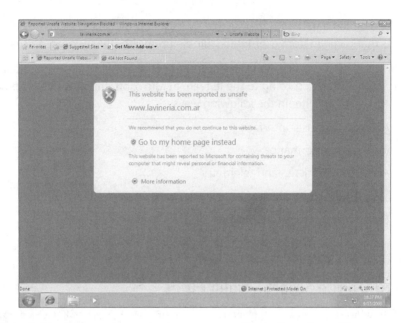

Figure 6.13 *No way to ignore the danger presented by the SmartScreen Filter.*

 LET ME TRY IT

Testing Your SmartScreen Filter

The following steps show you how to test your SmartScreen Filter. Once you complete these steps, you will see the warning messages provided for suspicious websites.

1. Open Internet Explorer and click the Safety button located on the top-right of your browser.

2. Select SmartScreen Filter and ensure your filter is turned on.

3. Search for a site that provides phishing information, such as www.phish-tank.com

4. Locate one of the recent submissions and copy the URL.

5. Paste the URL for the suspicious site into your address bar of a new tab or window.

Note the way your Internet Explorer responds with a reddish border and red address bar.

If you stumble upon a new phishing site or one you are suspicious of, you can click the Safety button, select SmartScreen Filter, and then then choose one of the following:

• Check This Website

- Turn Off SmartScreen Filter (not recommended)

- Report Unsafe Website

What Does "Advanced Heuristics and Telemetry" Mean?

Well, new scams are coming out all the time. And it is important to catch these scams and phishing attacks early so that others can be protected. Sometimes the SmartScreen filter sees something odd and actually requests feedback from you (see Figure 6.14). That feedback helps in determining if a site should be watched or blocked.

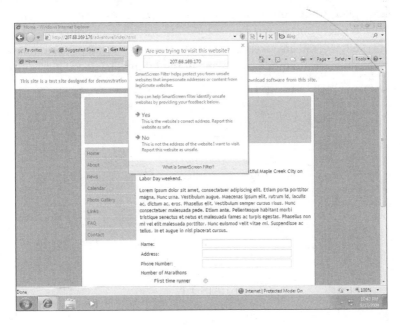

Figure 6.14 *Sometimes you can assist the SmartScreen Filter determine the reputation of a site.*

Why Do We Need Anti-Malware Support?

Some might have other assistance to protect against malware: Windows Defender, Windows Live OneCare, the Malicious Software Removal Tool, and so forth. However, if a site is known to distribute malware, the SmartScreen Filter protects you based upon the reputation of the URL. So this aspect is not meant to replace any of the tools you currently trust to protect you; it simply provides another layer or support.

InPrivate Browsing

There are times when you aren't working from your home system. You might be at a conference, at a training session for work, at an Internet café, and so on. And perhaps you want to protect yourself from IE storing information about your browsing session. In times past, you might have deleted your browsing history. (To delete your browsing history in IE8, click the new Safety button and choose Delete Browsing History at the top.) You can, however, use the new InPrivate browsing option to prevent IE from storing data (including cookies, temporary internet files, browsing history, and so forth) during your browsing session.

To turn it on, you can use a Jump List task for an immediate opening of IE with InPrivate already turned on. Another way to turn it on is from within IE8, where you can click the Safety button and choose InPrivate Browsing (or simply use the shortcut keys Ctrl+Shift+P). You are taken to a new browser instance, where you can clearly see you are in InPrivate mode by looking at the Address bar (see Figure 6.15).

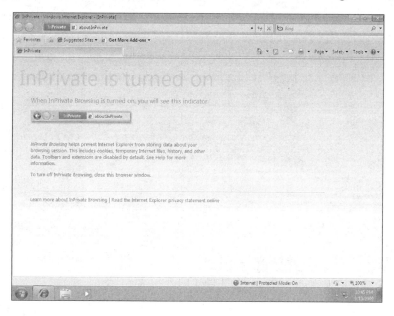

Figure 6.15   *Using InPrivate Browsing.*

 **LET ME TRY IT**

Starting an InPrivate Browsing Session

The following steps show you how to turn on InPrivate Browsing. Once it's activated, IE8 doesn't track the history or record of the websites you visit.

1. Open Internet Explorer and click the Safety button located on the top-right of your browser.

2. Select InPrivate Browsing and a new window opens.

Now you can surf wherever you like and then simply close the window to maintain your privacy.

InPrivate Filtering

Under the Safety button option, you might notice InPrivate Filtering. This is not the same as InPrivate Browsing. This is a separate feature you can enable that is designed to protect you from websites collecting information about you.

Perhaps you have seen this before. You go to a website and all of a sudden there are advertisements that are customized according to where you live. That can be a little odd. Some sites create a profile of you to be used to simply analyze what you click on or to create a targeted advertisement. Typically the advertisement you see is integrated directly with the site you visited.

If you do not want this kind of tracking, you can do one of two things. You can turn on the InPrivate Filter and let it automatically block a content provider for you, or you can manually choose which providers will receive your information and which ones will be blocked.

To turn this feature on, click the tools button and choose InPrivate Filtering. If it is the first time you are using this tool, you're asked if you want the tool to handle it automatically or if you want to perform the task manually. It is up to you. Once this is done, you can always go back and change your mind by selecting the InPrivate Filtering Settings link, which shows you the various options available to you (see Figure 6.16).

Want to see how InPrivate Browsing and InPrivate Filtering can protect you better while you surf? Then watch the following video.

SHOW ME   **Media 6.3—InPrivate Browsing and Filtering**
Access this video file through your registered Web Edition at
my.safaribooksonline.com/9780768695212/media.

Additional IE Features

The following section covers are a few more features we should mention so we don't leave important items out.

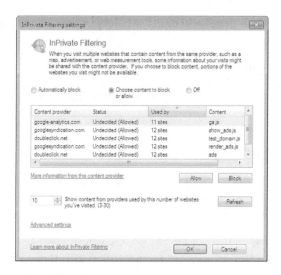

Figure 6.16   *Using InPrivate Filtering settings.*

Add-Ons

What exactly are Add-Ons? ActiveX controls, browser extensions, browser helper objects or toolbars, and so forth. Sometimes we love certain add-ons, such as Flash players, because it expands IE's ability to give us more animated or interesting content. However, some add-ons can cause problems. They might also cause pop-ups or they might contain spyware.

With IE8, you can actually start your browser with a No Add-Ons version of the browser. To do this, click Start, Programs Accessories, System Tools, Internet Explorer (No Add-Ons).

   LET ME TRY IT

Control Add-ons Allowed Within Internet Explorer

The following steps show you how to take full control of your add-ons. Enable or disable specific Add-Ons if your browser is running slow or crashes unexpectedly. This works great for troubleshooting problems in Internet Explorer.

1. Click the Tools menu and then choose Manage Add-Ons. The Manage Add-ons dialog box appears.

2. To see each add-on and its status, click each button on the left of the dialog box (see Figure 6.17). You can configure these add-ons from this window. These buttons include the following:

   • Toolbars and Extensions
   • Search Providers

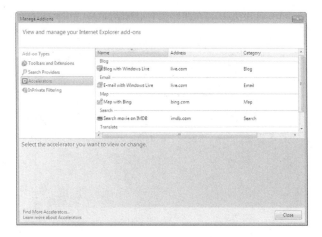

Figure 6.17 *Configuring add-on settings.*

- Accelerators
- InPrivate Filtering

3. You can also gain access to the Add-on gallery by clicking the Add-On type and then clicking the Find More link in the lower-left corner.

Pop-Up Blocker

Pop-ups are seen more as an annoyance than a security breach but we will include them here anyway. Under Tools, Pop-Up Blocker you will find the options Turn On/Off Pop-Up Blocker and Pop-Up Blocker Settings.

The Pop-Up Blocker Settings allow you to determine which website (if any) you want to allow as well as to choose Notifications and Blocking Level. You can enable a sound for when a pop-up is blocked. You can also show an Information Bar when a pop-up is blocked. Finally, you can set the Blocking Level to Low, Medium (the default), or High.

 LET ME TRY IT

Using Pop-Up Blocker

Modifying your pop-up blocker settings can help stop annoying pop-up windows. The following steps show you how to set the blocking level to low, medium or high and how to choose which sites you want to allow through Pop-Up Blocker.

1. Click the Tools menu, hover over Pop-Up Blocker and then select Pop-Up Blocker Settings. (This selection is unavailable if Pop-up Blocker is turned off.)

2. The Pop-up Blocker Settings dialog box appears (see Figure 6.18).

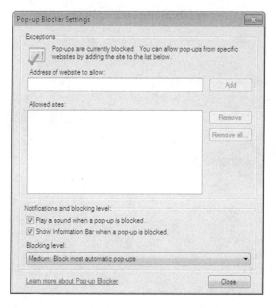

Figure 6.18 *Pop-Up Blocker settings.*

3. The top portion of this dialog box enables you to enter sites for which you would like to allow pop-ups. Type the site address and then click Add. The address now appears in the list of Allowed Sites.

4. You can also remove sites from the Allowed Sites list by selecting the site and clicking the Remove button. The Remove All button speaks for itself.

5. The lower portion of the dialog box is where you can enable/disable the following:
   • Play a Sound When a Pop-Up is Blocked
   • Show Information Bar When a Pop-Up is Blocked

6. At the very bottom of the dialog box you can set the Blocking Level:
   • High—Block All Pop-Ups
   • Medium—Block Most Automatic Pop-Ups
   • Low—Allow Pop-Ups From Secure Sites

Security Report

When you are on a site that shows a green bar (indicating that it's a site using website identification), you can click the lock to the right of the Address bar and it shows you if the site has been verified and by whom. You can find this same security report by clicking the Safety button and choosing Security Report. However, keep in mind that this feature isn't available on all sites. It's available only for those sites that have a report connected with their sites.

 TELL ME MORE   Media 6.4—A Discussion with Jack Blovits **About Some of the New IE8 Features**
Access this audio recording through your registered Web Edition at
my.safaribooksonline.com/9780768695212/media.

This chapter covers several security features integrated into Windows 7 and shows how to configure them.

7

Using Security Features in Windows 7

User Account Control (UAC) Improvements

You may be thinking, "Improvements? I don't know this feature at all, much less how it might now be improved." Well, with XP, we didn't have User Account Control (UAC). This was a newcomer in Vista and it received both praise and criticism depending on who was on the soapbox for the day. Let's review what UAC is designed to do and then we will show you the mini-improvements that makes this technology more palatable to users.

In-Depth Look at UAC

UAC was dubbed the "most hated new feature of Vista" and yet that was likely because users weren't really sure what its purpose was. To truly appreciate it, you have to think about pre-Vista Windows operating systems. Usually users were either provided with administrative privileges to make certain system changes or they were locked down so that they couldn't even change their system clock time without an administrator's help. There needed to be a balance. UAC strives to achieve that balance by giving standard users more abilities with their own systems without giving so much freedom that they expose their systems to security risks.

Here are a few of the new abilities that standard users now have:

- View system clock and calendar
- Change time zone
- Install Wired Equivalent Privacy (WEP) to connect to secure wireless networks
- Change power management settings
- Add printers and other devices that have the required drivers installed on their computers or have been allowed by an administrator in Group Policy
- Install ActiveX Controls from sites approved by an administrator

- Create and configure a Virtual Private Network connection

- Install critical Windows Updates

- Change the desktop background and modify display settings

- Use Remote Desktop to connect to another computer

All users (including admins) run in a standard mode. This is what frustrated admins working with Vista, but we will get to that soon enough. Let's first consider how this benefits admins and users alike. With Windows 7, users now have more ability and this allows them to do their work without having admin privileges and without bothering the administrator. In addition, standard users do not have the ability to do things that will hinder their machine or the network, so administrators have less to worry about. This not only prevents users from accidentally messing around with their systems or their networks, it prevents malware from sneaking into systems. If malware makes an attempt, a prompt appears and users cannot proceed without credentials.

This process we are talking about is called Administrative Approval Mode and it treats every user as if she is a standard user and then requests administrative credentials to proceed with certain operations that are considered admin-only type operations, even if you are an administrator, logged in already with your proper credentials.

So to access serious resources, standard users must provide the proper credentials, while logged-in administrators provide consent.

When a user attempts to perform an operation that requires administrative credentials, a dialog appears, showing a little shield graphic next to the option and prompting the users for credentials (see Figure 7.1). This has been called "over-the-shoulder" credentials because a user either knows the password for the admin or the admin can come over and type it for the user. Administrators can also disable this feature altogether; then the dialog box informs the user that she cannot perform the operation.

This sounds like a good thing, and it is a good thing. But it can be bothersome to an administrator. When an administrator is logged in to Vista and tries to access a resource that requires administrative credentials, the system still displays a dialog box that requires the admin to agree before moving forward (see Figure 7.2). In a normal workday, a standard user might go the entire day without seeing one of these. But admins see bunches of these every day.

Figure 7.1 *For a standard user, an action requiring administrative privileges calls for credentials.*

Figure 7.2 *For an administrator, UAC still requires confirmation.*

You might have noticed with UAC in Vista that more than a credential request was initiated. Your screen darkened—what Microsoft called a Secure Desktop mode. When your computer was in this mode, only trusted processes running as SYSTEM continued running. This prevented malicious applications from manipulating the prompt for the UAC and can still achieve a spoofing attack on you. You might think you are clicking a UAC button but it is really a fake. So, this Secure Desktop mode is just as important as the credential requests.

Here are some of the reasons you will see a prompt for elevated confirmation:

- Installing and uninstalling applications
- Working with Windows Firewall

- Installing drivers or configuring Windows Updates

- Adding, removing, or modifying user accounts

- Configuring parental controls, running elevated command prompts, and so forth

One danger in getting too used to seeing these prompts is that you might just agree without reading what you're granting permission for. So, you should take a moment to make sure you requested the application that's asking for permission. In addition, you should make sure your anti-spyware and antivirus applications are up to date so that nothing accidentally gets through. Most antivirus applications include an auto-update feature for both the application and virus definitions.

What's New with UAC?

Simply put, now you can control how UAC works without making extreme changes through the local policy, the registry, or Group Policy. There is a simple slider that you can use to select four different settings.

The slider options are located through the Action Center. You can open the Control Panel and then search for (or simply locate the applet for) the Action Center applet. Among the links on the left side Change User Account Control Settings. Click this link and the slider appears (see Figure 7.3).

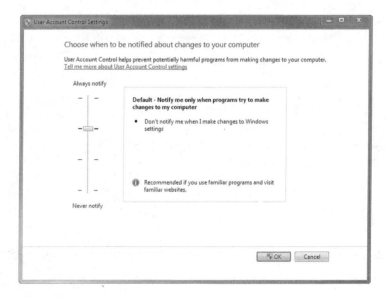

Figure 7.3   *The new UAC slider.*

SHOW ME   Media 7.1—Using the UAC Slider
Access this video file through your registered Web Edition at
my.safaribooksonline.com/9780768695212/media.

 LET ME TRY IT

Adjusting Your UAC Settings

The following steps show you how to adjust the UAC settings. While many users opt to turn it off, you might consider setting it to a low setting at first. You might find that a low setting might work well without being intrusive.

1. Click the Start orb and then click Control Panel.

2. Click Action Center.

3. From the links pane on the left, click Change User Account Control Settings. Simply move the UAC slider to your preferred setting.

> Another way to adjust UAC settings is through the User Accounts link in Control Panel. You can select users and adjust their settings.

There are four settings to choose from:

*   **Allows notify me when:** Programs try to install software or make change to my computer and (when) I make changes to Windows settings. (Recommended if you routinely install new software and visit unfamiliar websites.)

*   **Default—Notify me only when programs try to make changes to my computer:** Don't notify me when I make changes to Windows settings. (Recommended if you use familiar programs and visit familiar websites.)

*   **Notify me only when programs try to make changes to my computer (do not dim my desktop):** Don't notify me when I make changes to Windows settings. (Not recommended. Choose this only if it takes a long time to dim the desktop on your computer.)

*   **Never notify me when:** Programs try to install software or make change to my computer or (when) I make changes to Windows settings. (Not recommended. Choose this only if you need to use programs that are not certified for Windows 7 because they do not support User Account Control.)

> Keep in mind the option to not dim the desktop is basically turning off the Secure Desktop mode. As you learned earlier in this chapter, this is very important in the protection process.

UAC Within Your Network

User Account Control is certainly a positive solution for small offices, where you might not have a domain in place because you can create standard user accounts that allow users to log on to the system but don't allow them to make any major changes to the system if they don't have the correct credentials.

On an even higher level, UAC operates on a larger network level to protect computers in the enterprise. However, one concern is that administrators can be too easily tempted to give away their credentials in an effort to avoid the time-consuming task of providing the "over the shoulder" credentials that are needed.

If you have an application or device that requires administrative credentials and you don't want to constantly provide those for a user within your environment, you can use the Standard User Analyzer (SUA). It looks at the administrator credentials necessary for a standard user to run that particular application or hardware and then mitigates those permissions (loosens them up, so to speak) to allow that user perform that particular operation without requiring the user to call upon the administrator to intervene.

For more information on the SUA, visit http://technet.microsoft.com/en-us/library/cc766193%28WS.10%29.aspx.

The Action Center

The Security Center was included with the release of SP2 for XP. It encompassed a variety of tools that stood alone as features, with the Security Center providing a single access point to these features. It also monitored the system's state of protection. The Security Center was enhanced in Vista.

The Security Center in XP monitored only the firewall, antivirus (which isn't provided by Microsoft), and Automatic Updates. Vista improved the Windows Security Center (WSC) to provide for newer security features built-in to Vista. The Vista WSC still showed Firewall, Automatic Updates, and Anti-Virus status but included malware protection—which is actually the antivirus and spyware/malware section together—and a section for other security settings, such as Internet settings and User Account Control status. You could also monitor multiple vendor solutions running on a computer and indicate if they were enabled and up-to-date. By providing a single location for a user to check, WSC made it much easier for users to see if they were protected or vulnerable.

In Windows 7, the Windows Security Center has been renamed the Actions Center. In addition to a name change, the scope of what can be monitored is broadened to include maintenance (including backup/recovery features).

 **LET ME TRY IT**

Opening the Action Center

The following steps show you how to open the Action Center, which provides you with access to a centralized location for several security features.

1. Click the Start orb.

2. Click Control Panel.

3. Click System and Security (or, if you are looking at Control Panel icons, click Action Center).

4. Click Action Center.

As shown in Figure 7.4, Security and Maintenance are the focal points of the Action Center. Once you have the initial screen, note the Down arrows displayed in the Security and Maintenance sections. Click these arrows to see the state of the security and maintenance of your OS.

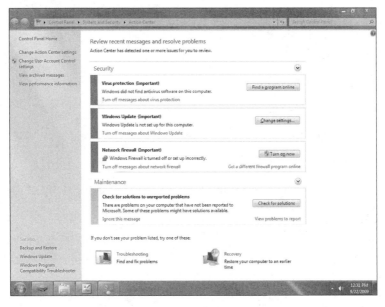

Figure 7.4 *The Action Center.*

In the Security section, click the Down arrow to reveal the status of the following settings (see Figure 7.5):

- Network Firewall

- Windows Update

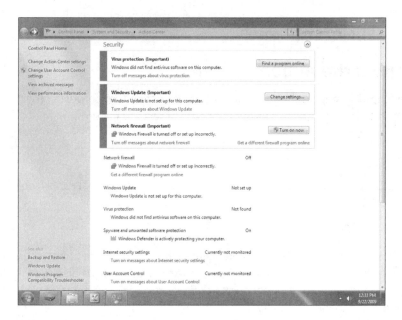

Figure 7.5   *The Security settings of the Action Center.*

- Virus Protection

- Spyware and Unwanted Software Protection

- Internet Security Settings

- User Account Control

- Network Access Protection

In the Maintenance section, click the Down arrow to reveal the status of the following settings:

- Check for Solutions to Problem Reports

- Backup

- Check for Updates

- Troubleshooting: System Maintenance

One of the interesting features under the Maintenance section is a feature called the Reliability Monitor. This was a feature introduced in Vista that was connected to the Performance Monitor, but it now exists separately. Click the View Reliability History link to display the Reliability Monitor, which shows a graph of the overall stability of your system over a period of time (see Figure 7.6). The red X icon reveals the type of issue that might have hindered your stability; it might have been a an application failure, a Windows failure, a miscellaneous failure, a warning, or an informational message. Details show you actions you can take to assist.

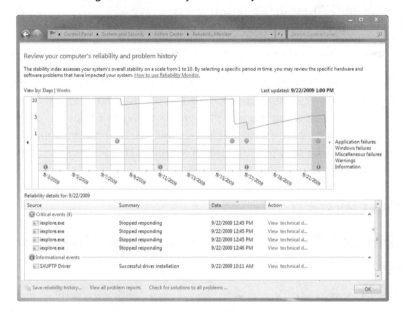

Figure 7.6   *The Reliability Monitor.*

 **LET ME TRY IT**

Viewing and Saving Data from the Reliability Monitor

The following steps show you how to access a stability index, which helps you assess your system's stability. Reports include application failures, Windows failures, warnings, and more.

1. Click the Start orb.

2. Click Control Panel.

3. Click System and Security (or, if looking at Control Panel icons, click Action Center).

4. Select Action Center.

5. In the Maintenance section, click the Down arrow.

6. In the Check for Solutions to Problem Reports section, click View Reliability History.

7. In the bottom-left corner, click Save Reliability History.

8. Browse to a location to where you would like to save the file.

9. Save the file name as First Report and click Save.

10. Navigate to the First Report.xml file you have saved and double-click it to open it. Your web browser opens the file for you to review.

An annoying feature to the Windows Security Center was the fact that it might alert you to issues you were already aware of. Telling you, for example, that you didn't have virus protection when you knew full well that you didn't have it (because you hadn't installed any). With the new Action Center, you have more control over what messages come your way. You can turn off messages that you feel are unnecessary or simply annoying.

 LET ME TRY IT

Turning Off Virus Protection Messages in the Action Center

The following steps show you how to change your notification settings in the Action Center for virus protection. This can help users who are using systems off the Internet and do not need to be notified about virus protection.

1. Click the Start orb.

2. Click Control Panel.

3. Click System and Security (or, if looking at Control Panel icons, click Action Center).

4. Select Action Center.

5. In the left pane, click Change Action Center Settings (see Figure 7.7).

6. In the Security Messages section, uncheck Virus Protection.

7. Click OK.

The Action Center is designed to assist you in securing your system. For example, even if security messages for an item are not enabled within your notification area, you can open the Action Center to see if items need to be enabled (like Windows Update) or installed (like with virus protection). The Action Center attempts to assist.

One way it does this with regard to virus protection is by offering you a Find a Program Online link that you can click to search for antivirus protection. You might already know of a solution you trust that you can install.

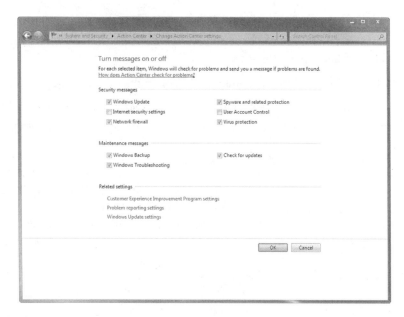

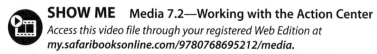

Figure 7.7   *Action Center settings.*

SHOW ME   Media 7.2—Working with the Action Center
Access this video file through your registered Web Edition at
my.safaribooksonline.com/9780768695212/media.

LET ME TRY IT

Downloading and Installing Free Antivirus Software

The following steps show you how to protect your system by downloading and installing a free version of AVG Anti-Virus. This software updates automatically and protects home computers from a variety of virus threats.

1. Start Internet Explorer.

2. In your Address bar, type **www.free.avg.com**.

3. On the AVG website, locate the download for the latest free version of AVG Anti-Virus.

4. Follow the download instructions.

5. Once you begin the installation, the software automatically checks for the latest updates before it runs the first scan of your computer.

6. During installation, a wizard verifies an installation point, reviews options, and recommends a timetable for scanning your computer. Unless you are an advanced user, accept the default settings.

7. On completion of the installation, a new icon appears in the Notification Area. From here, you can access the AVG Free User Interface, where you can configure your virus scan.

8. When you have finished examining this, open the Action Center.

9. In the Security group, under Virus Protection, you should see a green color indicating your computer has antivirus software installed and running.

Windows Update cis yet another way to keep your computer safe. You might think of Windows Update as the way Microsoft adds updates to the operating system in response to hardware changes and software compatibility. Yet another important role of Windows Update is as an early response to operating system threats that spring up on the Internet. These threats might fall out of the general range of spyware, viruses, Trojans, worms, etc., and more into the realm of software vulnerabilities that a hacker could potentially exploit. If you keep your Windows Update settings to automatic, Windows 7 downloads and installs the updates—usually unbeknownst to you.

Windows Defender

Spyware can do any number of things to annoy you and slow your system, such as displaying pop-up ads, altering your Internet settings, and even using private information without permission. Windows Defender is Microsoft's answer to spyware (keyloggers, bots, rootkits, etc.). Although it's included in Vista and Windows 7, you can download a free version for XP. It's a relatively simple tool (with an easy-to-use dashboard, as shown in Figure 7.8) you can use to perform an immediate scan of your system to look for the latest spyware and eliminate it from your system.

When it comes to anti-spyware software, you might think more is better. Actually, in most cases, the opposite is true. Having one very good anti-spyware application is better than having several installed and running. Why? Because many anti-spyware (and antivirus) scanners provide real-time monitoring to stop threats as they enter your system. When several of these applications are turned on, they all scan your system simultaneously. The result is a huge hit on the performance end, sometimes slowing your web browser to a crawl.

Behind the simple dashboard of Windows Defender, the underlying engine constantly works in the background to protect you, even silently looking into ZIP files (or other archive file formats) for harmful software within them, even before you open the files (which is a huge benefit because many spyware/malware creators use archive installers).

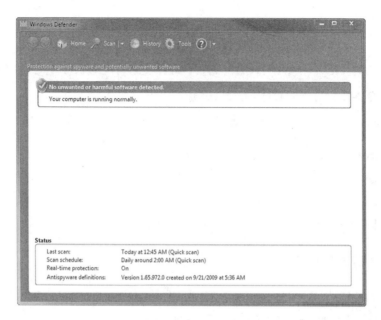

Figure 7.8   *The Windows Defender console.*

 **LET ME TRY IT**

Performing a Quick Scan with Windows Defender

The following steps show you how to scan your computer for spyware that might be located in the most common file locations. The default settings should not be changed for this scan.

1. Click the Start orb.

2. In the search field, type **defender**.

3. Click Windows Defender from the menu that appears.

4. Click the Scan button. By default, Quick Scan searches the most likely locations for any spyware.

> Wow! Talk about quick. When I ran Quick Scan on my computer manually, it took 45 seconds to scan 37,667 resources. Maybe they should have called it Turbo Scan!

 **LET ME TRY IT**

Performing a Full Scan of Your Computer from the Windows Defender Console

Similar to the previous steps, the following steps show you how to perform a full scan. Once again, leave all settings to their default configuration unless you have a specific requirement to change them.

1. Open Windows Defender.
2. Click the drop-down arrow next to the Scan button.
3. Select Full Scan. This scans all areas of the computer.

 LET ME TRY IT

Performing a Custom Scan of Your Computer from the Windows Defender Console

Similar to the previous steps, the following steps show you how to select exactly what is scanned. A Wizard lets you pick from selected drives and/or folders.

1. Open Windows Defender.
2. Click the drop-down arrow next to the Scan button.
3. Select Custom Scan. You are provided with several customizable scan options.

Some of us leave our systems on 24/7. If you don't, then you should know that Windows Defender is set up by default to scan your system at 2 a.m. each day. You might want to adjust this setting so it scans according to your computing schedule.

Windows Defender Tools and Settings

When you click the Tools button at the top of the Windows Defender dashboard, the Tools and Settings dialog box appears (see Figure 7.9).

 LET ME TRY IT

Changing When Defender Scans Your Computer

The following steps show you how to change the default time Windwos Defender scans your system. Note that on the Options page, you can select a checkbox to check for updated definitions before scanning. Select this to ensure the maximum protection before each scan.

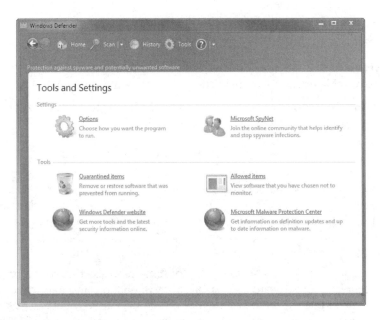

Figure 7.9   *Windows Defender Tools and Settings.*

1. Open Windows Defender.

2. Click the Tools button.

3. In the Settings group, click Options.

4. Using the drop-down arrows in the right pane, reset the scan time.

Options

After you click the Tools button, the Tools and Settings page appears. Click the Options link to configure how you want the program to run:

- **Automatic Scanning:** Configure your automatic scan settings (including frequency, time, and type).

- **Default Actions:** Choose an action you want to display or apply when items with Severe, High, Medium or Low alert levels are detected.

- **Real-Time Protection:** Allow Windows Defender to protect you while you work. It can scan downloaded files and attachments as well as scan programs that run on the computer.

- **Excluded Files and Folders:** Choose files or locations that you do not want Windows Defender to scan.

- **Excluded File Types:** Choose file types that you do not want Windows Defender to scan.

- **Advanced:** Configure Windows Defender to scan archive files, email, and removable drives; to use heuristics; or to create a restore point.

- **Administrator:** Configure how you want Defender to run with other users on the computer and what an administrator will see.

Windows Defender and Virus Protection

The name "Windows Defender" might imply that it's a one-stop PC protection software. Unfortunately, that is not the case. The primary role of Windows Defender is to block spyware and unwanted software from existing on your machine. As previously described, these range from annoying pop-ups to software that hogs system performance. These can be frustrating to deal with if they're unmonitored, but generally they're not too dangerous.

Virus protection software is looking for something else that is far more serious; it's looking for software that is maliciously targeting computers to exploit their resources in an effort to perform dishonest or illegal activities, such as harvesting credit card numbers, denial-of-service attacks, and worse. Many software companies have responded to these threats with virus protection software. Companies such as McAfee, Symantec, and AVG have full-system protection to ward off potential viruses. Microsoft itself has recently jumped into the arena with the beta version of Microsoft Security Essentials (MSE). This will replace Windows Live OneCare and will be a free offering. Early positive reviews cite the fact that it has a simple interface and uses little PC resources.

 LET ME TRY IT

Checking for Windows Defender Updates

Like all spyware protection software, Windows Defender is most effective after it has received the latest updates. The following steps show you how to download the latest updates.

1. Open Windows Defender.

2. To the right of the Help question mark icon is a drop-down arrow. Click this arrow.

3. Select Check for Updates. Defender immediately checks for and installs any new updates.

Microsoft SpyNet

After you click the Tools button, the Tools and Settings page appears. This is where you'll find the Microsoft SpyNet link One of the benefits to Microsoft being so large, with such a huge install base, is that users from all over the world (called SpyNet) are assisting in finding new spyware and other harmful programs and reporting them to Microsoft. SpyNet essentially allows for a voting option on software that hasn't been categorized as harmful or safe. By using SpyNet, you can see how other users have rated an application and what percentage of those users installed it (or didn't install it). This insight gives you greater opportunity to be in control of what you install on your system at a much earlier stage than what was provided with previous Microsoft operating systems. When Microsoft sees users uninstalling a particular type of software, they can check it out themselves and add that to their definitions of software that Windows Defender automatically detects.

You can choose to not be a part of it at all or you can choose basic or advanced memberships.

With a basic membership, Windows Defender sends Microsoft information regarding software it encounters on your system that isn't classified. You aren't alerted if Windows Defender detects software or changes made by software that have not been analyzed for risks.

With an advanced membership, Windows Defender notifies you if it detects software or changes made by software that have not been analyzed for risks. Windows Defender sends more information to SpyNet about spyware discoveries made on your computer, including file names and directories, how the software works, and changes that it makes to your computer—information that will be used to warn and protect other Windows Defender users.

 LET ME TRY IT

Changing Your SpyNet Membership

By joining Microsoft SpyNet, you can send selected information about spyware infections to Microsoft. The following steps show you how to view or change your current SpyNet settings.

1. Open Windows Defender.
2. Click Tools.
3. Click the Microsoft SpyNet link.
4. Select from one of the following:
   - Join With a Basic Membership
   - Join With an Advanced Membership
   - I Don't Want to Join Microsoft SpyNet at This Time
5. Click Save to enact your changes.

Tools

The tools you can use with Windows Defender include the following:

- **Quarantined Items:** Remove or restore software that was prevented from running.

- **Allowed Items:** View software that you have chosen not to monitor.

- **Windows Defender Website:** Get more tools and the latest security information online.

- **Microsoft Malware Protection Center:** Get information on definition updates and up-to-date information on malware.

One of the more interesting features in previous version of Windows Defender was a tool called Software Explorer. Software Explorer showed you the programs set to startup or those that are currently running. You could view network-connected programs and Winsock service providers as well. Alas, Software Explore is not included in Windows 7.

Windows Firewall

The Windows Firewall in Windows XP SP2 was a very simple tool to protect your system. You could turn it on or off and set exceptions to its behavior, effectively allowing some programs access while denying access by others. Vista significantly improved the firewall feature set by adding a new management console called Firewall with Advanced Security, which offered more advanced options and remote management.

Windows 7 continues to improve the firewall features, although it makes for a more complicated firewall feature. As shown in Figure 7.10, the firewall is broken into parts. There is a private side (for home or work networks) and a public side.

Having the private network broken into home or work allows you to configure your HomeGroup network to allow persons within the same Homegroup to easily share printers, libraries of files, pictures, music, videos and so forth.

Public networks (like an airport or a coffee shop) require a stricter level of protection. So rather than making changes on the fly, your system adjusts to the new network and is more protective based upon the settings you put in place for public networks.

You can click the Turn Windows Firewall On or Off link thinking you will see a very simple set of radio options. However, that link takes you to the Customize Settings page (see Figure 7.11). On this page, you can choose the following settings for both private and public networks:

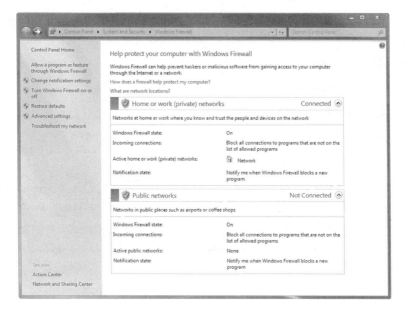

Figure 7.10   *Windows Firewall in Windows 7.*

- Block All Incoming Connections, Including Those in the List of Allowed Programs

- Notify Me When Windows Firewall Blocks a New Program

- Turn Off Windows Firewall (Not Recommended)

> If you are having trouble connecting to a network or resource, you might want to troubleshoot the problem by first turning off Windows Firewall temporarily. If you then succeed in connecting, it's safe to say that Windows Firewall was blocking the connection. You can then restore the firewall, letting the resource through as an exception.

 **LET ME TRY IT**

Turning Off Windows Firewall

The following steps show you how to turn off Windows Firewall. This can be done with little harm to computers that are not connected to the Internet. However, if your computer is connected to the Internet, you probably don't want to turn off

Windows Firewall. If you need to allow a valid application through the firewall, you will learn how to do this in the Let Me Try It section that follows this one.

1. Click the Start orb.

2. Click Control Panel.

3. Select System and Security.

4. Choose Windows Firewall.

5. In the left pane, clickTurn Windows Firewall On or Off.

6. To the right of the red shields in both the private and public network settings, select the Turn Off Windows Firewall (Not Recommended) radio buttons.

Figure 7.11 *Windows Firewall Customize Settings.*

 **LET ME TRY IT**

Allowing a Program or Feature Through Windows Firewall

By allowing a program through Windows Firewall, you can keep the firewall turned on while letting a specific application through. The following steps show you how to do this.

1. Open the Firewall.

2. In the left pane, click Allow a Program or Feature Through Windows Firewall (see Figure 7.12). The Allowed Programs page appears.

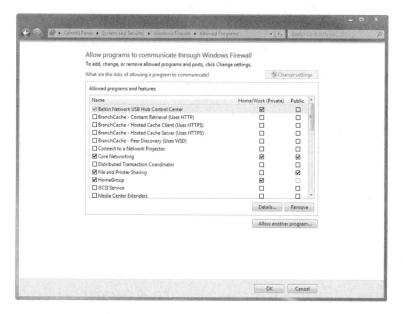

Figure 7.12 *Allowing programs through the Firewall.*

3. Select the Name of the allowed program or feature, select the Home/Work (Private) and/or Public network you want to allow it for, and then click OK.

From within the Firewall with Advanced Security (see Figure 7.13), you can see that profiles are used to help you and this is especially helpful with systems that move. Desktops sit still, but laptops move. It's the moving aspect that makes them vulnerable to new situations, like airport Wi-Fi connections or Starbucks T-Mobile hotspot locations. However, you can configure rules based upon the following three profiles (see Figure 7.13):

- **Domain Profile:** When your computer is connected to an Active Directory domain.

- **Private Profile is Active:** When a computer is connected to a network that has a private gateway or router.

- **Public Profile:** When a computer is connected directly to the Internet or to a network that isn't considered private or domain.

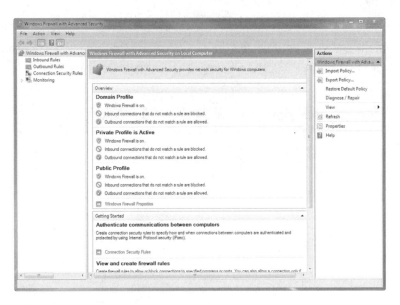

Figure 7.13   *Firewall with Advanced Security.*

 **LET ME TRY IT**

Opening Windows Firewall with Advanced Security

The following steps show you how to modify all aspects of Windows Firewall. Rules, profiles, and monitoring can all be configured and viewed from the Windows Firewall with Advanced Security window.

1. Click the Start orb.

2. Click Control Panel.

3. Select System and Security.

4. Choose Windows Firewall.

5. In the left pane, click Advanced Settings. The Windows Firewall with Advanced Security on Local Computer page appears.

The features on this page give you a tremendous amount of true control over your firewall settings—everything from creating rules for inbound and outbound connections to monitoring and much more.

You might also decide you would like to open specific ports on your firewall. Ports are a lot like channels on your television. So, your TV might have a single connection to the outside world, but by changing the channel, you can go to news stations, movie channels—really hundreds of options. Your computer is similar in that it might be connected to the Internet but different ports allow for different access.

For example, you have a port for sending email (Port 25), which uses a special protocol (Simple Mail Transfer Protocol or SMTP). You have a port for receiving email (Port 110 for the POP protocol). You have a port for your web browser to view web pages (Port 80 for the HTTP protocol), and so forth.

 LET ME TRY IT

Open Local Ports in Windows Firewall

Certain software requires a single open port in order to function correctly. The following steps show you how to accomplish this.

1. Open the Windows Firewall.

2. In the left pane, click Advanced Settings. The Windows Firewall with Advanced Security on Local Computer page appears.

3. In the left pane, click Inbound Rules.

4. In the right pane, click New Rule. The New Inbound Rule Wizard dialog box appears.

5. Select the Port radio button.

6. Click Next.

7. Choose Specific Local Ports and type the port number.

8. Click Next.

9. Verify that Allow the Connection is selected.

10. Click Next.

11. Confirm that all three boxes are checked.

12. Click Next.

13. In the Name field, type Custom Port Exception.

14. Click Finish.

You will now see on the right pane (in the middle) the rule Custom Port Exception.

The firewall is Network-Aware in the sense that, based upon the network (domain, private, or public), it can determine the settings necessary to protect the user for any given situation. But you are the one who needs to configure the policy that will be applied after the firewall determines your category network. Obviously, the more dangerous the situation (for example, a public Internet connection), the more strict the policy.

LET ME TRY IT

Restoring Windows Firewall Default Settings

The following steps show you how to restore the Windows Firewall settings to their default configuration. Some software already installed might stop working if it was set to gain access through the firewall; it might need to be reconfigured.

1. Open Windows Firewall.

2. In the left pane, click Restore Defaults.

3. On the Restore Default Settings screen, click the Restore Defaults button. This displays the Restore Defaults Confirmation dialog box.

4. Click Yes. The firewall resets to the default settings and returns to the main Windows Firewall screen.

Resetting the firewall to its default settings can have unintended consequences. If you have installed applications that Windows Firewall created exceptions for, these applications might stop working once you reset to default. You might need to once again let these programs through the firewall to keep using them. If the program has a simple installation program, it might be easiest to re-install it and allow it to set up the firewall setting again.

BitLocker Encryption

For those traveling on business, BitLocker is a feature that was a compelling reason to switch to Vista Ultimate Edition. Windows 7 simplifies this great security feature and adds a new twist. But before we discuss the changes, let's cover the basics.

Typically, if you lose your laptop or if it's stolen, the data you're carrying will be fair game to anybody who now possesses your laptop. With BitLocker enabled, the entire drive is encrypted and a thief won't be able to switch out the drive and attempt to crack through the encryption. BitLocker uses Advanced Encryption Standard (AES) as its encryption algorithm with configurable key lengths of 128 or 256 bits. These options are configurable using Group Policy.

Some of the frustrations with BitLocker in Vista were that it was too complicated to configure once the OS was installed. You needed to make a BitLocker partition and, if that wasn't done ahead of time, you had to jump through hoops by shrinking drives. This prompted Microsoft to release the BitLocker Drive Preparation Tool (part of the Ultimate Extras in Vista). That tool is included directly within Windows 7, so now you need only to turn BitLocker on (see Figure 7.14) through Control Panel, System and Security, BitLocker Drive Encryption. The tool will handle the rest.

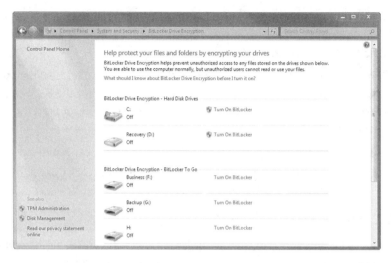

Figure 7.14   *BitLocker Drive Encryption applet.*

For BitLocker to work, you must have one of the following:

- A laptop that has the Trusted Platform Module (TPM) chip version 1.2. The TPM chip is like a smartcard that is embedded into the motherboard. It has a predefined number of unsuccessful attempts configured so that a thief cannot force his way in.

- A USB storage device, but your system's BIOS must be able to access USB devices prior to the boot-up of the OS.

 LET ME TRY IT

Setting Up BitLocker to Work on an Operating System

The following steps show you how to set up BitLocker encryption on a hard drive. You will be required to restart the computer, after which the drive will be encrypted. This process will take a while and will diminish performance until it's completed. Once it is done, you will receive a message stating that the process is complete.

1. Click the Start orb.

2. Click Control Panel.

3. Select System and Security.

4. Click BitLocker Drive Encryption.

5. On your operating system drive letter, click Turn On BitLocker. If your computer meets the requirements to run BitLocker, it automatically prepares the hard drive for encryption and reboots the computer.

6. The BitLocker Setup Wizard continues the installation. Choose where to store the recovery key from the following locations: Save the Recovery Key to a USB Flash Drive, Save the Recovery Key to a File, or Print the Recovery Key.

7. Click Next.

8. Verify the Run BitLocker System Check is selected and click Continue.

BitLocker to Go

BitLocker to Go encrypts USB storage devices. You can then restrict those drives with a passphrase so that even your portable storage is protected.

Administrators can determine the passphrase length and complexity. By using policy settings, administrators can also require users to provide apply protection to a USB drive prior to writing to them in the first place. You can also use a smartcard to unlock a drive. In the event you forget the passphrase to unlock your drive or lose your smartcard, you will be asked to create a recovery key (which can be saved to a file or printed) so that you can use the recovery key to access the drive.

 LET ME TRY IT

Setting Up BitLocker to Work on a Portable Drive

The following steps show you how to set up BitLocker on a portable drive. Upon completion of these steps, the drive will be encrypted.

1. Click the Start orb.

2. Click Control Panel.

3. Select System and Security.

4. Click BitLocker Drive Encryption.

5. Select the removable drive you would like to encrypt. This starts the BitLocker Drive Encryption Wizard.

6. Choose Use a Password to Unlock the Drive or choose Use My Smart Card to Unlock the Drive.

7. Click Next.

8. Choose where to store the recovery key from the following locations: Save the Recovery Key to a USB Flash Drive, Save the Recovery Key to a File, or Print the Recovery Key.

9.   Click Next.

10.   Click Start Encrypting.

The drive will now be encrypted, after which it will require the key to access the data.

Windows XP SP3 and Windows Vista systems can read devices encrypted with BitLocker to Go. On other systems, the device, when plugged in, will appear as a non-formatted device and you will not be able to access the data.

 SHOW ME   Media 7.3—BitLocker to Go
Access this video file through your registered Web Edition at
my.safaribooksonline.com/9780768695212/media

Windows Biometric Framework

This framework enhances support for the use of fingerprint biometric devices. In previous versions of Windows, these devices certainly existed and functioned but there was no inner support from the OS. The developers of the hardware device had to provide all the drivers, applications, and so forth for their device to work— often causing issues. Windows Biometric Framework establishes a core level of support, letting vendors work from that core so that there is some consistency in how these devices function and perform on Windows.

In addition, to make it easier to configure and work with biometric devices, Windows 7 provides a Biometric Devices applet in the Control Panel.

Your computer might not have a biometric device but you can still open the Biometric Devices dialog box through a hidden back door.

Opening the Biometric Devices Control Panel

The following steps show you how to gain access to any biometric devices on your machine through the Control Panel.

1.   Click the Start orb.

2.   Click Help and Support.

3.   In the search field, type **Biometric** and press Enter.

4.   Click Can I Use a Fingerprint Reader with Windows.

5.   Scroll to and click Click to Open Biometric Devices. The Biometric Devices page opens.

If you are having trouble with your fingerprint reader, such as an *unavailable* message displayed on the Biometrics Devices page, try locating the latest drivers from the manufacturer and installing them. If your hardware is not defective, this is the most likely cause of an inoperative reader. If you were thinking of accessing your fingerprint reader remotely, sorry to say this feature is not supported.

 TELL ME MORE   Media 7.4—A Discussion of Security in
Windows 7: Thumbs Up or Thumbs Down?
Access this audio recording through your registered Web Edition at
***my.safaribooksonline.com/9780768695212/media**.*

In this chapter, Windows 7 networking for the home environment is explored.

8

Networking with Windows 7

HomeGroups

Setting up a home network has never been astronomically difficult, but it's frustrating enough to novice users that they often give up or pay someone to come in and fix their networks. It's not the physical side that causes them pain. Walk into any store that sells computer equipment and you can pick up a wireless router or whatever else you need that will connect your home physically in a matter of minutes. But "sharing" your documents, printers, media and so forth is a bit more challenging if you do not know how to do this (and even more challenging if you have a hodge-podge of system types—some systems running XP and others running Vista).

With Windows 7, this pain point is addressed by HomeGroups, a feature that works only between systems running Windows 7). Obviously you can still network disparate systems together, but if you have an all-Windows 7 situation, the sharing is much easier to accomplish.

When you perform an installation of Windows 7, you can configure a HomeGroup at that time. But if you don't set it up then, you can use the HomeGroup applet found in Control Panel to get you started. You initially see a dialog that explains what a HomeGroup is for; click the Create a HomeGroup button (see Figure 8.1).

 LET ME TRY IT

Creating a HomeGroup

Complete the following steps to create a HomeGroup. On completion, you will have chosen what items to share and you will receive a password to share this data with other computers on your network.

1. Click the Start orb.

2. Click Control Panel.

3. Select Network and Internet.

4. Choose HomeGroup.

5. Click Create Homegroup to open the Create a HomeGroup dialog box.

Figure 8.1   *Creating a HomeGroup.*

6. Select what you want to share from the following and click Next.
    *   Pictures
    *   Music
    *   Videos
    *   Documents
    *   Printers

7. After the HomeGroup is created you will be provided a password for other computers to access the libraries in your HomeGroup. Write down the password.

8. Click Finish.

Keep in mind that you can always go back and easily make changes from the HomeGroup settings through Control Panel.

If you are having trouble creating a HomeGroup, make sure you check your version of Windows 7. Windows 7 Starter and Windows 7 Home Basic can join an existing HomeGroup but cannot start a HomeGroup. If you're having trouble connecting to a HomeGroup, verify your computer is actually connected to the correct network. If you have a wireless network connection, it can be very easy to connect to the wrong network inadvertently and spin your wheels trying to solve a connectivity issue.

After the HomeGroup is set up, you will receive a password (see Figure 8.2). This password is provided by default. You can write it down and share it with others in the family so they can access shared items (so long as they have Windows 7 on their systems) or you can change the password to something you would like.

Figure 8.2 *The HomeGroup password.*

 LET ME TRY IT

Locating a Lost HomeGroup Password

Follow these steps to retrieve your HomeGroup password. Once finished, you can print this password to save it for later reference or to distribute to others on your network.

1. Click the Start orb.

2. Click Control Panel.

3. Select Network and Internet.

4. Choose HomeGroup.

5. Click View or Print HomeGroup Password.

6. To print out the password, click Print this Page at the bottom right; otherwise click Cancel.

Some have asked why they cannot just create their own passwords right from the start. Apparently during the testing phase of Windows 7, the Windows development team discovered that users weren't aware they might be giving this password to others, so these users often used the same passwords they used to secure sensitive information. Rather than distribute this same password to others and potentially put their sensitive information at risk, users were given a starter password. This gave them the option of using this starter password or creating their own password.

After your HomeGroup is up and running, you can revisit your settings in the Control Panel and make additional changes, such as adjustments to your media streaming options (see Figure 8.3).

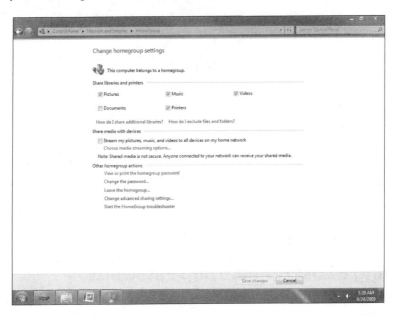

Figure 8.3   *Changing HomeGroup settings.*

 **LET ME TRY IT**

Accessing the HomeGroup Settings

Complete the following steps to change your HomeGroup settings.

1. Click the Start orb.

2. Click Control Panel.

3. Select Network and Internet.

4. Click the Choose Homegroup and Sharing Options link, which opens the Change Homegroup Settings screen.

Every system in a HomeGroup is considered a peer (or equal). Users can enter or leave the group by using the password, much like the use of a key to the home. Once in the group, they can access whatever is shared.

LET ME TRY IT

Changing the HomeGroup Password

Changing your password is an easy way to stop others from sharing your library. The following steps show you how to change your password. A later exercise shows you how to stop sharing individual library items in a HomeGroup.

1. Click the Start orb.

2. Click Control Panel.

3. Select Network and Internet.

4. Click the Choose Homegroup and Sharing Options link, which opens the Change HomeGroup Settings screen.

5. Click the Change the Password... link, which opens the Change Your Homegroup Password dialog box.

6. Verify that any current HomeGroup computers are on and not asleep or hibernating.

7. Click Change the Password. You will be prompted to accept the new password or change it.

8. Click Next.

9. Write down the password.

10. Click Finish.

One of the best parts to this is the use of Libraries. A folder such as Pictures is no longer a folder; it's a Library that can include multiple folders from multiple locations. You can control the addition of locations if you choose, but if Pictures is shared out, others can quickly view those new locations without finding a new way to connect to it. It will all come under the Library.

When it comes to sharing documents, the content is shared as read-only so that you do not have to fear items being changed without additional thought (although you can change this selectively, on a document basis, in Explorer; see Figure 8.4).

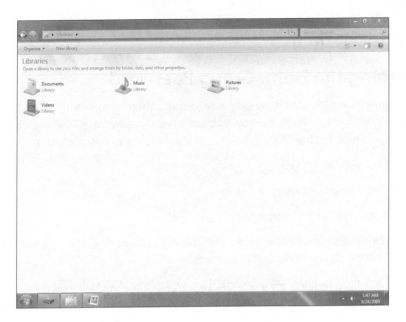

Figure 8.4   *Libraries that are shared with the HomeGroup.*

 **LET ME TRY IT**

Sharing Additional Libraries with the HomeGroup

The following show you how to share items to your HomeGroup. In addition to adding these items to your shared library, you can also modify how they are accessed (such as read-only or write).

1. Click the Start orb.

2. Select your user name. It should be in the right column at the top. This will open your personal folder.

3. Click on a folder you would like to share, but do not open it.

4. In the top menu, click the drop-down arrow to the right of Share With.

5. Select HomeGroup (Read/Write).

6. You might be asked for a confirmation of this. If so, click Yes.

7. To view which Libraries are being shared, click on a folder. Look to the lower-right of the screen, above the words Date Modified, and you will see State:Shared.

8. This folder is now being shared as a library with read/write access to users in your HomeGroup.

Be advised that when you add libraries to the HomeGroup, those libraries need to be present and connected in order to be accessed. For example, you can add a folder on a removable external hard drive as a library to your HomeGroup, but it can only be accessed when the external hard drive is connected to your computer.

If you would like to make a network resource as part of your HomeGroup, the folder to add as a library needs to be indexed. If it isn't, a quick workaround is to make the folder available offline. This indexes the folder as it creates offline versions. You can include the folder in a library once you make it available offline. Keep in mind that these offline versions of the files in the folder will be copied to your hard drive. Make sure you have enough room on your local hard drive to accommodate the offline files that you have added to your library.

 LET ME TRY IT

Removing Libraries from the HomeGroup

The following exercise shows you how to select exactly which library you would like to stop sharing with your HomeGroup.

1. Click the Start orb.
2. Click your user name (it should be in the right column at the top). This opens your personal folder.
4. Click once on a library you would like to stop sharing (but do not open it).
5. In the top menu, click the drop-down arrow to the right of Share With.
6. Select Nobody.

The library is now removed from your HomeGroup. However, it is still accessible from the local computer.

Another interesting aspect of the HomeGroup approach is that it allows computers that are typically connected to a domain at work (such as a company laptop) to access a home network. You can join a HomeGroup and see the items in the home but others will not be able to see back in to your system so your data is safe from prying eyes.

 LET ME TRY IT

Removing Your Computer From a HomeGroup

You can easily leave a HomeGroup. Follow these steps to accomplish this.

1. From the computer you want to remove from the HomeGroup, click the Start orb.
2. Click Control Panel.

3. Select Network and Internet.

4. Select HomeGroup.

5. Choose Leave the HomeGroup.

6. Click Leave the Homegroup.

7. Click Finish.

From within the HomeGroup options you can also access your media sharing settings and your Advanced sharing settings. Click Change Advanced Sharing Settings.

If you are having trouble with sharing in the HomeGroup, Windows 7 provides a HomeGroup troubleshooter (see Figure 8.5) to diagnose and locate potential problems. By default, the troubleshooter is configured to apply repairs automatically. This is a nice feature that helps minimize support calls and lets the operating system self-heal.

Figure 8.5   *The HomeGroup troubleshooter.*

 **LET ME TRY IT**

Using the HomeGroup Troubleshooter

The following steps how you how to identify issues with computers already connected to a HomeGroup. These steps work only on computers already connected to a Homegroup. To join a HomeGroup, visit the HomeGroup applet in the Control Panel to connect to an existing HomeGroup.

1. Click the Start orb.

2. Click Control Panel.

3. Select Network and Internet.

4. Click on HomeGroup.

5. In the Other Homegroup Actions section, click Start the HomeGroup troubleshooter. The HomeGroup troubleshooter dialog box opens up.

6. Click Next. The troubleshooter begins searching for problems and automatically fixes them (if possible).

7. Follow the wizard to complete the troubleshooter.

Public folder sharing (which is turned off by default) can be another easy way to share files and folders. Public folders are a quick and easy way to share a file without setting up an entire folder as a library. The weakness of public folders, however, is their inability to restrict users to seeing only the files in the Public folder. Also, there isn't much in the way of permissions. Generally speaking, if it can be seen in the public folders, it can be accessed. Still, if you want to share a file only temporarily with someone, public folders are the way to go.

 SHOW ME   Media 8.1—Working with HomeGroups
Access this video file through your registered Web Edition at
my.safaribooksonline.com/9780768695212/media.

 LET ME TRY IT

Turning on Public Folder Sharing

After you complete the following steps, members of your network will be granted access to all items located in your Public folder. They will have full rights to all files in the Public folder.

1. Click the Start orb.

2. Click Control Panel.

3. Select Network and Internet.

4. Click the Choose Homegroup and Sharing Options link. The Change HomeGroup Settings screen opens.

5. Click Change Advanced Sharing Settings.

6. Locate the Public Folder Sharing section.

You have two different profiles with Public Folder sharing options. One is the Home/Work profile (which is most likely where you want to turn on this feature) and the other is the Public profile (which you typically want to keep locked down a bit more, so you may not want to enable it here).

7. Choose Turn On Sharing So Anyone with Network Access Can Read and Write Files in the Public Folders.

8. Click Save Changes.

9. A UAC window might open. If so, click Yes.

Workgroups, HomeGroups, and Domains: What's the Difference?

For years, Windows networks have existed as either workgroups or domains. Now HomeGroups have been introduced with Windows 7. Domains, workgroups, and HomeGroups represent different methods for organizing computers in networks. The main difference among them is how the computers and other resources on the networks are managed.

Here's a brief look at each of the key features (source: Windows 7 Help and Support):

Workgroup

- All computers are peers; no computer has control over another computer.

- Each computer has a set of user accounts. To log on to any computer in the workgroup, you must have an account on that computer.

- There are typically no more than 20 computers.

- A workgroup is not protected by a password.

- All computers must be on the same local network or subnet.

HomeGroup

- Computers on a home network must belong to a workgroup, but they can also belong to a HomeGroup. A HomeGroup makes it easy to share pictures, music, videos, documents, and printers with other people on a home network.

- A HomeGroup is protected with a password, but you need to type the password only once, when adding your computer to the HomeGroup.

Domain

- One or more computers are servers. Network administrators use servers to control the security and permissions for all computers on the domain. This makes it easy to make changes because the changes are automatically made to all computers. Domain users must provide a password or other credentials each time they access the domain.

- If you have a user account on the domain, you can log on to any computer on the domain without needing an account on that computer.

- You probably can make only limited changes to a computer's settings because network administrators often want to ensure consistency among computers.

- There can be thousands of computers in a domain.

- The computers can be on different local networks.

Windows-based computers on a network must be part of a workgroup or a domain. Windows-based computers on home networks can also be part of a HomeGroup, but it's not required.

Computers on home networks are usually part of a workgroup and possibly a HomeGroup, and computers on workplace networks are usually part of a domain.

The Network and Sharing Center

The Network and Sharing Center was first introduced in Vista and has been slightly streamlined in Windows 7.

The main panel displays a compressed view of the network map, information about existing network connections, and any resources the user can locate on the network. You have links at the bottom of the center for the following:

- **Set up a New Connection or Network:** Set up a wireless, broadband, dial-up, ad hoc, or VPN connection; or set up a router or access point.

- **Connect to a Network:** Connect or reconnect to a wireless, wired, dial-up or VPN network connection.

- **Choose Homegroup and Sharing Options:** Access files and printers located on other network computers, or change sharing settings.

- **Troubleshoot Problems:** Diagnose and repair network problems or get troubleshooting information.

On the left side of the screen, you can click links to Manage Wireless Networks, Change Adapter Settings, or Change Advanced Sharing Settings.

Of course, to connect on the network, you need to have installed a network adapter. These come in several forms, including network cards, USB wireless networks, or integrated network adapters built into your laptop or desktop. Fortunately, most modern network adapters are plug and play and get you immediately connected to the network. But that might not be the case if you are upgrading to Windows 7 with older hardware.

If you have upgraded and suddenly disconnected from your network, there is a good chance your network drivers need to be updated. There are several ways to do this; one of these is from the aforementioned Change Adapter Settings link.

Here's a little conundrum: Your network adapter needs drivers to be updated so you can get on the Internet, but the only place to get these drivers *is* the Internet. The workaround for this could be a little tricky. The best answer is to download the drivers from another computer that can get on the Internet, then copy them to a portable jump drive to install them on the computer that has the outdated drivers. The next question is, "What type of network adapter do I have?" One way to find out is to look in Network Connections. Windows 7 might have recognized your network card but just might not have drivers for it. If you know you have a network adapter installed, you might have to consult with your computer manufacturer or take apart your computer to see the brand and model of your network card. If all this seems too difficult, buying an inexpensive plug-and-play USB network adapter is a low priced alternative.

 LET ME TRY IT

Upgrade Your Network Adapter Driver

The following steps show you how to upgrade your network adapter drivers. Internet access is recommended to complete this exercise.

1. Click the Start orb.
2. Click Control Panel.
3. Select Network and Internet.
4. Click Network and Sharing Center.
5. In the left pane, click Change Adapter Settings.
6. Point to the adapter you want to update, right-click, and select Properties.
7. If a UAC window opens, click Yes.
8. Click the Configure button.
9. Select the Driver tab.
10. Click Update Driver.
11. If you have a disk or other location where you have updated network driver software, select Browse My Computer for Driver Software.

12. Type the location (or click Browse to locate the drivers) and click OK.

13. Click Next.

14. Windows searches the location for updated drivers. If it finds more than one choice, it presents you with all options. Pick the closest one to your specific hardware.

15. You might receive a notification that your drivers have not been digitally signed. Read the message carefully before proceeding. In many cases, the drivers will work. However, you will have to decide whether to use them or not.

16. Upon successful completion and connection to the network, return to Network Connections to see an icon for your new connection.

When updating drivers, your hardware manufacturer might not yet have released drivers for Windows 7. If drivers for Vista are available, install those instead. Oftentimes, drivers between the two systems are interchangeable. If and when Windows 7 drivers for your hardware are released, they most likely will be available as an optional download in Windows Update.

One newcomer to the Network and Sharing Center is View Your Active Networks, which is located just below the basic network map. Here you will see all the networks you can connect to along with any to which you are currently connected.

Another nice touch is a refinement to the Connect to a Network dialog box. This is the second link under the heading Change your Network Settings. Click this to bring up a new pop-up box called the View Available Networks (VAN) interface. This is similar to the Connect to a Network pop-up used to connect to networks in Vista. A subtle revision here is the removal of one layer of display messages. The menu pops up above the network icon and shows up like a jump menu.

When the pop-up appears, it not only shows you what network you are connected to, but a Change button gives you one-click access to previously established connections. This is a simple yet effective upgrade.

Setting Up Your Network Location

You might have noticed each time you connect to a network a dialog box appears, asking you to select your network location. This feature was first introduced in Vista. The purpose of this dialog box is to automatically configure your firewall and security settings depending on your location. Here are the four network locations and an explanation for each one:

- **Home Network:** There are two instances when you choose this setting. One is for home networks and the other is when you know and trust the users and devices on the network. Because computers on a home network can belong to a HomeGroup, there is much greater access allowed to available network resources. Network discovery is turned on for home networks, which allows you to see other computers and devices on the network and allows other network users to see your computer. This setting offers the easiest connectivity between computers and network devices.

- **Work Network:** Select Work Network if the network you are connected to is a small office or similar workplace network. You will be visible to other computers since network discovery (which allows you to see other computers and devices on a network and allows other network users to see your computer) is on by default. One restriction with this setting is that you cannot create or join a HomeGroup.

- **Public Network:** Choose Public Network for networks in public places (such as cafés, airports, or networks offering free Wi-Fi). This setting keeps your computer from being visible to other computers around you and is the most restrictive in terms of security and visibility. Use this setting on a public network to help protect your computer from any malicious software from the Internet. You cannot connect to a HomeGroup is on public networks and network discovery is turned off. Also consider using this option if you're connected directly to the Internet without using a router. A router serves as an additional layer of insulation from all Internet attacks. Without a router, your firewall needs to be set to a highly secure state. Also use Public Network if you have a mobile broadband connection. This also requires high security and firewall protection.

- **Domain:** If you see this setting, it is unchangeable and controlled by your network administrator.

When connecting to a secured network, the only requirement now is to enter the network security key (passphrase). If you are switching from Windows XP to Windows 7, this is a welcome change because you no longer have to specify the encryption type (WEP, WPA, or WPA2).

Although it's not part of the network map, the network folder is closely related to it. From here you can view all available network resources (see Figure 8.6). This can be opened by clicking Network from any Explorer window, which shows the computers and other resources you have access to on the network. A link back to the Network and Sharing Center is on the top menu. Clicking on any of the computer icons shows any shared resources on these devices you can share.

Figure 8.6 *Setting up a connection or network.*

 **LET ME TRY IT**

Setting Up a New Broadband Connection to the Internet

To complete the following steps, you will need a broadband connection to the Internet along with the ISP-assigned user name and password. Upon successful completion, you will have established a high-speed connection to the Internet.

1. Click the Start orb.

2. Click Control Panel.

3. Click Network and Internet.

4. Select Network and Sharing Center.

5. Click Set up a New Connection or Network. This opens the Set Up a Connection or Network dialog box.

6. Click Connect to the Internet.

7. Click Next.

8. You are asked, "How do you want to connect?"

9. Select Broadband. The Connect to the Internet configuration screen opens.

10. Type your User Name and Password.

11. Select Remember This Password.

12. Click Connect to establish your new connection.

> Network printers were once a part of business networks exclusively, but low cost and improved technology have made network printers an attractive option for the home as well. Once installed on a wireless home network, users can print from anywhere within the wireless network range. Very convenient!

 SHOW ME Media 8.2—The Network and Sharing Center
Access this video file through your registered Web Edition at my.safaribooksonline.com/9780768695212/media.

Connecting to a Printer Share from Another Computer

The following steps show you how to connect to another computer (with a printer connected to it that is shared) and then access the shared printer. When you finish this exercise, you will be able to print from the shared printer.

1. Click the Start orb.

2. Click Computer.

3. In the left pane, click Network.

4. In the top menu, click Add a Printer. The Add Printer dialog box appears.

5. Click Add a Network, Wireless or Bluetooth Printer and click Next. Windows searches the network for available printers.

6. When it finds the network printer you want to connect to, select it and click Next.

7. If a printer driver suitable for use with Windows 7 is available, the printer is installed. If not, Windows uses Windows Update to search for a driver online.

8. Upon successful installation of your printer drivers, your network printer is now ready for use.

Utilizing the Network Connectivity Status Indicator (NCSI)

The NCSI (a feature we saw implemented originally in Vista) is the little networking icon that sits in your Notification Area. It has four different states you can use to quickly see if there is a connectivity problem.

It will either tell you No Connectivity where it has a little Red X, or "Connectivity Problem" which has a little warning caution sign over it, or Local connectivity which has only the computers, and then Internet Connectivity has the Globe on top of it indicating that you have access to the Internet.

Another enhancement to this icon is the fact that if you have a notebook computer and there is a network card built in and then also a wireless network card, you would, in the past, have two network status icons. One of might appear broken all the time because you don't usually have both plugged in and available.

With Windows 7 (actually, starting with Vista), one of the benefits with the new NCSI icon is the fact that it consolidates all your network connections to one icon. So if there is something going on with two separate connections and you hover over one connection, you'll see the two distinct network connections listed there individually.

If your network is always on, you might not need the icon in the Notification Area.

Removing the Network Icon from the Notification Area

The following steps show you how to remove the networking icon from the Notification Area. Take note of the other modifications you can make in this window while in this section.

1. Right-click the Start orb.

2. Select Properties.

3. Select the Taskbar tab.

4. In the Notification Area, click Customize.

5. Locate the Network icon, click the drop-down for Behaviors, and select Hide Icon and Notifications.

6. Click OK.

The icon is removed from the Notification Area taskbar.

The Network Map

At the top of the Network and Sharing Center, you might have noticed a mini-map of your connection to the Internet with a connecting router shown between your computer and the Internet. If you select the See Full Map option, you will see an expanded display of your computer and everything your computer is connected to, including any network connections (wired and wireless), any computer-to-computer connections (called *ad hoc*), and any connections to the Internet (see Figure 8.7). The map shows you any problems between connections as well, so you can begin diagnosing connectivity issues visually before you make corrections physically.

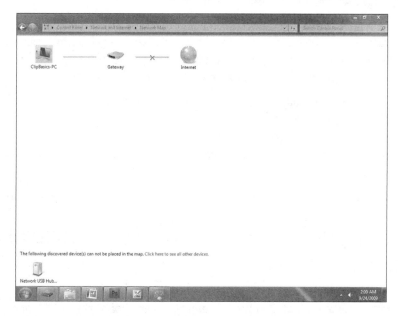

Figure 8.7   *The Network map indicating an Internet connectivity issue.*

One little-known feature of the network map is the ability you have to click on a problem area to start Windows onboard diagnostics. This was first introduced in Vista and has been slightly revised and updated for Windows 7. For example, if you see an X over the connection between your computer and the Internet, click the X to diagnose the problem. This opens Windows diagnostics and attempts to solve the problem for you.

Viewing the Network Map

The following steps show you how to view the Network Map in a few easy steps.

1. Click the Start orb.

2. Click Control Panel.

3. Click Network and Internet.

4. Click Network and Sharing Center.

5. In the right corner, click See Full Map.

6. Windows creates and displays the Network Map.

> The Network Map looks similar to the one in Vista but it functions a bit better and seems to have an easier time locating devices on the network, even presenting you with ones that it cannot integrate into the map. This helps in understanding the network topology.

Advanced Sharing Settings

Selecting Advanced Sharing Settings brings you to the options for different network profiles. Here you can choose the Home or Work profile or the Public profile. And then you can set the following options:

- **Network Discovery:** When Network Discovery is on, this computer sees other network computers and devices and it is visible to other network computers.

- **File and Printer Sharing:** When File and Printer Sharing is on, files and printers that you have shared from this computer can be accessed by users on the network.

- **Public Folder Sharing:** When Public Folder Sharing is on, users on the network, including HomeGroup members, can access files in the Public folders.

- **Media Streaming:** When Media Streaming is on, users and devices on the network can access pictures, music, and videos on this computer. This computer can also find media on the network.

- **File Sharing Connections:** Windows 7 uses 128-bit encryption to help protect file-sharing connections. Some devices don't support 128-bit encryption and must use 40- or 56-bit encryption.

- **Password Protected Sharing:** When Password Protected Sharing is on, only a user who has a user account and a password on this computer can access shared files, printers attached to this computer, and the Public folders. To give other users access, you must turn off Password Protected Sharing.

One distinct setting between Private and Public settings is the HomeGroup connections setting (which you cannot use on the Public network side).

Media Streaming is one option that media lovers will get excited about. Enabling this option allows you to turn your Windows 7 into a streaming media source for your network. By default, this feature is turned on, but you can customize it here in Advanced Sharing Settings. Click Choose Media Streaming Options to access these options.

There are a ton of possibilities with this:

- Listen to music on your Windows 7 machine from another computer on the other side of the house.

- View your videos on an Xbox 360 connected to the TV in a spare bedroom.

- Access your photo galleries stored on your Windows 7 machine on another computer.

Parents who are concerned with what content can be accessed are welcome to take control of this by clicking the Customize link. Here you can customize the content rating you will permit streamed to media programs and remote connections.

One other aspect of Media Streaming is that it runs independent of your file and print sharing security configuration. That means you can enable media streaming to multiple devices on the network without easing up the file and print sharing setup you have on the same machine.

Troubleshoot Problems

When you click the Troubleshoot Problems link off the Network and Sharing Center, this tool initially searches for troubleshooting packs and then presents them to you for both network and Internet options.

Accessing the Troubleshooting Packs

The new Troubleshooting packs in Windows 7 are easy to locate and use (see Figure 8.8). The following steps show you how to find them.

1. Click the Start orb.

2. Click Control Panel.

3. Click Network and Internet (unless you have icons showing in Control Panel, in which case you can simply click the Troubleshoot link).

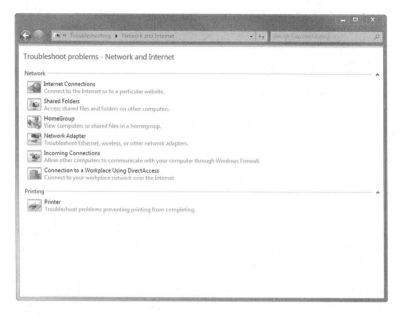

Figure 8.8 *Troubleshooting packs.*

4. Click Network and Sharing Center.

5. Click the Troubleshoot Problems link, which opens the troubleshooting pack.

Selecting anyone of the options provided opens a troubleshooting tool that is designed to specifically detect problems related to your choice. The benefit here is that you no longer need to search for every type of problem in the universe if your connection is giving you trouble—especially if you know that the problem is coming from the network adapter specifically or the Internet side of your network connection.

The network diagnostics automatically run a set of troubleshooting tools that analyzes all elements of the network or Internet item you've chosen and provides a systematic diagnosis of connectivity problems. It then automatically resolves the problems it finds or at least will walk you through simple solutions.

Accessing the Internet Connections Troubleshooting Pack

Complete the following steps to access a simple troubleshooting wizard that looks at your Internet connectivity and tries to locate any issues. If it can't find a problem, the troubleshooter takes you to Windows Help and Support for further analysis.

1. Click the Start orb.

2. Click Control Panel.

3. Click Network and Internet.

4. Choose Network and Sharing Center.

5. Click the Troubleshoot Problems link, which opens the Troubleshooting pack.

6. Click the Internet Connections button, which opens the Troubleshooting pack for Internet Connections.

7. Click Next. The wizard then attempts to diagnose potential problems.

8. Click Troubleshoot My Connection to the Internet. It then checks for problems in web connectivity, name resolution, and network gateway configuration.

9. If the troubleshooter can't solve the problem automatically, you are presented with the most likely problem and a series of steps to correct it.

10. If this still does not solve your problem, click the Why Can't I Connect to the Internet link to open Windows 7 Help and Support. You can review additional solutions to your problem there.

Accessing the Shared Folders Troubleshooting Pack

Complete the following steps to access a simple wizard that looks at the shared folders you are trying to connect to and fixes any issues connecting to them. If it can't find a problem, the troubleshooter takes you to Windows Help and Support for further analysis.

1. Click the Start orb.

2. Click Control Panel.

3. Click Network and Internet.

4. Choose Network and Sharing Center.

5. Click the Troubleshoot Problems link, which opens the Troubleshooting pack.

6. Click the Shared Folders button, which opens the Troubleshooting pack for Shared Folders.

7. Click Next.

8. Using the following sample format, type the network location you would like to access in this format: \\MarketingPC\Resources\Data.

9. Click Next. The wizard attempts to detect name resolution and network gateway configuration problems.

10. If the troubleshooter can't solve the problem automatically, you are presented with the most likely problem and a series of steps to correct it.

11. If this still does not solve your problem, click the link Why Can't I Connect to the Internet link to open Windows 7 Help and Support.

12. You can review additional solutions to your problem there.

Accessing the HomeGroup Troubleshooting Pack

Complete the following steps to access a simple troubleshooting wizard that looks at your HomeGroup and tries to locate issues connecting to it. Follow the troubleshooting instructions to locate and resolve issues.

1. Click the Start orb.

2. Click Control Panel.

3. Click Network and Internet.

4. Choose Network and Sharing Center.

5. Click the Troubleshoot Problems link, which opens the Troubleshooting pack.

6. Click the HomeGroup button, which opens the Troubleshooting pack for HomeGroup.

7. The UAC window might appear. If so, click Yes.

8. Click Next. The HomeGroup diagnostics begin.

9. Different messages will display, depending on your issue.

10. If the diagnostics apply a solution, you are asked if the problem is fixed. Select the appropriate answer to proceed.

Accessing the Network Adapter Troubleshooting Pack

Complete the following steps to access simple wizard that looks at your network adapter and tries to locate any issues. If the troubleshooter can't resolve the issue, it takes you to other options for solving the problem.

1. Click the Start orb.

2. Click Control Panel.

3. Click Network and Internet.

4. Choose Network and Sharing Center.

5. Click the Troubleshoot Problems link, which opens the Troubleshooting pack.

6. Click the Network Adapter button, which opens the Troubleshooting pack for Network Adapter.

7. Click Next.

The troubleshooter attempts to solve the problem and presents a possible solution. If it is unable to locate a problem, you will are presented with an opportunity to explore additional options or close the troubleshooter.

Accessing the Incoming Connections Troubleshooting Pack

Complete the following steps to access a simple wizard that looks at your incoming connections and tries to locate any issues. If the troubleshooter can't resolve the issue, it takes you to other options for solving the problem.

1. Click the Start orb.

2. Click Control Panel.

3. Click Network and Internet.

4. Choose Network and Sharing Center.

5. Click the Troubleshoot Problems link, which opens the Troubleshooting pack.

6. Click the Incoming Connections button, which opens the Troubleshooting pack for Incoming Connections.

   7. Click Next.

   8. Select from one of the four choices:
   - Share Files or Folders
   - Connect to this Computer Using Remote Desktop Connection
   - Find this Computer on the network
   - Something Else

   9. Click Next.

   10. A series of diagnostics runs, attempting to solve the problem. You are pre-sented with the results.

Accessing the Connection to a Workplace Using DirectAccess Troubleshooting Pack

Complete the following steps to access a simple wizard that looks at your Direct Access configuration and tries to locate any issues. If the troubleshooter can't reslove the issue, it takes you to other options for solving the problem.

   1. Click the Start orb.

   2. Click Control Panel.

   3. Click Network and Internet.

   4. Choose Network and Sharing Center.

   5. Click the Troubleshoot Problems link, which opens the Troubleshooting pack.

   6. Click the Connection to a Workplace Using DirectAccess button, which opens the Troubleshooting pack for Connection to a Workplace Using DirectAccess.

   7. Click Next.

   8. Read the DirectAccess compatibility requirements.

   9. Click Next.

   10. Connection to a Workplace Using DirectAccess diagnostics attempts to locate and solve the problem automatically. The results are displayed.

   11. The results display.

Accessing the Printer Troubleshooting Pack

Complete the following steps to access a simple wizard that looks at your printer and tries to locate any issues. If the troubleshooter can't resolve the issue, it takes you to other options for solving the problem.

1. Click the Start orb.

2. Click Control Panel.

3. Click Network and Internet.

4. Choose Network and Sharing Center.

5. Click the Troubleshoot Problems link, which opens the Troubleshooting pack.

6. Click the Printer button, which opens the Troubleshooting pack for Printer.

7. Click Next.

8. Diagnostics assess your printer situation.

9. Select the printer you would like to troubleshoot.

10. Click Next.

11. The troubleshooter diagnoses any problems and presents possible solutions.

Configuring Your TCP/IP Settings

There is a certain form of standardization in the networking world that allows our hardware to communicate with machines all over the world. Transmission Configuration Protocol/Internet Protocol (otherwise known as TCP/IP) serves as the prime communication language for our computers.

TCP/IP has evolved over the years. Windows 7 supports the latest version, IPv6. While this version supports more IP addresses than IPv4, the fundamentals of the IP stack have not changed. That's great news because that means there is little or no need for users to manually configure IP settings. For the vast majority of home users, changing TCP/IP settings is rarely—if ever—done.

Because you almost never have to configure TCP/IP settings these days, you might have forgotten some of the basics about them. In Windows 7, you access these settings in the Local Area Connection Properties dialog box (see Figure 8.9).

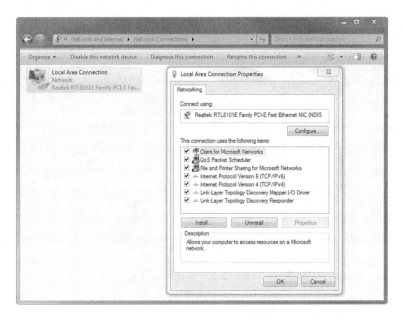

Figure 8.9   *The Local Area Connection Properties dialog box.*

Opening Local Area Connection Properties

Follow these steps to see the settings for all the network adapters connected and recognized by the sytem.

1. Click the Start orb.

2. Click Control Panel.

3. In the Network and Internet group, click the View Network Status and Tasks link.

4. In the left pane, select Change Adapter Settings.

5. From an active network connection, right-click and choose Properties. (If a UAC window opens, click Yes.) This brings up the Local Area Connection Properties dialog box.

Dynamic Host Configuration Protocol (DHCP) is a critical part of most modern networks. Simply put, DHCP allows a computer (typically a server) or router (such as a wireless network router) to handle all the heavy lifting when it comes to creating and maintaining the network. A DHCP server provides the TCP/IP address to host devices on the network. The address is supplied in octet form (such as 192.168.0.1) and provided to devices on the network. Once DHCP is established and address are assigned, the network operates pretty much on its own. Windows 7 is set up out of the box to run in a DHCP environment.

There are occasions when some computers or devices might require what is called a static IP. This is a fixed address that never changes. This might be a requirement, for example, when connecting to certain network printers or copiers. Or port forwarding might be required on a certain machine. By and large however, static IP addresses are seldom seen in mainstream home networks.

If you are asked to configure your TCP/IP settings, it's a good idea to know what your settings are. Then, if you have some trouble, you can restore those settings. A quick way to see your IP settings is to use the command prompt.

Checking Your TCP/IP Settings from a Command Prompt

Upon completing these steps, you will be able to see the TCP/IP settings for all network adapter on your computer. This exercise accesses these settings through the command prompt.

1. Click the Start orb.
2. In the search field, type **cmd** and then press Enter. A black screen opens to a command prompt.
3. Type **ipconfig** and press Enter.
4. Locate the IP address for your active network connection.

When working from a command prompt, you should be able to see the version of your IP address. (If not, you might need to scroll up on the command window to view all the IP information.) It might be an IPv4 address. The number appears in octet form (such as 192.168.0.3). You also have listed here the subnet, default gateway, and DNS information. This data is required if you ever need to establish a static IP.

The command prompt is another fast way to test your Internet connection when you have connectivity problems. For example, simply type **ping www.google.com** to send a ping request to Google. If it succeeds, you receive a reply with a status of the packet speed. If it fails, you receive a failure message, such as Ping Request Could Not Find Host.

The command prompt used to be a crucial part of Windows. With each successive version, as more and more elements have become parts of the graphical interface, I tend to use the command prompt less and less.

If you need to change your TCP/IP address, first determine the type of address you have (IPv4, IPv6, or both). Once you know that, you can configure your new address.

SHOW ME   Media 8.3—Configure Your TCP/IP Settings
Access this video file through your registered Web Edition at
my.safaribooksonline.com/9780768695212/media.

Changing a Network Adapter to Use a Static IPv4 Address

This exercise shows you how to change your IP settings from DHCP to static and how to insert an IPv4 address into your network adapter settings (see Figure 8.10).

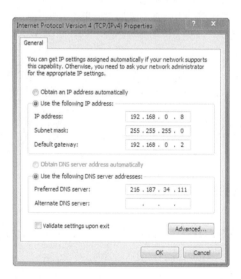

Figure 8.10   *Configuring a static IP address.*

1. Click the Start orb.
2. Click Control Panel.
3. In the Network and Internet group, click the View Network Status and Tasks link.
4. In the left pane, click Change Adapter Settings.

5. From an active network connection, right-click and choose Properties. (If a UAC window opens, click Yes.) The Local Area Connection Properties dialog box appears.

6. Click the correct Internet Protocol Version and click Properties. The Internet Protocol Version Properties dialog box appears.

7. Use the Following IPv*X* Address radio button.

8. In the IPv*X* Address box, type the new IP address.

9. Complete the information for Subnet Prefix Length box and the Default Gateway box, respectively.

10. Complete the information for the Preferred DNS Server box.

11. Click OK.

Today, routers are inexpensive and usually easily obtained. But a situation could arise where there is no router available. What if you find yourself in a situation in which you have several computers, but only one connected to the Internet? Does Windows 7 provide a way to connect them all to the Internet? Yes, there is: it's called Internet Connection Sharing (ICS). ICS is not used frequently, but it is good to know about it in case the need arises. The minimum hardware you will need to make it work is a computer connected to the Internet (host) and a wired hub. Be sure the host can connect to both the Internet and the wired hub simultaneously.

I set up an ICS environment without a wired hub by using a wireless router. To do this, I had to dumb down the router and turn off DHCP. This turned it into a simple router. After plugging in the ports to local computers, I used the ICS host to set up the network. Not the best solution, but better than nothing.

 **LET ME TRY IT**

Setting Up Internet Connection Sharing on a Wired Network

The following steps show you how to set up ICS. Upon completion, computers on your network can access the Internet through the local system.

1. On the host computer with a connection to the Internet, click the Start orb.

2. Click Control Panel.

3. Choose Network and Internet.

4. In the Network and Sharing Center, click View Network Status and Tasks.

5. In the left pane, click Change Adapter Settings.

6. Right-click the connection to the Internet and choose Properties. If it's a Local Area Connection, the Local Area Connection Properties dialog box appears.

7. Click the Sharing tab. (You won't see this tab if you have only one network connection.)

8. Select the Allow Other Network Users to Connect Through This Computer's Internet Connection check box.

9. Click OK.

10. Verify your Internet connection is operating correctly.

11. Connect the first computer you want to share the Internet with to the hub.

12. Make sure the newly connected computer is set to receive IP addresses automatically.

13. Test the connection to the Internet.

14. Add additional computers sharing the Internet in the same way.

A no-no when using ICS: Do not use ICS on networks that have DHCP servers, DNS servers, domain controllers, or gateways. Remember, your wireless router likely is also your DHCP server, so make sure you are disconnected from it before setting up ICS. Having these up on the network at the same time creates conflicts and brings your network to a grinding halt.

 TELL ME MORE   Media 8.4—A Discussion of the Ease of **Networking with Windows 7**
Access this audio recording through your registered Web Edition at **my.safaribooksonline.com/9780768695212/media.**

This chapter delves into advanced networking features of Windows 7, showing advanced users how to get the most out of them.

Using Windows 7 on the Network

In this chapter, we discuss the more advanced networking features of Windows 7 and we review of modern network topology. Domain networking is standard in most mid- to large-sized organizations. This type of network is briefly examined and you also learn how to connect one.

Other aspects of Windows 7 networking explored in this chapter are DirectAccess, BranchCache, AppLocker, Local Group Policy Settings, and remote connection applications already integrated within Windows 7.

Domain Networking

If you have never worked in a corporate setting, phrases such as domain, domain controller, and Active Directory might have little or no meaning to you. These expressions are all components of larger networks called domains. What is a domain?

To start with, for a domain to exist, there must be at least one or more computers functioning as servers. These machines are called domain controllers in a Windows world. At a minimum level, these domain servers authenticate which machines can access the domain.

A Domain Controller (DC) is a Windows Server (2000/2003/2008) running Active Directory services. What exactly does a domain controller do? There are many functions that a DC must perform, but from the angle of a user who logs into the domain, the DC validates the login and issues a token that can be used to grant or deny permissions to access resources within the domain (or perhaps across domains). Responding to security authentication requests is one of the key responsibilities of a DC.

The Logon Process and Tokens

When you log onto your domain, you provide a user name and password. The domain controller you connect to confirms your credentials, considers settings that apply specifically to you or groups you belong to, and provides you with a token.

That token must be presented (behind the scenes) to objects you attempt to access, like when you want to access a folder on a server. Gaining access is dependent on your token and the objects list.

A Discretionary Access Control List (ACL) is maintained on the objects themselves so that when a person/device/process attempts to access an object (file, printer, and so forth), the subject presents a token that includes groups the subject is a member of. The object compares that token to the list. If any group has a Deny setting attached, the object is denied. Denied settings are kept at the top of the list so that denial is quickly determined. If access is granted, that access includes a list of permissions as to what type of access can be granted.

Joining a Domain

Obviously you cannot simply walk into an office that has a domain set up, plug your laptop into an open RJ-45 network connection. and join a domain. Where would the security be in that? You must have the proper credentials on the domain and you must have been registered ahead of time within the domain.

The actual process for joining a domain is pretty straightforward, however.

 LET ME TRY IT

Connecting to and Joining a Domain

Getting on the domain network requires authentication to the domain. The following steps show you how to accomplish this.

1. Click the Start orb.
2. Click Control Panel.
3. Choose System and Security.
4. Click System.
5. In the Computer Name, Domain and Workgroup Settings group, click the Change Settings link.
6. If a UAC window appears, click Yes. The System Properties dialog box appears.
7. Click the Network ID button. The Join a Domain or Workgroup dialog box appears (see Figure 9.1).
8. Click Next.
9. Click Next again.
10. Verify you have all the account information listed and click Next.

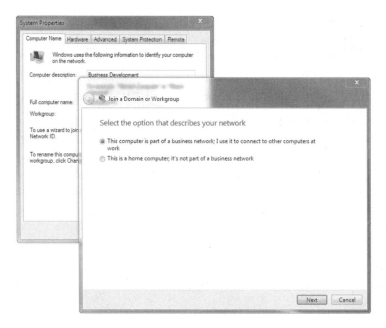

Figure 9.1 *The Join a Domain or Workgroup dialog box.*

11. Type your User name, Password and Domain name.

12. Click Next.

The Wizard completes by attempting to connect you to the domain with the credentials you have provided.

There is a distinction between your user account on the domain and your user account on the computer. The computer can allow multiple users to sit down and hit Ctrl+Alt+Delete and log into the domain if they have the correct user credentials to do so. You, however—assuming you have the correct user credentials—can log into the domain from any location within the domain (barring any security settings that might prevent you from doing so or additional security features that you don't have configured for your account (for example, a fingerprint scanner).

Log-in flexibility is helpful to your network administrators. So if a network administrator is troubleshooting a software issue on a certain computer, he doesn't have to carry all his software around each time he wants to solve a problem at a particular desktop. He can login with his username and password from his own workstation to access all his technical resources, such as network drives and public drives containing software.

SHOW ME   Media 9.1—Joining a Domain
Access this video file through your registered Web Edition at
my.safaribooksonline.com/9780768695212/media.

Domain-Joined Computers and HomeGroups

Many of us may use laptops at work and bring those systems home with us. You might have a need to be on a domain at work yet still need to access media content from your HomeGroup at home. This is possible in Windows 7 because your domain-joined laptop can see the HomeGroup and access those items within; however, none of the other HomeGroup members can see in to your work laptop, so to speak. So the sensitive corporate data on your laptop is locked from unapproved eyes.

The capability to join a HomeGroup can be disabled by the domain administrator at will. So although you have the ability, you might not have the permissions from above.

How does the computer know where you are? Network Location Awareness (NLA) is a feature by which the system can see if you have changed network locations and it can tag locations (with your help) as Home, Work, or Public. Windows 7 can switch profiles depending on which location you are using.

Changing Advanced Sharing Settings

If your computer is joined to a domain, you probably won't be able to change the network location to Home or Work. It's still a good idea to configure your network options. This is easily done by changing your advanced sharing settings (see Figure 9.2).

 LET ME TRY IT

Manually Configuring Advanced Sharing Settings

The following steps show you how to configure several different sharing options. On completion, you will have customized how items are shared.

1. Click the Start orb.
2. Click Control Panel.
3. Choose Network and Internet.
4. In the Network and Sharing Center group, click View Network Status and Tasks.
5. In the left pane, click Change Advanced Sharing Settings.

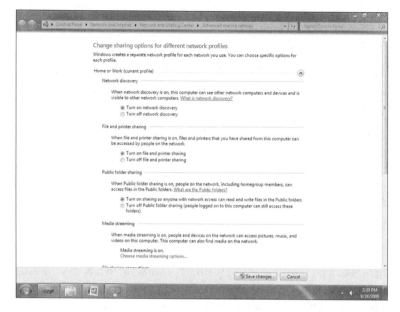

Figure 9.2 *Configuring Advanced Sharing Settings.*

6. If not opened, click the Down arrows on the right to show your choices.

7. You may configure options in the following groups:

> Network Discovery
>
> File and Printer Sharing
>
> Public Folder Sharing
>
> Media Streaming
>
> File Sharing Connections
>
> Password Protected Sharing
>
> HomeGroup Connections

8. After making your choices, click Save Changes.

9. If a UAC window appears, click Yes.

> The Password Protected Sharing option is not available on domain networks. To use password-protected sharing, you must know the username and password of the other system for access.

Naturally, the great thing about a domain is the connectivity to domain resources: other computers, printers, and so on. Connecting to other computers on the domain is not hard; you just need to know the name of the computer you want to access. Do you know your name?

LET ME TRY IT

Viewing Your Computer Name and Domain

The following steps show you how to view your computer name and the name of the domain it is joined to.

1. Click the Start orb.
2. Click Control Panel.
3. Choose System and Security.
4. Click System.
5. In the Computer Name, Domain, and Workgroup Settings section, you will see your computer name.

Sharing files can be one of the best features of working in a domain environment. Some companies provide public network drive space. That could be good or bad depending on the file you want to share.

For example, if you want to make a company policy document available for all to read, you could share it in a public folder. However, maybe someone in Accounting needs to share a file that includes company salaries with someone in Human Resources, but that type of sensitive information shouldn't be available to the entire company. Windows 7 provides the Share With menu, a new means of sharing files that solves problems like this. The Share With menu lets you share individual files and folders, and even entire libraries, with other people.

LET ME TRY IT

Sharing a File as Read-Only with Someone Else on the Domain

The following steps show you how to share files from your library with someone else on the same network.

1. Click the Start orb.
2. Navigate to the file within your personal folder you would like to share with another user on the domain.
3. Right-click the item you want to share and choose Share With.
4. Click Specific People. The File Sharing Wizard appears.
5. Click the arrow next to the text box and choose the user you would like to share the file with.
6. Click Add. The name appears in the list below the textbox.

7. Verify that the Permission Level for this user is set to Read by clicking on the Down arrow to the right of Read.

8. Click Share.

9. If a UAC window opens, click Yes.

10. You receive confirmation that the file has been successfully been made available for sharing.

11. Click Email to send a link to this share to the user or copy the link, open an email client, paste the link into the body of the message, and then send it to the user.

12. Click Done.

> If you are having trouble sharing an item, it could be due to one of the following factors:
>
> Only files from within your personal folder can be shared by default.
>
> If you don't see the Share With menu, you might be trying to share an item on a network or other unsupported location.
>
> If you're trying to share something in a Windows 7 Public folder, the Share With menu displays an Advanced Sharing Settings option. This option takes you to Control Panel, where you can turn Public folder sharing on or off.

Advanced file sharing lets you share more than just your libraries. If you choose, you can share the entire contents of your drive on a domain. For security reasons, this feature is turned off. If you feel you really must do this, use caution with who you give permission to access it.

 LET ME TRY IT

Using Advanced Sharing Settings to Share a Folder Outside Your File Library

The following steps show you how to share files from outside your library with someone else on the same network.

1. Click the Start orb.

2. Navigate to the file outside your library you would like to share with another user on the domain.

3. Right-click the folder you want to share and choose Share With.

4. Click Advanced Sharing.

5. Select Advanced Sharing.

6. If a UAC prompt appears, click Yes or entire credentials to accept. The Advanced Sharing dialog box appears.

7. Select the Share This Folder check box.

8. Click Permissions.

9. Select Add or Remove.

10. Choose a user or group to share your folder with.

11. Select the check boxes for the permissions you want to assign for that user or group.

12. Click OK.

13. Click OK again.

Remember sharing your entire hard drive (or root) with C$ in the old days? You might have wondered where this has gone. By default, Vista and Windows 7 prevent local accounts from accessing administrative shares through the network. To enable administrative shares, you have to make this registry change.

Hive: HKEY_LOCAL_MACHINE

Key: Software\Microsoft\Windows\CurrentVersion\Policies\System

Name: LocalAccountTokenFilterPolicy

Data Type: REG_DWORD

Value: 1

After rebooting, the hidden share is accessible from other computers.

Looking at DirectAccess and BranchCache

DirectAccess and BranchCache are two new features to Windows 7. Actually, these features will not function without the release of the Server 2008 R2 release as well.

DirectAccess

With Windows 7 and Server 2008 R2, mobile users can access their corporate networks from any Internet connection (drum roll) without a Virtual Private Networking (VPN) connection.

Typically, within a business network, users with mobile systems receive updates and policy changes only when they connect to the network. With DirectAccess, users do not even need to log-in; as long as they have Internet access, the changes from IT can be applied.

This will prove to be a real improvement for administrators in maintaining users on the go. Now, regardless of their location, administrators can be sure that even remote mobile users are guaranteed secure connections to their enterprise networks regardless of location.

> DirectAccess uses IPv6-over-IPsec for encrypted communications over the Internet and does not work with IPv4.

BranchCache

The name actually says what it does. Branch offices usually contain users who access data that might not be held locally (at the main office). Using BranchCache, a user at a branch office can access various content that might be at the main headquarters. If, perhaps, another user at the branch attempts to access that same content, the second user can access that content faster because the the content accessed by the first user can be cached on the server.

You can set BranchCache to work in one of two modes:

- Hosted Cache mode: The server itself retains the cached files.

- Distributed Cache mode: Clients retain copies of the cached files. The server still ensures content is fresh, still maintains the latest version of files, and still maintains the permissions for accessing those files.

This type of feature requires various forms of security and some of the technologies in place include Secure Sockets Layer (SSL), Secure Message Block (SMB) Signing, and IPsec.

AppLocker

The greatest risk to any network comes from the inside, from users who have downloaded or installed unauthorized software and files which may contain viruses and malware. That is why AppLocker (see Figure 9.3), an update from the Software Restriction policies in Vista can really help to curtail those security risks.

AppLocker includes policy settings that can be configured to prevent unapproved software from running on a computer. These rules can be applied within Group Policy settings that can restrict all the way down to an application's version number.

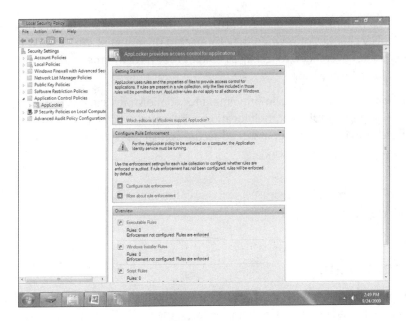

Figure 9.3   *AppLocker—New to Windows 7.*

Windows AppLocker contains several new features:

- Audit-only mode

- Wizard to create multiple rules at one time

- Policy import or export

- Rule collection

- PowerShell support

- Custom error messages

- Rule scope can be configured for a specific user or group

- Default rule action deny

There are three types of rules:

- **Path Rules:** Allows you to restrict program execution to a path (which will work if all applications launch from the same paths).

- **Hash Rules:** Uses a cryptographic hash to ensure that the application is the right application—which works great so long as you don't have to constantly update the .exe file for the applications you use (because that changes the hash).

- **Publisher Rules:** Uses a digital signature from the publisher to identify the applications you approve.

 LET ME TRY IT

Open AppLocker to Configure Rules

The following steps show you how to access AppLocker, followed by an explanation of rule creation.

1. Click the Start orb.

2. Click Control Panel.

3. Choose System and Security.

4. Click Administrative Tools.

5. Double-click Local Security Policy.

6. If the UAC dialog box appears, click Yes.

7. In the console tree on the left pane, double-click Application Control Policies.

8. Double-click AppLocker.

A scenario where you might use AppLocker is if you wanted to create a rule to allow only those in the Finance department to execute certain financial applications.

You would begin by creating new rules. Right-click Executable Rules and begin with one of the following:

- **Create New Rule:** Launches a Wizard that helps you create an AppLocker rule.

- **Automatically Generate Rules:** Automatically creates rules for all installed applications.

- **Create Default Rules:** Creates three rules that allow the execution of applications in both the Windows and Program Files folders.

AppLocker also has three enforcement modes:

- **Not Configured:** Rules and Group Policy Objects (GPOs) override this default setting.

- **Enforce Rules:** Enforces the configured rules.

- **Audit Only:** Allows you to preview which application is affected by a policy before enabling it. An event log records all data for review before enforcing a rule.

You can begin working with these features either through Group Policy settings or through the Local Security Policy on your desktop. Auditing your rules first lets you vary the effectiveness of the rule. In order for AppLocker to be enforced on a computer, the Application Identity service must be running.

 **LET ME TRY IT**

Starting the Application Identity Service and Configuring AppLocker to Audit Rules

The following steps show you how to start the Application Identity service. Next, you open AppLocker and configure it to audit rules.

1. Click the Start orb.

2. In the search field, type **service**.

3. In the Programs group, click Services.

4. If a UAC window opens, click Yes.

5. Right-click Application Identity.

6. Select Properties.

7. Using the drop-down arrow, change Startup Type to Automatic.

8. Click OK.

9. Right-click again on Application Identity.

10. Select Start.

11. Close the Services window.

12. Click the Start orb.

13. Click Control Panel.

14. Choose System and Security.

15. Click Administrative Tools.

16. Double-click Local Security Policy.

17. If the UAC dialog box appears, click Yes.

18. In the console tree on the left pane, double-click Application Control Policies.

19. Double-click AppLocker.

20. In the right pane in the middle section, click the Configure Rule Enforcement link. The AppLocker properties dialog box opens.

21. On the Enforcement tab, in the Executable Rules section, select the Configured checkbox.

22. In the Executable Rules section, click the drop-down arrow next to Enforce Rules and choose Audit Only.

23. Click OK.

Using AppLocker's audit function allows you to see how applications would behave if your rules were enabled. It displays a list of all the files that will be enforced by the rule. As you examine this, you can spot any troubles that might crop up before deploying the rule.

Local Group Policy Settings

Local Group Policy settings have existed since the introduction of Windows 2000. From a network perspective, policies help administrators control groups of computers and users. But on a local level, you can still use a policy (the local policy) to control users who log on to that particular machine.

Vista included the Multiple Group Policy Objects feature, which provided for the use of more than one local policy. Multiple Group Policy Objects (GPOE) can be created to control the computer or users that log-in. So, you can create a policy that affects an individual user or a policy that affects all standard users (called non-Administrators when configuring the policy). It is up to you.

You need to access Local Group Policy settings (see Figure 9.4) from the Microsoft Management Console (MMC). When you add the GPOE snap-in, the Group Policy Wizard begins.

This isn't the same as opening the policy with gpedit.msc (which opens the actual local policy itself). You are looking to configure a different policy here.

 LET ME TRY IT

Opening MMC and Saving the Local Group Policy Editor Snap-In

The following steps show you how to add the Local Group Policy editor snap-in to the Microsoft Management Console and save it. After this is completed, you can return to this saved configuration and open it directly.

1. Click the Start orb.

2. In the search field, type **mmc** and press Enter.

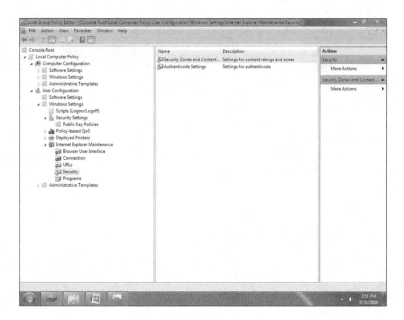

Figure 9.4   *Browsing through Internet Explorer policy options.*

3. If the UAC dialog box appears, click Yes.

4. After the MMC dialog box appears, click File.

5. Choose Add/Remove Snap-In.

6. In the left pane, click Group Policy Object Editor.

7. Click the Add > button. This opens the Group Policy Wizard.

8. Local Computer is selected by default. Click Finish.

9. Click OK.

10. In the center pane, click Local Computer Policy.

11. In the top menu, click File and choose Save As.

12. Browse to a location where you can easily locate this file.

13. In the File Name box, type **Local Group Policy Editor.msc**.

14. Click Save.

From here you have the choice of setting policies for Computer Configuration or User Configuration. Past that, there are extensive choices to audit (see Figure 9.5) or to lock down the machine even further.

You might notice in entries in your policy for your users that you never put there. This happens sometimes when you activate a security feature. For example, if you set up parental controls for a user, an individual user policy object is created behind the scenes. This policy then shows up in the policy editor even though you never explicitly added it here.

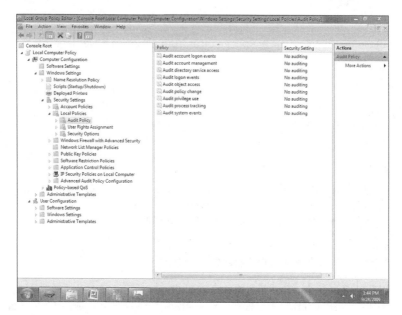

Figure 9.5 *Setting up auditing in Local Group Policy.*

Select the user or group (admin or non-admin) to work with; then you will have the MMC console with the user-configuration options that you can configure.

 **LET ME TRY IT**

Creating a 90-Day Password Policy Using Local Security Policy Editor

The following steps show you how to create a 90-day password policy.

1. Click the Start orb.

2. In the search field, type **security**.

3. Click Local Security Policy.

4. If a UAC window opens, click Yes.

5. Double-click Account Policies.

6. Double-click Password Policy.

7. Double-click Maximum Password Age in the right pane.

8. In the Local Security Setting tab, type **90** in the box.

9. Click Apply.

10. Click OK.

11. Close the Local Security Policy editor. Your changes have been made.

> To use the Local Security Policy, you must be a member of the Administrators group on the local computer or you must have been delegated the appropriate authority to useit. If the computer is joined to a domain, members of the Domain Admins group will likely be able to perform this procedure.

 SHOW ME Media 9.2—Using Local Group Policy Settings
Access this video file through your registered Web Edition at
my.safaribooksonline.com/9780768695212/media.

Remote Desktop Connections

Accessing your computer remotely is increasing in demand as more and more users are working from home. Early on, PcAnywhere and now GoToMyPC.com have become major developers of this technology. Windows 7 brings us the latest Remote Desktop Connection Version 6.1, as seen in Figure 9.6.

The Remote Desktop Connection client that comes with Windows 7 is equipped with new and enhanced features, including the Remote Desktop Protocol (RDP) version 7. Enhancements to the Remote Desktop Connection client include the following:

- Windows 7 Aero support

- Direct 2D and Direct 3D 10.1 application support

- True multi-monitor support

- RDP Core Performance Improvements

- Multimedia enhancements

- Media Foundation support

- DirectShow support

- Low Latency audio playback support

- Bi-directional audio support

Figure 9.6   *New features in Remote Desktop Connection include multi-monitor support.*

 **LET ME TRY IT**

Opening Remote Desktop Connection

The following steps show you how to quickly open Remote Desktop Connection.

1. Click the Start orb.

2. In the search field, type **remote**.

3. Click Remote Desktop Connection. This opens the Remote Desktop Connection application.

4. In the lower left, click Options to view the following tabs:

> General
>
> Display
>
> Local Resources
>
> Programs
>
> Experience
>
> Advanced

Despite its simple interface, Remote Desktop Connection is a very powerful tool. It simplifies your efforts to work on your laptop by giving you the ability to access all of your work-related programs, files, and network resources as though you were sitting in front of your computer at work.

Before you can begin working with Remote Desktop Connection, both the computer you sit at (client) and the computer you connect with (host) require some configuration. Microsoft has forced you to manually configure the program in an effort to provide a greater degree of security. Forcing manual configuration of the program—rather than enabling access by default—ensures unwanted guests do not have access to computers to do as they please.

 LET ME TRY IT

Configuring Remote Desktop Connection Permission on a Host Machine

The following steps show you how to modify the connection settings for Remote Desktop Connection (see Figure 9.7). After completing these steps, you will be ready to connect with another system.

1. Click the Start orb.
2. Click Control Panel.
3. In the search field, type **system**.
4. In the Control Panel group, click System.
5. In the left pane, click Remote Settings.
6. If a UAC window appears, click Yes.
7. The Remote tab of the System Properties dialog box opens.
8. Select the second radio button, Allow Connections from Computers Running Any Version of Remote Desktop(Less Secure).
9. Click Select Users.
10. Add a user name. (If you are an administrator of the machine, by default you will be able to connect.)
11. Click OK, and then click OK again.

To access a remote machine through Remote Desktop Connection, the machine needs to be out of sleep or hibernation mode. Make sure the settings for sleep and hibernation (if available) are set to Never.

Figure 9.7 *Enter an IP address to connect on your local area network.*

 LET ME TRY IT

Connecting with Another Computer on the Same Network

With the system properly set up from the previous exercise, the following steps show you how to connect with another computer using Remote Desktop Connection.

1. Click the Start orb.

2. In the search field, type **remote**.

3. Click Remote Desktop Connection. This opens the Remote Desktop Connection application.

4. In the Computer text box, type the computer name (or IP address, if you're on a local network).

5. In the User Name text box, type the user name.

6. Click Options button in the lower-left of the application. Select the Allow Me to Save Credentials checkbox.

7. Click Connect.

8. Log-in with credentials.

9. On acceptance, you are logged into the machine.

With the host computer properly configured, you can now access this computer from the client (provided you know the computer name or IP address).

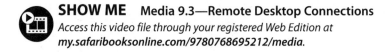 **SHOW ME**   **Media 9.3—Remote Desktop Connections**
Access this video file through your registered Web Edition at
my.safaribooksonline.com/9780768695212/media.

RemoteApp and Desktop Connections

Windows 7 also features RemoteApp and Desktop Connections (see Figure 9.8), a new way to connect remotely to your computer. The focus here is on corporate networks. With this application, you can use access programs and desktops (remote computers and virtual computers) made available to you by your IT department.

Figure 9.8   *Connect remotely with a URL through the new RemoteApp and Desktop Connections.*

When you're at home, you can access all the programs and computers that you normally would be accessed only at work. By utilizing RemoteApp and Desktop Connections rather than Remote Desktop Connection or other means to connect, your network administrator can publish resources available for you to access and give you either a special file or URL to set up the connection. Then he can update these resources, which are then automatically passed on to you. With a connection, all of these resources are located in one easy-to-access folder on your computer. Using these resources is almost the same as if they were on your local network or on your computer.

Starting RemoteApp and Desktop Connections Using a URL

The following steps show you how to use RemoteApp and Desktop Connections to connect your corporate network.

1. Click the Start orb.

2. In the search field, type **remote**.

3. In the Control Panel group, click RemoteApp and Desktop Connections.

4. In the left pane, click Set Up a New Connection with RemoteApp and Desktop Connections. This opens the Set Up a New Connection with RemoteApp and Desktop Connections dialog box.

5. In the Connection URL text box, type the web address provided by your administrator and click Next.

6. The Ready to Set Up the Connection dialog box opens.

7. Read the security warning provided and then click Next.

Adding Connection Resources opens and verifies the connection to start downloading the data.

 TELL ME MORE   Media 9.4—A Discussion of New Networking **Features in Windows 7**
Access this audio recording through your registered Web Edition at
my.safaribooksonline.com/9780768695212/media.

This chapter goes through the Control Panel and highlights the top features of several of the applets.

10

Control Panel Features in Windows 7

Using the Control Panel

The Control Panel has been an integral part of Windows since the very beginning; however, starting with Windows 95, we saw the Control Panel take on its modern form as a folder with shortcuts to applications (called *applets* in earlier versions of Control Panel).

You might recall that Control Panel had different views to work with: a Classic view that showed all your applet shortcuts, and a default Home view that showed you categories of options.

In Windows 7, the Control Panel offers your computer adjustment tools in a Category view to start with (see Figure 10.1). You can adjust the size of the icons by clicking the Category down-arrow in the upper-right corner. Figure 10.2 shows Large Icons selected.

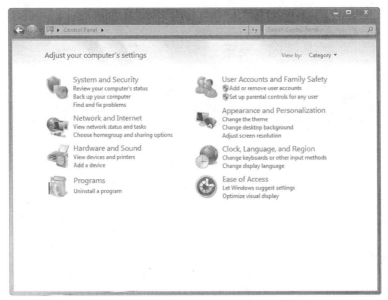

Figure 10.1   *Accessing the Control Panel using the Category view.*

An alternative way to find Control Panel items (as they are now referred to as) is to search for them by name. If you have forgotten the name, simply type a letter or two of the name and Search returns a list of several items in the Control Panel—ideally what you're looking for.

Figure 10.2   *Control Panel with Large Icon view.*

One thing you might want to do is have your Control Panel options expand off the Start menu to help you work a bit faster.

SHOW ME   Media 10.1—Using the Control Panel
Access this video file through your registered Web Edition at
my.safaribooksonline.com/9780768695212/media.

Expanding the Control Panel from the Start Menu

The following steps show you how to create a shortcut that puts the Control Panel applications on your Start menu.

1. Right-click the Start orb.

2. Choose Properties. The Taskbar and Start Menu Properties dialog box opens to the Start Menu tab.

3. Click the Customize button and locate Control Panel.

4. Select the Display as a Menu radio button to allow Control Panel to expand out as a menu.

5. Click OK.

6. Click OK again.

Another alternative way to access the Control Panel is to turn it into a Jump List from the Taskbar. You can do this when you have an instance of Control Panel running. Right-click the Control Panel icon in the Taskbar and choose Pin This Program to the Taskbar. Now when you right-click this icon on the Taskbar, a Jump List of recently used Control Panel items appears. This list will dynamically change depending on which Control Panel applets you frequently access.

The Item Lineup

If you are looking at Control Panel in Windows 7 and you are a former Windows XP user, you will note a lot of change. If you are a Vista user, you will note some change, but not too much. Let's take a look at each applet.

In some cases, an item has already been discussed (or will be discussed in a future chapter) and we will mention that when we discuss the item here.

The Action Center

As discussed in Chapter 7, the Action Center replaces the Security Center for XP and Vista users as the one-stop location for your security (and now) maintenance dashboards. The Action Center is located in the System and Security group.

Administrative Tools

This is less of an item and more of a shortcut to Administrative Tools that you might need to use, such as Computer Management, Event Viewer, and Services (all of which we discuss in greater detail in Chapter 12). The Administrative Tools are located in the System and Security group.

AutoPlay

Use AutoPlay to change default settings for CDs, DVDs and devices so that you can automatically (per your specifications) play music and movies, view pictures, and so forth.

This item gives you a single location (see Figure 10.3) to determine the desired result you want when putting in different types of media. You can configure a DVD to automatically play within Windows Media Center or some other application. Or you can determine that pictures or audio files use specific options.

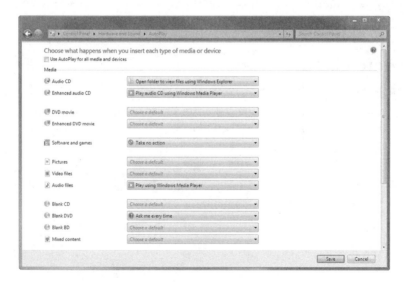

Figure 10.3   *The AutoPlay item.*

LET ME TRY IT

Modifying Your Picture, Video and Audio Autoplay Options

The following steps show you how to change the computer's behavior when you insert media such as CDs and DVDs.

1. Click the Start orb.

2. Select Control Panel.

3. Choose Hardware and Sound.

4. Click AutoPlay.

5. In the Pictures media type, click the drop-down arrow and select a new action to take.

6. Select new actions to take for Video Files.

7. Select new actions to take for Audio Files.

8. Click Save.

The AutoPlay options include settings for enhanced audio CDs or enhanced DVD movies. What are these? Well, sometimes artists include additional items on their CDs, like music videos and so forth. Basically these are CDs or DVDs that have different format types on them, requiring additional settings.

Backup and Restore

This is Windows 7 integrated tool for backing up and restoring your files and/or system (see Figure 10.4). Vista introduced a Backup and Restore Center tool for performing your own backup. Windows 7 has expanded and enhanced its feature set. The new Backup and Restore application is a bit more intense and 'work-oriented' than we saw in Vista.

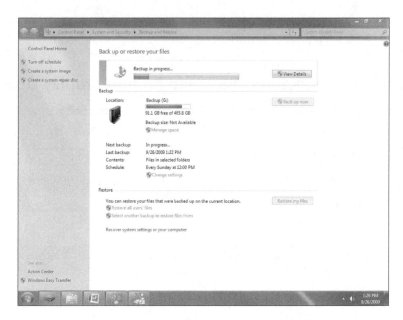

Figure 10.4   *Backup and Restore in progress.*

Backup and Restore (or Recovery) involves different approaches because you might be referring to different aspects of restore. For example, you might want to recover an entire system, or perhaps you might want to simply recover files that have been corrupted. You might want to just go back to a point in time and restore to that point in terms of system changes but not file changes.

From within Control Panel there is a new Backup and Restore item that allows you to perform the following:

- Create a schedule and turn it on or off
- Create a system image
- Create a system repair disc
- Create a new, full backup
- Restore all user files
- Restore your system

The backup features in Vista asked you to choose between backing up files or backing up the entire computer. With Windows 7, if you choose Let Me Choose when configuring your backup, you're provided with a few more options. You can determine if you want a library, a folder, a drive, or other items. You can even include a system image (which is a copy of the drives required for Windows to run and can be used to restore your computer if Windows stops working). If you choose Let Windows Choose, every user will be backed up and a system image will automatically be created.

 LET ME TRY IT

Setting Up a Scheduled Backup of Selected Data Files and Creating a System Image

The following steps show you how to create a backup schedule for data you choose. In addition, you learn how to create and save a system image.

1. Click the Start orb.

2. Select Control Panel.

3. Choose System and Security.

4. Under the heading Backup and Restore, select the link Back Up Your Computer.

5. In the Backup and Restore window that opens, click Set Up Backup.

6. If a UAC window appears, click Yes.

7. Locate the drive you want to back up to and then click Next.

8. Select the Let Me Choose radio button and then click Next.

9. Using the checkboxes, select folders you want backed up. Notice that the Include a System Image of Drives: (C:) is selected.

10. Click Next.

11. Review your backup settings and then click the Change Schedule link.

12. Using the drop-down arrows, change any preferences for How Often, What Day, or What Time you'd like to run your backup.

13. Click OK.

14. Click the Save Settings and Run Backup button and your backup begins.

15. Click View Details to open another window with more information on your backup progress.

16. On completion, you will find a backup file and an image folder in the backup location.

With your first backup complete, your next backup will occur according to the schedule you created. The only changes made will be with files that have changed since the last back up, an incremental backup. The system image will not be created again automatically.

Restoring your files is a painless process. You can restore backed-up versions of files that are lost, damaged, or changed accidentally. You can also restore individual files, groups of files, or all of the files that you have backed up.

 LET ME TRY IT

Restoring Your Files

1. Click the Start orb.

2. Select Control Panel.

3. Choose System and Security.

4. Under Backup and Restore, click the Restore Files from Backup link.

5. In the Backup and Restore window that opens, click the Restore My Files button. This opens the Restore Files dialog box.

6. Click Browse for Files.

7. Choose the files you want restored and click Add Files.

8. Choose the location you would like the files restored to and then click Restore. A window opens, showing you the progress of your restore.

9. On completion, your files will be restored as they were last backed up.

After making several backups over a period of time, the files might grow in size to a point where you would like to delete some of them to save space. In the Backup and Restore window is a link to Manage Space. This link allows you to view backups in date range, see what size they are taking up, and remove unnecessary ones.

Also in this section you can administer the amount of space taken up by system images. You can choose for Windows to manage the space or you can choose to save only the latest system image.

Another feature new to Windows 7 is native .iso burning. This allows you to save files in .iso format as an image burned onto a CD/DVD. Disc images of backups can be saved as .iso files. By keeping these backups offline, it can help in restoring files in the event of a system failure.

To open Windows Disc Image Burner, right-click any existing .iso file and choose Burn Disc Image. A simple dialog opens, letting you choose your disc burner drive. To start burning the disc image, click Burn. This simple yet effective utility we've been waiting for is now here.

For additional recovery methods you can choose the Recovery item in Control Panel to access an option to go to System Restore. Or you can select the Advanced Recovery Methods link, which takes you to two options:

- Use a system image you created earlier to recover your computer. If you have created a system image, you can use it to replace everything on this computer (including Windows, your programs, and all your files) with the information saved on the system image.

- Reinstall Windows (requires Windows installation disc). This option reinstalls Windows on your computer. Afterward, you can restore your files from a backup. Any programs you've installed must be reinstalled using the original installation discs or files. Existing files might remain in the Windows.old folder on your hard disk after the reinstall completes.

One last item in this section to consider is on the Create a System Repair Disc link located in the left pane of the Backup and Restore center. A system repair disc can be used to boot your computer in case it goes down. This disc also contains Windows system recovery tools that can help you recover Windows from a serious error or restore your computer from a system image.

After clicking the Create a System Repair Disc link, a very simple menu is presented, letting you choose which CD/DVD drive to burn the disc to. After you select it, click Create Disc. Hopefully, you'll never have to use it.

BitLocker Drive Encryption

As discussed in Chapter 7, this item helps you to configure BitLocker encryption for your entire system or with the new BitLocker to Go option to encrypt USB drives. The BitLocker item can be located in the System and Security group.

Color Management

The Color Management item was introduced in Vista but was also available as a downloadable XP PowerToy. This tool is designed to establish a better screen-to-print match and to provide support for more reliable printing with today's powerful color devices (such as digital cameras and modern printers).

Keep in mind that whether you're working with the scanner/camera, the computer, or the printer, you are dealing with different devices that have different characteristics and capabilities with colors. Additionally, even software programs have different color capabilities. For example, the same picture opened by two different photo viewing applications might produce different results to the viewer.

Color Management maintains consistency between different devices and applications to produce a more uniform appearance. It's a tool that will mostly appeal to digital photographers who are serious hobbyists or experts in the field.

One of the simpler features of Color Management is calibrating the display.

 LET ME TRY IT

Using Color Management to Calibrate Your Display

The following steps take you through a Wizard that helps calibrate your display colors. This requires you to adjust several on-screen sliders to set various color levels.

1. Click the Start orb.

2. In the Search field, type **color**.

3. Select Color Management.

4. Click the Advanced tab.

5. In the Display Calibration section, click the Calibrate Display button.

6. If a UAC window appears, click Yes.

7. The Display Color calibration box opens. If you use multiple monitors, make sure you are viewing this box on the display you are attempting to calibrate.

8. Click Next.

9. Click Next again.

10. Click Next again.

11. Using the slider on the left, adjust the gamma level.

12. Click Next.

13. Click Next again.

14. Using the controls on your display, set the Brightness higher or lower until you can distinguish the suit from the shirt with the X that is barely visible.

15. Click Next.

16. Click Next again.

17. Using the contrast control on your display, set the Contrast as high as possible without losing the ability to see the wrinkles on the shirt.

18. Click Next.

19. Click Next again.

20. Move the slider bars to adjust the Color Balance, removing any color from the gray bars.

21. If you prefer, use the Previous Calibration button and the Current Calibration button to compare the display.

22. At the end of this dialog, a box is checked by default that initiates the ClearType Tuner that ensures text appears correctly. Leave the box checked or uncheck it (depending on your preference) and click Finish.

Credential Manager

This is a new tool in Windows 7 that allows you to save your credentials (such as your usernames and passwords) for websites you log into and other resources you connect to (such as other systems). These credentials are saved in the Windows Vault (see Figure 10.5). One of the coolest features here is that you have the ability to backup and/or restore the vault.

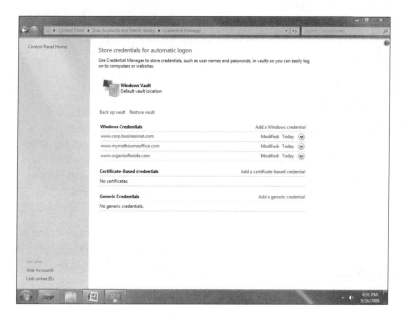

Figure 10.5 *The Credential Manager and the Windows Vault.*

On first glance, this might look like you will have the ability to use this feature for all of your website login information (Gmail, Twitter, Facebook, and so on). However, it works only with sites that can interact with Credential Manager and the Windows Vault.

SHOW ME Media 10.2—Credential Manager
Access this video file through your registered Web Edition at
my.safaribooksonline.com/9780768695212/media.

LET ME TRY IT

Adding Website Credentials to Windows Vault

The following steps take you into Credential Manager. To complete the steps, you will need the name of a website that you would like to add your credentials to along with the username and password required to log into the website.

1. Click the Start orb.

2. Select Control Panel.

3. Click User Accounts and Family Safety.

4. Click Credential Manager.

5. In the Windows Credentials section, click Add a Windows Credential.

6. In the Internet or Network Address box, type the address of the website or network location. Type your User Name and Password information. Click OK.

Your newly added credentials are listed. If you prefer, repeat this process with both Certificate-Based Credentials and Generic Credentials. When completed, click Back Up Vault to choose a location to backup your stored logon credentials. Interestingly, instead of a Save button, you are asked to press Ctrl+Alt+Delete. This secures the Desktop during the save process and requires you to add a password to the backup file you are saving.

Date and Time

As mentioned in Chapter 2, this item is used to (logically) configure the Date and Time on the Date and Time tab. Here you can configure the date, time, and time zone for your system. However, it is the Additional Clocks feature (introduced in Vista) that is really helpful. You can configure two additional clocks with their own time zones. When you hover your mouse over the time, you will see the time in these other locations. The Date and Time item can be located in the Clock, Language and Region group.

Default Programs

This is a quick place to find your default program associations and file-to-program associations. For example, if you are tired of your MP3 files opening up with Media Player and you want them to open with WinAmp or some other player, you can make the changes here.

There are four options when you open up the Default Programs item. (Keep in mind you can also open the Default Programs item by clicking the Start orb and clicking Default Programs.)

- **Set Your Default Programs:** Need to choose between Firefox and Internet Explorer as your default browser? Here is where you can tell Windows 7 which one is your go-to application. The same is true for your email, contact management information, media files, and photos.

- **Associate a File Type or Protocol with a Program:** For an expanded view of all file types and protocols and their associated applications, you can select this option to ensure all your file types can be opened by the application you prefer.

- **Change AutoPlay Settings:** This option opens the AutoPlay item discussed previously in this chapter.

- **Set Program Access and Computer Defaults:** This is yet another way to specify which programs access certain information. You can choose the following: Computer Manufacturer (this appears only if a manufacturer established preconfigured settings), Microsoft Windows (for an all-Microsoft default world), Non-Microsoft (allows you to use only non-Microsoft programs; access to Microsoft programs will be removed unless you select Custom), and Custom (for a mix and match of applications—it's the most logical choice for most of us, and that's why it's selected by default).

Changes made under the Set your Default Programs settings are unique per user. They won't affect other users on your computer. By contrast, the options you select for Set Program Access and Computer Defaults' apply to all users on the system.

Desktop Gadgets

This item opens up your Desktop Gadgets dialog box, providing you with options to use as gadgets as well as a link to download additional ones.

Device Manager

We first encountered Device Manager back in Windows 95 and it has moved around a bit from one version of the OS to another until, starting with Vista, it was given an item within Control Panel (although you can still access it from the Computer Management tool). It's one of the best tools to utilize when you have a hardware issue because you can quickly see which devices or drivers are not functioning properly.

Try as you might, you won't find printer information in the Device Manager, instead, look in Devices and Printers located on the Start menu.

To access Device Manager, click the Start orb, Control Panel, Hardware and Sound, and under the Devices and Printers section, click Device Manager. With Device Manager you can see which devices are installed and functioning properly. You can right-click the system and choose one of two options:

- **Scan for Hardware Changes:** This option checks for any PnP hardware already installed. A good use for this is in troubleshooting devices. Sometimes we might right-click a device and actually delete it from Device Manager. But, because it is still physically connected, the scan will find that device again and ask us to supply drivers for it. Sometimes this can help us find out the source of a hardware problem.

- **Add Legacy Hardware:** If you select this option, the Hardware item runs, asking you to choose between searching for the drivers or allowing you to choose your own drivers.

The Windows Compatibility Center website is a great place to go to find out if your hardware is compatible with Windows 7. To find the Windows Compatibility Center, go to www.microsoft.com and search for *windows compatibility center*. Here you will find a comprehensive list of devices that have already been tested and approved to work with Windows 7. If you are unsure if a device will work or not with Windows 7, check here before installing it.

You can also update drivers by right-clicking an item and choosing Update Driver Software. We can modify settings from within the Properties of the hardware devices we have. Then you can use:

- **Driver Rollback:** From the Properties of any given device you can go to the Drivers tab. There is an option here to roll back the driver. When you have a problem with a device after you have installed an updated driver, you can select this driver to roll it back to its previous version.

- **Device Conflicts:** Sometimes two hardware devices require the same resources from your system and they will compete for these resources, causing a hardware conflict. You can use Device Manager to disable devices you do not need or want. You can also resolve the conflict by going into the Properties of a device and clicking the Resources tab for a manual resolution to the problem.

Like XP and Vista, Windows 7 uses a driver-signing process to make sure drivers have been certified through Microsoft to work correctly. Sometimes we purposely choose to install devices that have not been verified. Other times maybe we didn't know. If you click the Start orb and type sigverif.exe in the Search field, the Signature Verification Tool scans your system for any unsigned drivers. This is not to say that all of these are bad drivers, but when you are troubleshooting a problem, it helps to have all the facts.

Devices and Printers

This feature shows you all the devices connected to your computer. Depending on the device, you can see items related to that device. For example, in Figure 10.6, you can see your Devices, Printers and Faxes, and any Unspecified items. By selecting the Microsoft XPS Document Writer, it shows you some options in the Menu toolbar, such as See What's Printing, Print Server Properties, and more.

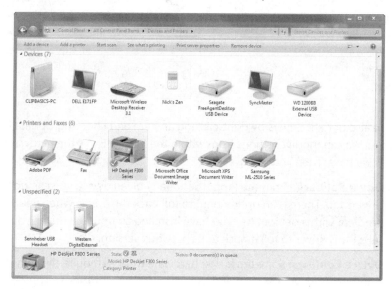

Figure 10.6 *Devices and Printers.*

Device Stage

Where Devices and Printers really shines is in its interaction with Device Stage. This is a new way to interact with items you plug into your computer, such as your phone, digital camera, printer, or portable media player. It works for USB devices and Bluetooth and Wi-Fi devices as well.

When you first plug in a device, drivers are loaded (if Windows 7 has them) and your device is soon up and running. If a driver isn't found, Windows 7 searches for the driver on Windows Update. Device Stage shows you all the applications, services, and information for a device. The manufacturer can create a device that supports Device Stage so that it appears on the Taskbar with the correct image of the device and offers Jump List displays for things you can do with the device.

This is quite a change from previous operating systems. In the past, you had to locate an application that went along with a device (such as a scanner). That meant clicking through various menus and applications to try to locate the feature you needed. If you didn't use the features for a while, it could digress into a lengthy search on how to perform a simple task. Now, with Device Stage, the device becomes the focus (see Figure 10.7).

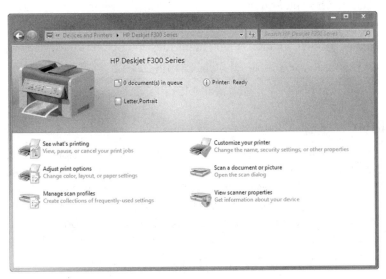

Figure 10.7   *Device Stage shows you features available by device.*

Because Device Manager features a device and all it can do, you now need only to click on a device and all features associated with it will appear front and center. The result is a far more logical approach to utilizing your hardware. Instead of searching for the scanner application, you can simply click Devices and Printers and locate the scanner. The entire experience makes Device Stage one of the most significant additions to Windows 7 and quickly makes for a 'must-have' feature.

LET ME TRY IT

Using Device Stage to View a Device and Its Corresponding Jump List

The following steps show you how to access Device Stage. In order to view a device, you must have device hardware already attached to your computer.

1. Click the Start orb.

2. Select Control Panel.

3. Click Hardware and Sound.

4. Click Devices and Printers.

5. Locate an enhanced device icon and double-click it. Device Stage items appear, including various menu items (depending on your device).

6. On the Taskbar, right-click the device icon.

7. A Jump List opens, showing available tasks you can perform with this device.

Display

These settings were discussed in Chapter 2 and they are accessible through both the Control Panel or by right-clicking your Desktop and choosing Screen Resolution. The initial screen shows you ways to adjust the size of text and other items on your screen by using radio buttons (see Figure 10.8). On the left of the page, you will find links for the following options: Adjust Resolution, Calibrate Color, Change Display Settings, Adjust ClearType Text, and Set Custom Text Size (DPI).

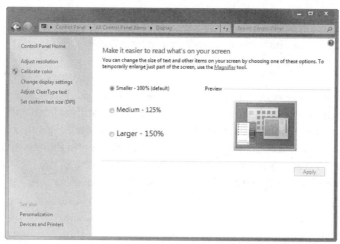

Figure 10.8 *Display options.*

Ease of Access Center

In Windows XP, this item is called Accessibility Options. It was renamed Ease of Access Center in Vista and it retains the same mission as it did when it was known as Accessibility Options: to enhance the functionality for users with limited vision, hearing, manual dexterity, or reasoning abilities. Microsoft has made some excellent efforts in these areas. We applaud their efforts, and for those of us who have loved ones who require these settings, there is nothing better than seeing them succeed as a result of these features.

When you open up the Ease of Access Center from the Control Panel, you see immediately that there are several tools you can configure (see Figure 10.9). If you are not sure which tool might be the right one, a special survey is available that might be able to put you in the right direction from the start.

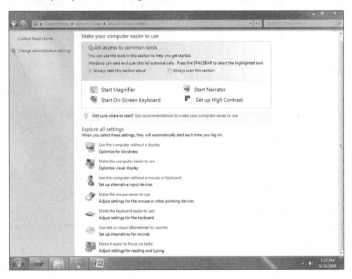

Figure 10.9   *The Ease of Access Center.*

 **LET ME TRY IT**

Getting Recommendations to Make your Computer Easier to Use

The following steps show you how to open the Ease of Access Center. You can choose among several options to make your computer easier to use.

1. Click the Start orb.

2. Choose Control Panel.

3. Select Appearance and Personalization.

4.   Click Ease of Access Center.

5.   In the center of the page, in a yellow box, click the Get Recommendations to Make Your Computer Easier to Use link. The first page that displays is specific to Eyesight.

6.   Read through the statements in each page and select each statement that applies to you. Click Next after each page, which progresses you to pages for Dexterity, Hearing, Speech, and Reasoning, respectfully If you would like to go back to review or change any answers, click the blue arrow in the upper-left corner of any page.

7.   When you have completed all five pages, click Done.

8.   The Recommended Settings page opens, presenting you with customized choices that are based on your selections. Review the recommended settings and select the options you would like to use.

9.   Click Apply.

10. Click OK.

> Some settings require you to log-off and log-on again to use them.

At the top of the Ease of Access Center page is the Quick Access to Common Tools feature, which provides you with access to Magnifier, Narrator, On-Screen Keyboard, and High Contrast tools. You can turn them on with a mouse click or you can hear the options read out loud to you (which occurs by default). You can press your spacebar to choose one of these options. Any options you choose will stay with you until you log off.

- **Magnifier:** Magnifier enlarges different parts of the screen. This comes in handy when you are viewing objects that are hard to see. It also allows you to see the whole screen more easily.

Select from three modes:

- **Full-Screen Mode:** With full-screen mode activated, your entire screen is magnified. Magnifier can follow the mouse pointer for you.

- **Lens Mode:** When you select Lens Mode, the area around the mouse pointer is magnified. Moving the mouse pointer causes the part of the screen that's magnified to move along with it.

- **Docked Mode:** By choosing docked mode, only a portion of the screen is magnified. Everything else on your display is normal size. This gives you control over which area of the screen is magnified.

Unless you are using the Aero theme, Magnifier works only in Docked Mode. Full-Screen Mode and Lens Mode are not available.

- **Narrator:** Narrator is a simple application that reads aloud any text on the screen and requires that your speakers work. There are several available options, including changing the narrator's voice.

- **On-Screen Keyboard:** This lets you use the mouse to enter text on screen. With the On-Screen Keyboard turned on, you can still use your traditional keyboard.

- **High Contrast:** This provides choices from several High Contrast windows themes. A link here takes you to the Personalization menu, where you can select a High Contrast theme at the bottom of the page.

Located at the bottom of the Ease of Access Center is the Explore All Settings section. The options presented here help you utilize special tools to make Windows more accessible:

- **Use the Computer Without a Display:** This presents you with two main sections. The first, Hear Text Read Aloud, gives you an option to have Narrator open each time you log on.

- **Make the Computer Easier to See:** This feature optimizes your visual display so the computer is easier to see.

- **Use the Computer Without a Mouse or Keyboard:** This allows you to work with alternative input devices. One of these devices controls your computer through Speech Recognition.

- **Make the Mouse Easier to Use:** You can increase the size and contrast of the mouse pointer, helping you more easily see it onscreen. You can also use Mouse Keys, which is a way to use the numeric keypad to move the mouse around the screen.

- **Make the Keyboard Easier to Use:** You can turn on features such as Sticky Keys, which allows you to enter keyboard shortcuts (such as Ctrl+Alt+Del) one key at a time.

- **Use Text or Visual Alternatives for Sounds:** Turn on visual cues and visual warnings here.

- **Make it Easier to Focus on Tasks:** These options make it easier for you to type and manage windows, among other things.

Folder Options

For the most part, the options available in Folder Options remain the same as those available in Vista. They include three tabs: General, View, and Search.

On the General tab, you can configure how you want to browse folders and you can configure how you want to open items (using a single click or using a double-click). There are two new checkboxes in the Navigation Pane section that are worth noting. By default, when you are working with Explorer, Windows 7 navigation shows you important items but not necessarily *all* of your items that you might be used to. If you select Show all Folders, then you will see them all. You can also select Automatically Expand to Current Folder.

The View tab has a variety of options to choose from and they are pretty straight-forward. However, because many users do not know these options exist, we recommend that you scan through the options to gain a better understanding before you use them. The Search tab has a few different groups of settings, such as What to Search, How to Search, and When Searching Non-Indexed Locations.

Fonts

Fonts displays all the fonts installed on the computer. Windows 7 has made some improvements to the Fonts dialog by showing you previews. Each thumbnail for the font shows three characters of the alphabet on the icon (see Figure 10.10). In addition, fonts of a combined set no longer take up different slots. They will appear as one font that you can double-click to view other options.

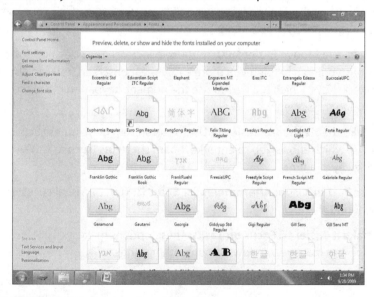

Figure 10.10   *Font improvements.*

You can also toggle fonts on or off if you prefer (also known as hiding fonts). By default, Windows 7 hides fonts based upon regional settings, but you can also manually hide them. The Font section is part of the Appearance and Personalization group.

A new font to look for is Gabriola Regular. It is a beautiful script font and supports a variety of advanced OpenType functions.

Getting Started

In Vista, this item is the Welcome Center. It is easy to locate in Windows 7. Simply click the Start orb and type **getting started** in the Search field. You can also access it in the Control Panel by typing **getting started** in the Search Control Panel box.

As shown in Figure 10.11, the Getting Started center shows you new features in Windows 7 and offers links to either tools or online information. PC vendors might use this area to personalize the welcome information to their particular needs.

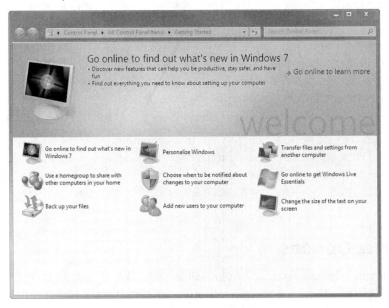

Figure 10.11   *Getting Started replaces the Welcome Center.*

HomeGroup

Discussed in detail in Chapter 8, the HomeGroup settings allow you to configure a smaller set of networked Windows 7 systems to share files (documents, pictures, music, videos) and printers as well as stream media to and from devices. All of these features are new in Windows 7 and facilitate home networking and sharing. The HomeGroup item can be accessed from the Network and Sharing Center.

Indexing Options

To speed up searches, there is an indexing feature in Windows 7 that is turned on by default. However, there are predefined locations that are indexed by default, such as Internet Explorer History, Offline Files, Start Menu, Users folder, and Windows Live Mail.

To access Indexing Options, simply click the Start orb and type **index** in the Search field. You can also access it in the Control Panel by typing **index** in the Search Control Panel box. When you click Indexing Options item and then click the Modify button at the lower-left of the Indexing Options dialog, you can quickly add locations to the index. Keep in mind, however, that adding to the indexing increases the workload on Windows 7 in its effort to keep those areas up to date. But it makes for faster searches when you are looking for something that isn't on the standard index path.

Through Advanced Options you can also determine if you want to index encrypted files, rebuild the index (if it is giving you problems), and you can find the location of the index file. You can also determine file types to include or exclude, among other options in the Advanced Options dialog box.

From time to time you are going to find that your index will crash, so to speak. If you find yourself in Outlook searching for an email that you know you have and you cannot get any results from your search or any search, you should rebuild the Index. It will take a few moments but it will fix the problem.

Internet Options

The Internet Options group is located within Network and Internet on the Control Panel. Basically, these are your IE8 settings—they aren't really your Internet Options. You can configure them from within IE by going to your Tools, Internet Options or you can configure them here. Obviously, if you use another browser (such as Firefox or Safari), the vast majority of the settings you configure here will not apply at all to those other browsers.

Keyboard

To open the Keyboard item, simply type **keyboard** in the Search Control Panel box and then click Keyboard. Nothing new to report here. In the Keyboard Properties dialog that appears, use the Speed tab to configure the Character Repeat settings and the Cursor Blink Rate. Click the Hardware tab to access hardware information and properties.

Location and Other Sensors

To open the Location and Other Sensors item, simply type **location** in the Search Control Panel box and then click Location and Other Sensors. This is where you can configure the Windows-based sensors that can detect your location and the orientation of your system. So, essentially, Windows 7 supports both hardware and software sensors that can be designed for systems. Examples of hardware sensors are a GPS, a microphone, an accelerometer, or a motion detector. Software sensors might be based on information coming through the network or Internet.

One simple use for these types of features might be the support of ambient light sensors (ALS) so that the system will automatically control the brightness based upon the available ambient brightness detected.

Mouse

The Mouse item is found in the Hardware and Sound group on the Control Panel. After you click Hardware and Sound, you will see the Mouse link under the Devices and Printers group. Much like Keyboard, there is not much new to report. One item to take note of is ClickLock (which isn't new—it's been around since ME), which is located on the Buttons tab. If you have a hard time holding the mouse button down to move items and highlight text easily, ClickLock will help you. The other point to take note of is the fact that Windows 7 supports enhanced Wheel support. In the Mouse Properties dialog boxt, click the Wheel tab to configure Horizontal Scrolling.

Network and Sharing Center

As discussed in detail in Chapter 8, the Network and Sharing Center is your one-stop location for all of your network configuration options. The Network and Sharing Center is located in the Network and Internet group on the Control Panel.

Notification Area Icons

This option allows you to configure the settings for your Notification Area (also called the System Tray) to show or hide certain icons or notifications. You can find Notification Area Icons by typing **notification** in in the Control Panel Search box.

Parental Controls

Parental controls can be accessed in the User Accounts and Family Safety group on the Control Panel. Parental Controls were made available to us in Vista, but Windows 7 excludes the onboard Activity logging and the Internet settings (because those items have been moved over to the Windows Live download features). However, Parental Controls still provides you with the ability to set times that users can use the computer and also gives you control over what games and programs other users can use.

Performance Information and Tools

You can find the Performance Information and Tools item by typing **performance** in the Control Panel Search box. Discussed in greater detail in Chapter 11, this option takes you to your Windows Experience Index, where you can see an assessment of your system components on a scale of 1.0 to 7.9. You can also see links to all sorts of performance-oriented settings that can help improve the performance of your system, including adjusting visual effects, indexing options, power settings, and more.

Personalization

As discussed in Chapter 2, the Personalization settings can be accessed by the Control Panel and by right-clicking the Desktop and choosing Personalize. Here you can select a theme to quickly change the Desktop background, window color, sounds, and screen saver all at once. Or you can make changes to these items individually.

There are links that take you to other settings, such as Change Desktop Icons, Change Mouse Pointers, and Change Your Account Picture.

Phone and Modem

Remember how annoying the Location Information dialog used to be? It would come up when you chose Phone and Modem Options and it wouldn't budge until you put in an area code? Well, that's one thing that hasn't changed in Windows 7. It's the same annoying dialog. The settings themselves haven't changed; they include the country/region you are in, the area code, the carrier code, an outside line number, and the phone system uses tone or pulse dialing. You can find the Phone and Modem item by typing **phone** in the Control Panel Search box.

Power Options

These settings are always under scrutiny and constantly improving to meet the needs of a 'Green IT' effort. Reducing power that is wasted will save the environment from unnecessary harm and will also save a company from unnecessary spending. As shown in Figure 10.12, Windows provides several power plans to choose from.

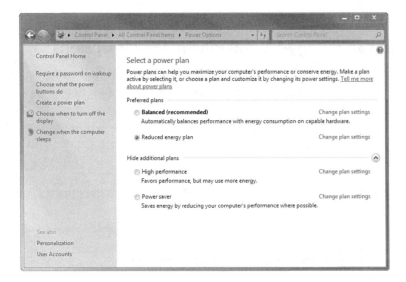

Figure 10.12 *Create your own power configuration and "go green" with Power Plans.*

The following power plans are designed to configure hardware and system settings to accommodate different power objectives:

- **Balanced:** This offers full performance when you need it and saves power during periods of inactivity. This is well suited for most configurations.

- **High Performance:** This increases the screen brightness and, in some cases, might increase the computer's performance.

- **Power Saver:** This conserves power by reducing system performance and screen brightness. If you need to get the most out of a single laptop charge, this is the plan for you.

If you are used to earlier power options, these power plans aren't new; they were formerly known as schemes. The difference is that now you can easily select one of three default options unless you want to get more involved.

You can configure the options in any one of those default plans or configure a personal plan that suits you. By selecting the initial link to edit settings, you will be selecting when to Turn Off the Display and when to Put the Computer to Sleep. If you select Change Advanced Power Settings, you are taken to a much more involved dialog with all sorts of options for password settings, when to turn the hard disk off, adapter settings, and much more.

 LET ME TRY IT

Creating an Energy-Saving Plan in Power Options

The following steps show you how to create an energy-saving power plan. Laptop users will have additional choices to select that are not shown here.

1. Click the Start orb.

2. Choose Control Panel.

3. Select Power Options.

4. In the left pane, click Create a Power Plan. This opens the Create a Power Plan page.

5. Select Power Saver.

6. In the Plan Name box, type **Reduced Energy Plan**.

7. Click Next.

8. On the Change Settings for the Plan page, there are two drop-down menus. From the Turn Off the Display: drop-down, select 2 Minutes.

9. From the Put the Computer to Sleep: drop-down, select 10 Minutes.

10. Click Create.

Your new reduced energy plan is now in effect.

To change the way the power buttons respond on your computer, in the left pane of the Power Options page, click Choose What the Power Buttons Do. When you press the Power button or Sleep button, you can have the computer shut down, sleep, hibernate, or do nothing at all. This page is also where you can configure your password protection on your Wakeup options.

Programs and Features

If you are coming to Windows 7 from XP, you might still be looking for the Add/Remove Programs item. In Vista, it was replaced by Programs and Features, which added the ability to Turn Windows Features On or Off (see Figure 10.13) in addition to uninstalling or making changes or repairs to installed applications.

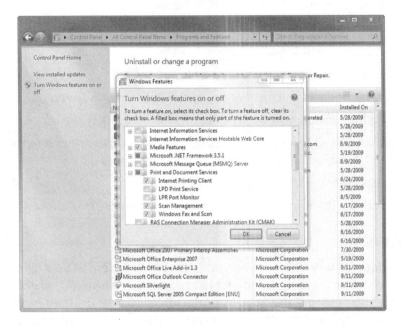

Figure 10.13   *Turning on Windows Features.*

Some programs and features included with Windows 7 need to be turned on before they can be used. Certain other features are turned on by default, but you can turn them off if you don't use them.

In versions of Window prior to Vista, there was no 'Turn-off' feature. To turn off a Windows feature (like Internet Explorer 8 or Windows Media Player) meant uninstalling it completely from your computer. In Windows 7, turning off a Windows feature does not uninstall it, nor does it reduce the amount of hard disk space used by Windows. The features actually remain stored on your hard disk so you can 'flip the switch' and turn them back on again. This applies only to Windows features, however; all other applications still require the traditional install/uninstall routine.

Turning on Windows Scan Management

The following steps show you how to add extra Windows 7 features that were not installed by default. While performing this exercise, note the other options available to install.

1. Click the Start orb.

2. Choose Control Panel.

3. Select Programs.

4. In the Programs and Features group, click Turn Windows Features On or Off.

5. If a UAC window appears, click Yes.

6. The Windows Features dialog box opens. Click the plus sign next to Print and Document Services.

7. Select the Scan Management checkbox.

8. Click OK. The Scan Management feature is now enabled.

Recovery

A new location for your System Restore options, Recovery can be used to resolve many system problems by going back to a point in time where you can undo recent system changes and more. This is discussed in further detail in Chapter 11. You can find the Recovery item by typing **recovery** in the Control Panel Search box.

Region and Language

You can access Region and Language settings in the Clock, Language and Region group on the Control Panel. This tool has changed only slightly from the way it worked in XP and Vista. There are four tabs to work with to configure the following:

- **Formats:** Configure the default way your computer renders number, currency, date, and time. You can choose a specific format based on a country in the world and the options adjust accordingly. You can also choose to customize that format.

- **Location:** This setting assists with some programs that provide local news and weather.

- **Keyboards and Languages:** Configure an input language and a display language. An input language involves changing the keyboard layout to support other keyboard layouts. You can read and edit documents in multiple languages by selecting the proper keyboard layout. You can even try different

US keyboard layouts, such as the Dvorak keyboard, for improved type speed. You can change the display language as well.. The display language is the language used for Wizards, dialog boxes, and menus.

- **Administrative:** For welcome screen and new user accounts, you can view and copy your international settings. You can also configure the language for non-Unicode programs.

RemoteApp and Desktop Connections

To find RemoteApp and Desktop Connections, type **remote** in the Control Panel Search box. As discussed in Chapter 9, this is a new Control Panel feature that you can use to access programs and/or desktops (remote computers or virtual systems) that have been made available by your network administrator. This feature is also connected with the new Windows Server 2008 R2 features for RemoteApp and Desktop Connections where RAD feeds provide a set of resources and these feeds are presented through this tool in Windows 7.

Sound

Customizing your sounds is a nice way to personalize your Windows 7 environment settings. The Sound group, found in Hardware and Sound, is where you can configure sound and recording options depending on the sound devices you have installed. The Playback, Recording, and Sounds tabs are the same as they were in Vista.

New to Windows 7 is a Communications tab that helps Windows to automatically adjust the volume of different sounds when you are using your PC to place or receive telephone calls. You can mute all other sounds, reduce the volume by 80 or 50 percent, or you can do nothing at all.

Speech Recognition

Do you remember in *Star Trek IV* when Scotty goes back in time to 1980s earth? He winds up in front of a computer, picks up the mouse, and starts using it like a microphone, saying "Computer. Hello, Computer!" Scotty must have been thinking the computer had Windows 7 Speech Recognition.

Speech Recognition has two primary functions:

- To allow you to control the computer by giving specific voice commands.
- To allow you to dictate text (see Figure 10.14) or have text read back to you in a Text-to-Speech (TTS) manner. The Speech Recognition tools provide you

with the ability to train your computer to work with your voice or simply to train yourself to use the right commands to operate your computer.

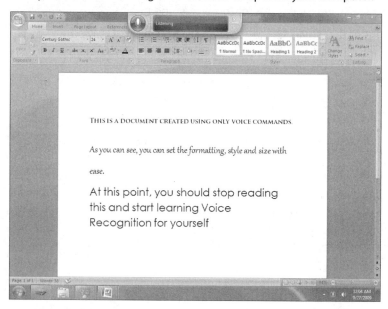

Figure 10.14 *Dictate to your computer and let it do the work of your hands.*

Do you type fast? If not, pay attention to this section. For many, Speech Recognition works a whole lot faster than typing. If you're dictating, it gives you a chance to close your eyes and just talk to the computer, concentrating on your topic as the computer types every word you say. Later on, when you have the main points down on the page, you can go back and correct any mistakes by using your keystrokes.

Before you start with Speech Recognition, your microphone has to be set up properly. In Control Panel, click Ease of Access Center and then choose Set Up Microphone. Complete this Wizard to set up your microphone. If you have a choice between two microphone styles, go with a headset. This works much better with speech recognition and doesn't pick up as much background noise.

Once you have completed the setup, go straight to the Speech Tutorial. Here's why: The tutorials let you see how speech recognition works from all angles. Even better, you need to speak the commands to make it work. Meanwhile, as you get familiar with the commands, you not only learn the program, the program learns you. Speech Recognition begins to keep a voice profile on how you speak. Your accent, tone, pace and style is "learned" by Speech Recognition. In fact, if someone else speaks into the microphone, the accuracy Speech Recognition drastically declines. The system literally knows your voice.

Speech Recognition is available only in English, French, Spanish, German, Japanese, Simplified Chinese, and Traditional Chinese. You can change the language setting from the Advanced Speech options in the Control Panel.

Some users might want to set up their microphones and just jump right into Speech Recognition. The following Let Me Try It shows you a a few things to do to get started right off the bat. (This exercise requires Word 2007.)

 LET ME TRY IT

Using Speech Recognition

The following steps show you how to use only your voice to control your computer and dictate a paragraph to it. You need a computer microphone to complete this exercise.

1. Make sure your microphone is plugged in and working correctly.
2. Click the Start orb.
3. Select Control Panel.
4. Choose Ease of Access.
5. In the Speech Recognition group, click Start Speech Recognition.
6. Move the Speech Recognition bar to the top of your screen.
7. Clearly speak Start Listening into your microphone. This turns on the Speech Recognition. The Speech Recognition readout will say Listening.
8. Say "Open Word 2007." Word 2007 opens with the cursor blinking.
9. Say "Watch the computer type when I speak."
10. Say "Select Sentence." This highlights your entire sentence.
11. Say "Bold." The sentence changes to boldface.
12. Now dictate a paragraph to your computer and see how accurate it transcribes it.

In Windows 7, Speech Recognition allows users to interact with applications that are not specifically written with speech recognition in mind. If you are using a Microsoft product, such as Word, the tools work flawlessly (for a speech-to-text application, that is). If you are using other applications that are not compatible, a separate text box opens. You can speak into it and then innsert the text to your application afterward.

Previous users of Speech Recognition will find that the voice commands are large-ly—if not entirely—unchanged. And while the speech recognition was very good in Vista, Windows 7 seems to raise the bar a notch. For new users, print out the Speech Reference Card available in the Speech Recognition Group in Control Panel. From here you will find simple commands to control your computer and com-mands to use during dictation.

If you still want even greater accuracy, select 'Train your computer to better under-stand you' in the Speech Recognition group in Control panel. This will help improve dictation accuracy.

During computer downtime, Speech Recognition can optionally review docu-ments and email on your computer for commonly used words and phrases. This, too, can help improve recognition accuracy. A privacy statement is available online to help ease your 'Big Brother' fears.

In the left pane of the Speech Recognition group, you can configure your recogni-tion options by clicking the Advanced Speech Options link, which opens the Speech Properties dialog box. If more than one person will use Speech Recognition from the same user account, the Recognition Profiles area includes a New button you can click to add a new user's voice profile.

Sync Center

We are a synchronizing generation. We sync our Desktop to our server, our digital cameras, our email, our cell phones, our portable media players, our camcorders, our PDAs, our laptops, and so forth. With the Sync Center, you now have a single item that helps you know how you're doing—how in-sync you really are.

Through the Sync Center (see Figure 10.15) you establish sync partnerships with devices you use and then you have a behind-the-scenes relationship with your device that allows the center to display information like a progress bar and a report of any problems or conflicts.

If you have a mobile device, a simple way to see the connection status without opening the Mobile Device Center is to open the Sync Center.

To open the Sync Center, open Control Panel, type **sync** in the Control Panel Search box, and click on the Sync Center that appears on the left of the screen. By design, the Sync Center has a very simple layout. There are just a few links in the left pane and a main view window.

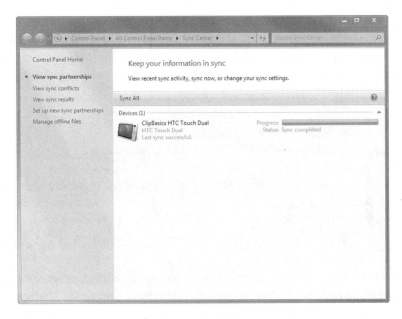

Figure 10.15   *Keep your data synchronized in the Sync Center.*

- **View Sync Partnerships:** Sync your device, view recent sync activity, or change your sync settings.

- **View Sync Conflicts:** View any files that had conflicts during the sync process. If there are conflicts, you can resolve them one at a time as you view details for each conflict.

- **View Sync Results:** Review errors, warnings, and other sync information.

- **Set Up New Sync Partnerships:** Before you can sync with anything, you need to set up a new partnership for it.

- **Manage Offline Files:** This opens the Offline Files dialog box. Four tabs let you configure several options:
  - **General:** Disable offline files, open the Sync Center, or view your offline files.
  - **Disk Usage:** Provides a visual graphic of your available offline file space and temporary file space. Two options on this tab are changing your space limits and deleting temporary files.
  - **Encryption:** A simple Encrypt button lets you do just that to your offline files.
  - **Network:** Set the interval at which the Sync Center checks for a slow connection.

If you are concerned with security, you might want to turn on encryption. File encryption works independently of the NTFS file system. It provides an additional level of access protection—above and beyond permissions that you have established. If your computer is ever lost or stolen, encryption can safeguard files that contain sensitive or confidential information.

The Encryption tab isn't available if your version of Windows 7 does not include the Encrypting File System (EFS). If EFS is available and you want to encrypt your offline files, be advised that you encrypt only the offline files stored on your computer; you don't encrypt the network versions of the files. Also, you do not need to decrypt an encrypted file or folder stored on your computer before using it. This is automatically done by Windows. The whole process is transparent to the user.

Another nice feature of Sync Center is that you can schedule your synchronization. So, for Offline Files, although you normally might sync, then go on a business trip, then re-sync (perhaps manually doing the syncs), you can use Sync Center to work more on a schedule.

If you were looking for your Offline Files item, this is actually where Windows 7 has been moved. While many tools have been added to Control Panel for easy access, this one has been buried one level deeper in the Sync Center. Open the Sync Center and, in the left pane, you will see the Manage Offline Files link.

If you are wondering why you should use Offline Files, here are three reasons:

- You can keep working when the network goes down. With Offline Files, it doesn't matter if the network becomes unavailable. If this happens, Windows automatically opens offline copies of files stored locally and you can continue working. When the network returns, the offline files are synchronized back on the network.

- You can get the latest version of the network file. Just click to sync with your network folder and get the updated file.

- You can speed up work over slow connections. If your network has a slow connection, you can switch to working with offline copies of your network files. When you're done with the file, synchronize it with the network folder.

One issue that concerns some users when they're working with Offline Files is the synchronization process. The worry is that somehow, a file will not get updated correctly when it is modified offline and, when the file is synchronized with the network, how will Windows know which version is correct? Simply put, if you are away from the network and have changed a file that someone has already changed on the network while you are gone, a sync conflict occurs when you are back on the network.

Windows prompts you that there is a conflict and asks you which version to keep. If you know in advance that the file you are working on will be updated before you get back on the network, rename the file so you can keep your work and merge it with the network version when you get back on the network.

System

The System item, discussed in greater detail in Chapter 11, shows you basic information about your system to begin with. It is more of a portal to other information. For example, you can change settings regarding your computer name, domain, or workgroup settings. You can also access the Device Manager, Remote Settings, System Protection, and more Advanced System Settings. You can access the System item by clicking the System and Security group in Control Panel.

Taskbar and Start Menu

We discussed this item in great detail in Chapters 1 and 2. This item gives you control over the appearance and working behavior of the Taskbar and Start menu. You can open Taskbar and Start Menu from the Appearance and Personalization group in Control Panel.

Troubleshooting

This item in Control Panel is more of a station that leads off to all the troubleshooting tools within Windows 7. Open it by typing **trouble** in the Control Panel Search box and then clicking Troubleshooting on the left. Consider it an easy place to go when you are having a problem but don't know where to begin.

Figure 10.16 shows how diverse the Troubleshooting tools are.

However, the Troubleshooting packs you see initially are not representative of every pack that exists. If you click the View All link in the left pane, you will see all of your packs and their descriptions.

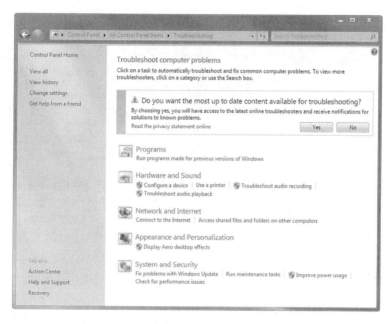

Figure 10.16   *Troubleshooting anything and everything.*

You can click the View History link to show you which tools you have run and when you ran them. You can clear the history, view details, search for help, or delete your history.

You can click Change Settings' to alter settings that relate to Computer Mainte-nance. For example, you can turn off the System Maintenance troubleshooter, which checks for routine maintenance issues and notifies you. In the Other Settings group, you can select checkboxes to:

- Allow users to browse for troubleshooters available from the Windows Online Troubleshooting service.

- Allow troubleshooting to begin immediately when started.

Last, but not least, you can click Get Help from a Friend, which takes you to the Remote Assistance tools. This allows a connection from another person who can help to fix your problem. There is also a link at the bottom of the Remote Assis-tance page to Offer Remote Assistance to Help Someone.

At the bottom of the Remote Assistance page there is a link to the Problem Steps Recorder, which is covered in the next section.

Problem Steps Recorder (PSR)

The Problem Steps Recorder (PSR) is a new feature in Windows 7 that should go over well with both users and IT departments alike. The purpose of the PSR is to help identify what has led up to a particular computer issue. For example, you might have a problem printing from a specific point in an application. In the past, this might have required a call to your helpdesk support, who might attempt to walk you through the problem over the phone (if they recognized the problem). The PSR (see Figure 10.17) simplifies this process.

Figure 10.17 *The small but handy Problem Steps Recorder.*

If you click your Start orb and type **recorder** in the Search field, you will see two items: the Sound Recorder and Record Steps to Reproduce a Problem. Click the latter to access the Problem Steps Recorder. As you learned in the previous section, you can also locate a link to it from Remote Assistance, which is logical because the two do work hand in hand.

With the PSR, you turn it on and run through all the steps that led up to the problem. You can click Add Comment at any point to highlight the problem and to make notes. A pre-packaged zip file contains all the data from your recording in the form of screenshots and computer data all put into one tidy MHTML document that you can open in Internet Explorer. Open this MHTML document and you will see all the items you selected as screenshots with green boxes surrounding the items you clicked. You also see any comments you added. In addition, you are shown a step-by-step in the Additional Details section. You can email this document to someone else so they can help troubleshoot the issue you are having.

 LET ME TRY IT

Using the Problem StepsRecorder

The following steps show you how to record a series of steps and then review them with the Problem Steps Recorder.

1. Click the Start orb.

2. In the Search field, type **psr**.

3. Click psr.exe. This opens the Problem Steps Recorder.

4. Click the Start Record button.

5. Navigate through Windows to repeat the problem you are having. (For the purposes of this exercise, open the Control Panel, click System and Security, and open the Action Center.)

6. Click the Stop Record button. The Save As dialog opens.

7. Navigate to a location to save the zip file, typea File Name of Action Center, and click Save.

8. Browse to the location of the Action Center zip folder and double-click it. Double-click the MHTML document. Internet Explorer opens, showing you the Recorded Problem Steps taken to access the Action Center.

Notice among the links near the top of the page there is a link to Review the Recorded Problem Steps as a Slide Show.

One other feature of the PSR is located on the recorder itself. To the right of the question mark is a small drop-down arrow that lets you configure settings and gives you the option of sending your PSR zip file as an attachment though Outlook.

By default, the Problem Steps Recorder saves up to 25 screen captures per recording. If your recording takes more than 25 steps, the PSR keeps recording screen captures, but saves only the final 25. So if you took 30 steps to get to a problem, only steps 6-30 are saved. You can capture more than 25 screen shots by increasing the number in the PSR settings.

User Accounts

On home systems or systems that do not connect to a domain you can use the User Accounts item to help you to create new accounts and configure various aspects of those accounts.

If you are working on a system that is connected to a network domain, you will not be using this item because your user accounts are configured by an administrator for you. An exception to this would be if you wanted to configure local accounts on the system.

There are three types of accounts that can be created in Windows. Each one can have a password. Like Windows XP and Vista, a visual logon screen shows each user's account. The types of user accounts are:

- **Standard User:** Gives you access to typical daily Windows functions but still maintains a measure of restriction.

- **Administrator:** Gives you full control over the computer.

- **Guest:** Gives you very limited access to the machine.

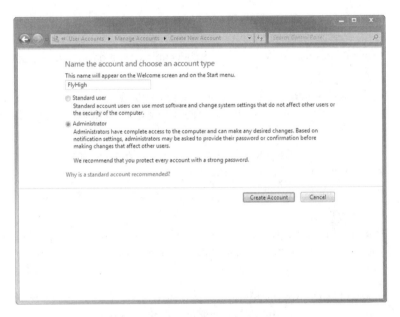

Figure 10.18 *Adding a new user account takes just a few seconds.*

 **LET ME TRY IT**

Adding a User Account

The following steps show you how to add a user account in Windows 7. You will be asked to create either a Standard User or an Administrator account.

1. Click the Start orb.

2. Select Control Panel.

3. Click the User Accounts and Family Safety group.

4. Click User Accounts.

5. Click Manage Another Account.

6. If a UAC window appears, click Yes.

7. Click Create a New Account.

8. In the text box, type a New Account Name for this account.

9. Choose between Standard User or Administrator.

10. Click the Create Account button.

After the account is created, you can configure a few options for it by clicking on the user on the Manage Accounts page:

- **Change the Account Name:** The name you type here will appear on the Welcome screen and Start menu.

- **Create a Password:** In this dialog, you can create a password and password hint.

- **Change the Picture:** You are not limited to Windows-only pictures. Click the Browse for More Pictures Link at the Bottom of the Choose Picture page to select your own picture to display.

- **Set Up Parental Controls:** This opens the Parental Controls item, allowing you to customize the configuration of the account.

- **Change the Account Type:** Select between Standard User or Administrator accounts.

- **Delete the Account:** Before deleting the account, you will be prompted if you would like to save the user's personalized data (such as documents, favorites, music, pictures, and more).

From time to time a user might forget the password he uses to log-on to Windows 7. Without the password, there is no logging on the system—plain and simple. To ward off a potential problem, it's recommended that each password-protected user account create a password reset disk. Bear in mind, however, that the password reset disk needs to be created from the account requesting the password reset disc disk. You cannot create a disk from another account. That means this needs to be made *before* a password is lost.

 LET ME TRY IT

Creating a User Account Password Reset Disk

The following steps require you to log-on to the account you wish to create the password for. An optional USB drive can be used to save the password.

1. Log-on to the account you want to create a password reset disk for.

2. Click the Start orb.

3. Select Control Panel.

4. Click the User Accounts and Family Safety group.

5. Click User Accounts.

6. In the left pane, click Create a Password Reset Disk. This opens the Forgotten Password Wizard. (If you intend to save this to a USB drive, insert that drive now.)

7. Click Next.

8. Select the location where you want to create the password key disk from the drop-down menu.

9. Click Next.

10. Type your account password in the text box.

11. Click Next. A progress indicator will appear as the key is being saved.

12. When the indicator stops at 100%, click Next.

13. Click Finish. You can locate your key on the media you saved it to by finding the file *userkey.psw*.

Another quick way to reset your account password is to have someone who has an administrator account to log-on and manually replace your password. Then you can log-on with the password they provide and change the password.

If you are an administrator doing this on behalf of a user, be careful, there is a potential risk involved. When you use an administrator account to reset a password for another user, that user will lose access to their encrypted files, encrypted email messages, and stored passwords for websites or network resources.

This same risk does not apply if a user uses a password reset disc to reset her password.

From time to time you might have the need to delete a user account. Like the other aspects of User accounts, this is easily done. The key to completing this is logging on with an administrator account.

 LET ME TRY IT

Deleting a User Account While Keeping the User's Files

The following steps show you how to delete a user account while keeping its data. On completion of the steps, the data will be saved in a folder on the Desktop.

1. Log-on to an administrator account.

2. Click the Start orb.

3. Select Control Panel.

4. Click the User Accounts and Family Safety group.

5. Click User Accounts.

6. Click Manage Another Account.

7. If a UAC window appears, click Yes.

8. Select the account you would like to delete by clicking on it.

9. Click Delete the Account.

10. You will be asked to either Delete Files or Keep Files. Click the Keep Files button.

11. You will be asked to confirm the deletion along with a message that the users files will be saved in a folder that is placed on your Desktop. Click the Delete Account button.

12. Minimize the Manage Accounts page and locate the saved data in the folder Windows created on your Desktop.

Windows CardSpace

Windows CardSpace is new to Windows 7 and can be found by typing **card** in the Search Control Panel box. Discussing the concept of digital identities is so difficult with the average computer user. One writer mentioned that we have different forms of personal identity (for example, a passport, a driver's license, a credit card, a social security card, a birth certificate, and so forth). Each is used in different situations and some can be used in multiple situations (such as when buying items, you can use that credit card more than once).

Your online identities are important to maintain as well. And we have no shortage of these as well. So the problem comes in that there are a variety of digital identities provided by a variety of sources and there will never be a way to control all of that. So instead of trying to control it, Microsoft has decided that what's really needed is an "identity metasystem." Microsoft and others have been working together to create this metasystem to define the standards necessary to make this work. The end result is CardSpace. Microsoft says their goal in promoting this system and encouraging vendors and others to use it is to "let people on any machine, running any operating system, use digital identities as easily, as effectively, and as securely as they today use their identities in the physical world."

Imagine it like a wallet. Your wallet contains a variety of identities you use in the real-world. The wallet isn't a new form of identity, it holds the identities. CardSpace allows you to choose from a portfolio of digital identities. Some you perhaps created yourself, others you perhaps obtained from merchants, banks, and so forth. This is a new technology, so it might take a while for it to catch on.

Keep in mind that CardSpace works only when a site requests a card.

Windows Defender

Discussed in great detail in Chapter 7, Windows Defender is a tool that provides protection from spyware and malware in real time on your system. You can configure to run quick scans or full scans either on a schedule or manually. Type **defender** in the Control Panel Search box to locate the Windows Defender application.

Windows Firewall

Also discussed in great detail in Chapter 7, Windows Firewall is a tool that helps to protect your system from unwanted access—access fromboth from the outside world trying to come into your computer or from unauthorized applications that might be running on your system that you don't want to allow out from your computer. Type **firewall** in the Control Panel Search box to locate the Windows Firewall application.

Windows Mobile Device Center

PDA and Smartphone users will find that they have an extra item in the Control Panel after installing their devices—the Windows Mobile Device Center (WMDC; see Figure 10.19). First introduced in Vista, the Windows Mobile Device Center is a replacement for all previous versions of ActiveSync.

When Vista first burst onto the scene, users decried the lack of hardware compatibility for their legacy devices. In its first incarnation, Windows Mobile Device Center didn't help. Instead of having the ultimate operating system to synchronize with, many PDA users found they were unable to connect. Soon they were scurrying back to Windows XP, grumbling every step of the way. Subsequent releases of Windows Mobile Device Center have widely expanded the amount of devices able to connect and sync. However, if you have a very old PDA or Smartphone, there's a good chance it might never connect. Here a few tips to try before you give up:

If you are using a USB cable different from the OEM one provided by your manufacturer, be advised that despite looks, not all USB cables are created equal. I recently had to troubleshoot a device only to discover that both USB cables that I tried to connect with (they work with every other USB device I have) were no good—only the OEM cable connected.

Try searching through Internet forums to see what workarounds other users have used. Search through forums like www.brighthand.com with the keywords **Windows Mobile Device Center** and your device name (for example, Hp Ipaq 3735).

If you find there is no support for your hardware, it might finally be time to upgrade that ancient relic.

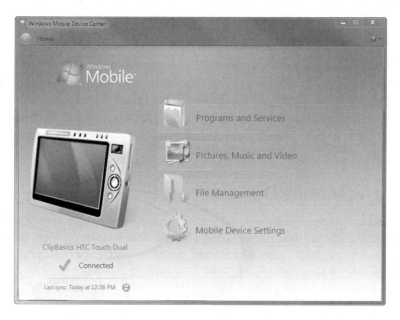

Figure 10.19 *The Windows Mobile Device Center—Ready for your handheld.*

There are two connection styles you can choose from when you first sync:

- Creating a Partnership
- Connecting Without Setting Up Your Device

With a partnership, Windows automatically synchronizes data from your device that you select. You can choose to sync contacts, calendar appointments, email, files, and more. Every time you plug in the device, the WMDC opens and syncs the data. This feature can be a lifesaver if the device's battery dies or you accidently delete data on your mobile device. Instead of losing the data permanently, it is 'backed-up' by being synchronized with your machine. Just plug it in, sync again, and your mobile data is restored.

 LET ME TRY IT

Setting Up a Partnership with Your Windows Mobile Device

The following steps show you how to create a partnership between your device and your computer. To complete this exercise, you will need a Smartphone or PDA running Windows Mobile.

1. Plug in your mobile device. Windows 7 will find new hardware and install drivers for it.

2. After drivers are successfully installed, the WMDC starts. (If the WMDC does not started automatically, click the Start orb, click Control Panel, click Hardware and Sound. Click Windows Mobile Device Center).

3. Look for a green check in the lower left along with the word Connected. (If you do not see this, unplug the device and turn it off. Reboot Windows 7. After Windows 7 has completely booted up, turn on the device and plug it back in. The Windows Mobile Device Center will auto start.)

4. On the right, click Set up your Device and the Set up Windows Mobile Partnership dialog box opens.

5. Select which items you would like to synchronize. (Note: Though it will be visible, you will be unable to select email unless you have already configured Outlook. A version of Outlook is provided with many mobile devices in order to utilize this feature.)

6. Click Next.

7. In the Device Name text box, type a name for your mobile device. This name will show up every time you open the WMDC.

8. Click Set Up. Windows establishes the partnership and attempts to sync the data. When completed, you will see a date and time of the last sync under the word Connected.

After a partnership has been established, new options appear in the WMDC:

- **Programs and Services:** Here you will find links to Add/Remove Programs, which opens a new dialog for installing or removing Windows Mobile applications. Also in Programs and Services are links to Microsoft resources, such as updates and help. The options here will vary from one device to another depending on the manufacturer.

- **Pictures, Music and Video:** Hover your mouse of this and an interactive window opens. Click the blue More button to reveal all your choices. The first link tells you how many media items exist on your device that have not been synchronized. Pictures/Video Import Settings brings up a dialog to fine-tune your import features, including giving you the ability to delete the item from the device after import. A third choice is to Add Media to your Device from Windows Media Player.

- **File Management:** Select this to browse the contents of your device. If your device has a storage card, it can be accessed from here.

- **Mobile Device Settings:** Clicking the More button opens up a bevy of links—Change Content Sync Settings, Manage a Partnership, Connection Settings, and more.

The other option you have when first synchronizing the device is Connecting Without Setting Up Your Device. This limits you to file sharing on the host system or using your device to share mobile broadband. This choice is a good option if you need to quickly connect to a machine to share data. For example, if you have a storage card on your mobile device, you can use it like a Jump Drive by plugging-in your device to a host machine, starting WMDC, and selecting Connecting Without Setting Up Your Device. Once connected, the device will show up in Windows Explorer with access to your storage card.

Mobile broadband lets users tether a cell phone to a computer and access the Internet through the cell phone's network connection. To use this, you need a data card (SIM) and a mobile broadband data plan with a provider. This can be a great solution to get connected to the Internet in remote locations or areas that do not provide broadband service.

Windows Update

Windows Update is a way to connect to a Microsoft database that has drivers, patches, security fixes, and so forth to keep your OS installation up to date. Updates and software from Microsoft for Microsoft products are free as part of its maintenance and support services. If you choose not to configure Windows Update (see Figure 10.20), a large red shield will try to persuade you to turn it on, as will warnings in the Action Center.

If you share your computer with other users, every user gets the same update, regardless of who uses them. Users who are administrators by default can install updates. You can also allow users with Standard User accounts to have permission to install updates. This allows standard, non-administrator users to install updates manually.

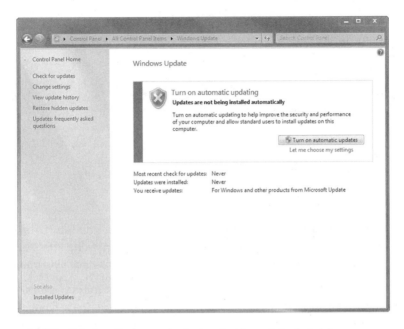

Figure 10.20 *Windows Update makes it clear that it wants to do its job.*

For a home system, you can configure your Windows Update setting to connect to Microsoft and update your system or you can do it manually. If you are a network admin, consider using Group Policies to configure these settings for your workplace. And, if you have a large enough environment and a small enough network connection to the Internet, you might want to consider setting up a Windows Update Server. This will go out and download updates and then your network systems will check in with the server and download from the internal system. It's a great way to ensure that all your systems are protected with the latest security patches and fixes.

SHOW ME   Media 10.3—Windows Update
Access this video file through your registered Web Edition at
my.safaribooksonline.com/9780768695212/media.

With Windows Update, you configure your system to work on a schedule of your choosing (or none at all if you prefer to handle checking for updates manually, which is not recommended). What many disliked about Windows Updates in the past was that updates usually required reboots and these reboots pushed a request box at you every 10 minutes until you complied with the request. Now you can choose longer periods of time (up to four hours) before that dialog box appears; the dialog simply is not as intrusive.

In Vista, we first saw Windows Update removed as a web application and made part of the operating system. Windows 7 carries this on. The functionality is part of the Control Panel and checks in with a database at Microsoft. Now your Windows Defender and Windows Live Mail get updated through the update process so that new anti-spyware lists and junk mail filters are in place.

There are four different Windows Update classifications:

- **Important:** As the name suggests, these updates are important. They can improve security, privacy, and reliability. Generally speaking, these updates should be installed when they are available and can be installed manually.

- **Recommended:** These updates can range from fixes for non-critical problems to enhancements to your computing experience. These can be installed automatically.

- **Optional:** These can include drivers for your hardware or new software enhancements from Microsoft (such as language packs). These must be installed manually.

Windows Update will deliver the following different styles of updates:

- **Security Updates:** These contain fixes for product-specific, security-related vulnerabilities.

- **Critical Updates:** These are broadly released patches for specific critical but non-security issues.

- **Services Packs:** Consider these as all of the above and more rolled up in one. Service Packs could also have a few requested design changes or features.

The status of Windows Update can appear in the Notification Area as a pop-up window letting you know there are updates available and what their status is. For most users, leaving the settings on Install Updates Automatically works best. Advanced users might want to set their update configuration to either Download Updates But Let Me Choose Whether to Install Them or Check for Updates But Let Me Choose Whether to Download and Install Them.

 **LET ME TRY IT**

Configuring Windows Update to Download But Not Install Updates

The following steps show you how to configures how Windows Update behaves. Upon completion, updates will be downloaded but not installed unless they are authorized by the user.

1. Click the Start orb.
2. Click System and Security.
3. Click Windows Update.
4. Click the Change Settings link.
5. From the Important Updates drop down, select Download Updates But Let Me Choose Whether to Install Them.
6. Click OK.
7. If a UAC window appears, click Yes.

Now when an update arrives, you can choose whether to install it or not. You will be notified when updates arrive will be able to view and select which ones you want installed. Updates will appear here as well for Microsoft Office applications and can include Office Service Packs, notifications, and more.

Every now and then, an update fails. This occurs for a variety of reasons. There are a couple of steps that must take place for an update to happen. These range from scanning your machine for needed updates to downloading and then installing the update. Failure to complete any one of the steps will cause an update failure. Before giving up, try to install the update manually.

 LET ME TRY IT

Manually Installing Optional Updates

Windows Update generally has several optional updates for Windows 7. The following steps show you how to choose optional updates to install.

1. Click the Start orb.
2. Click System and Security.
3. Click Windows Update.
4. Click the View Available Updates link.
5. Choose the updates you want to install by selecting the check boxes on the left.

6. Click Install.

7. If a UAC window appears, click Yes.

8. With some updates, additional dialogs might open with license terms for you to accept or deny.

9. Windows update provides a status report of your updates and finishes by listing the number of failed /successful updates.

To review installed updates, go to the left pane in Windows Update and click the View Update History link. Here you will find listed Name, Status, Importance, and Date Installed (or attempted install).

From time to time you might find your system doesn't react quite right after an update. Though rare, there might be an occasion you need to uninstall an update. The following Let Me Try It shows you how to do this.

 LET ME TRY IT

Viewing and Uninstalling an Update

The following steps show you how to view past Windows Update installations and then uninstall an update of your choice. This exercise requires you to have first connected to Windows Update and installed an update.

1. Click the Start orb.

2. Click System and Security.

3. Click Windows Update.

4. In the lower-left of the page, click the Installed Updates link.

5. Click the update you wish to remove.

6. From the top menu, click Uninstall. A dialog appears, asking you to confirm the uninstall.

7. Click Yes to uninstall the update.

In some cases, network users might be unable to remove an update. It might be that your computer is connected to a network where updates are managed by Group Policy. Or, if an update applies to a security-related area of the operating system, you might not be able to remove it. Get in touch with your system administrator or your IT department if you think an update that you can't remove is causing problems.

 TELL ME MORE   Media 10.4—A Discussion About Some of the New Control Panel Items in Windows 7
Access this audio recording through your registered Web Edition at
my.safaribooksonline.com/9780768695212/media.

This chapter examines Windows 7's on-board monitoring tools and shows you how to utilize them in day-to-day situations.

11

Managing and Monitoring Windows 7

Performance Information and Tools

The Windows Experience Index (WEI) was first introduced in Vista. It returns largely unchanged in Windows 7 (see Figure 11.1) save for a few subtle refinements. The purpose of the WEI is to measure the capability of your computer's hardware and software configuration. After testing it out, the WEI expresses this measurement as a Base score number. The higher the base score, the better.

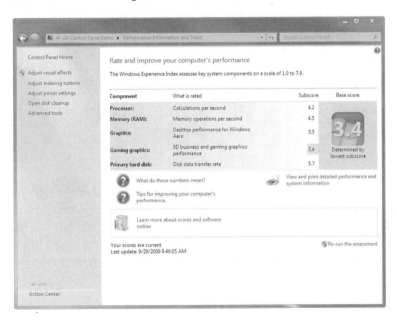

Figure 11.1   *The Windows Experience Index (WEI).*

 **LET ME TRY IT**

Running the Windows Experience Index Assessment

Before starting this exercise, shut down any applications running on your system. These could potentially slow system performance and return a lower score. The following steps show you how to run the Windows Experience Index assessment (see Figure 11.1).

1. Click the Start orb.

2. Click Control Panel.

3. Click System and Security.

4. Click System.

5. Click Windows Experience Index.

6. In the lower right, select Re-Run the Assessment. If a UAC window opens, click Yes. The test runs and updates your base score.

The Base score rating is a number that is based upon the five Subscore ratings for the following categories:

- Processor
- Memory (RAM)
- Graphics
- Gaming Graphics
- Primary Hard Disk

The final rating is not, as you might expect, a compilation of all the ratings. It's actually the lowest of the Subscore ratings. For someone using basic computer functions (such as surfing the Internet), a score of 4.0 would be just fine for them to use these basic functions. On the other hand, someone playing the latest hardware-intensive games would typically need a much higher score, perhaps 7.0 or above.

WEI scores range from 1.0 to 7.9. The high score was 5.9 in Vista, so the adjustment to 7.9 accounts for faster hardware since Vista was released. In response to experience and feedback comparing closely related devices, Windows 7 updated the scoring rules that Vista used.

Can you get a higher base score on some components without upgrading your hardware? Yes. The improvement to your score won't be huge, but you can do a few things to definitely make it better. Here are a couple suggestions to improve your computer's performance. Not all of these will affect the base score, but they will contribute to improved performance overall.

Close all running applications: Before running WEI, shut down as many applications as possible. These could have an impact on performance. If you really want to prepare the machine for the test, reboot it before running WEI. During the test, don't start or use applications.

Configure visual effects: Changing how menus and windows display can have an effect on performance.

Adjust power settings: These, too, can have an effect on your computer's speed. Select the High Performance option before running the test. If you are running this test on a laptop, make sure it is plugged in. Using a laptop with a battery draining down can cause some CPUs to enable a reduced power mode that slows the calculations in an effort to save energy. This can affect your Processor Subscore.

Clean up your hard drive: This is always a good idea and there are some good hard-drive cleaning tools in Windows 7, such as Disk Cleanup and Disk Defragmenter.

By knowing your base score, you can make better software purchasing decisions. The key is purchasing titles that are equal to or below your base score. For example, the hottest game on the market might require a high-performing graphics card. By understanding your Gaming Graphics Subscore, you can determine if your machine can handle it or not. If your Gaming Graphics Subscore falls short yet you still want to try a game that requires a high-performing graphics card, your system might be sluggish it might not run at all.

Seeing exactly how your hardware rates gives you a good feel for what needs to be upgraded next. In the neverending upgrading world of computers, it's only a matter of time which component will be next on your shopping list.

Windows System Assessment Tool (WinSAT)

The Windows System Assessment Tool (WinSAT) is the behind-the-scenes application that creates your WEI.

For the most part, when you install an OS like XP, you get XP in all its glory, regardless of the box you are running it on. So, although the underlying DLLs might be different, the OS options should be the same, right? Or should they? Does it really make sense that two systems—one which is a $200 cheap-o box with cheesy hardware—should be put in the same position to handle the OS features of a mega system? Well, Windows 7 has a little underlying tool that helps to differentiate between the two, called WinSAT.

When you first install Windows 7, but before the first log-in, WinSAT runs its testing process to see what your individual system can handle. It uses that information to determine which operating system features should be enabled or disabled by default. For example, if your system cannot handle Aero features, the settings on your OS will reduce itself to basic mode.

The WinSAT utility creates its output in the system directory: %systemroot%\Performance\WinSAT\DataStore. Each time your run WinSAT, a new XML file is generated in this folder with the date of the assessment stuck at the beginning of the file-name—for example, 2010-01-01 12.00.00.000 Assessment (Formal).WinSAT.xml. There is also a file in this directory with the word *Initial* inside the bracketed part of the filename.

Advanced Tools

The Performance Information and Tools page includes an Advanced Tools link to the left. Clicking this option takes you to the Advanced Tools page (see Figure 11.2).

This page displays any Performance Issues you can address to improve performance as well as a variety of tools you can use to monitor or improve your performance. These tools include the following:

- **Clear All Windows Experience Index Scores and Re-Rate the System:** Forces a complete re-run of all Windows Experience Index tests.

- **View Performance Details in Event Log:** Displays details of problems affecting Windows performance.

- **Open Performance Monitor:** Displays graphs of system performance and collects data logs.

Figure 11.2 *Advanced Tools for performance.*

- **Open Resource Monitor:** Displays real-time system resource usage and manage active services and applications.

- **Open Task Manager:** Displays information about the programs and processes that are currently running on your computer.

- **View Advanced System Details in System Information:** Displays details about the hardware and software components on your computer.

- **Adjust the Appearance and Performance of Windows:** Provides settings to change visual effects, processor and memory usage, and virtual memory.

- **Open Disk Defragmenter:** Displays the schedule used to automatically defragment your hard disk; you can modify this schedule to better suit your needs.

- **Generate a System Health Report:** Displays details about system health and performance.

The Reliability Monitor

In Vista, the Reliability Monitor and the Performance Monitor were combined with the Resource Monitor. These have been split up in Windows 7 so that each one stands on its own. The overall functionality within each is the same, however; they just look a little differently (and have a few new features) because they have been restructured to work alone.

What is your standard method for determining the reliability of your system? Most of us determine our system's reliability by how long it has been since it has blue screened on us or forced us to reboot. Unfortunately, that isn't the most "technically sound" way to assess reliability.

The main goal of the Reliability Monitor is to keep track of "reliability events," which have been defined as changes to your system which could alter the stability or other events that might indicate system instability (see Figure 11.3). Events monitored include:

- Windows updates

- Software installs and uninstalls

- Device driver installs, updates, rollbacks, and uninstalls

- Application hangs and crashes

- Device drivers that fail to load or unload

- Disk and memory failures

- Windows failures, including boot failures, system crashes, and sleep failures

The Stability Index rating gives you a visual of how reliable your system performs over time. You are given an overall Stability Index score. Ten is perfection, one is the lowest. The Reliability Monitor retains up to a year's worth of data so you can really see how your system has been performing over time.

The Reliability Monitor displays a Stability Index rating 24 hours after installation and provides specific event information.

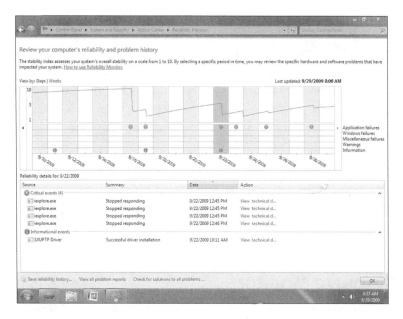

Figure 11.3   *Reliability Monitor.*

If you see a drop in stability, you can check the date the drop began and then see if the decline was due to one of the following issues:

- Application failures

- Windows failures

- Miscellaneous failures

- Warnings

- Information

Since the main purpose of the Reliability Monitor is to display data, there is limited functionality. The menu at the bottom of the page allows you to save your history as an .xml file, view all problem reports, and check for solutions to all problems. Another option is to find solutions for individual events.

SHOW ME   Media 11.1—The Reliability Monitor
Access this video file through your registered Web Edition at my.safaribooksonline.com/9780768695212/media.

Using Reliability Monitor to Check for a Solution to a Specific Application Problem

The following steps show you how to run the Reliability Monitor to check for a solution to an application failure. A connection to the Internet is required.

1. Click the Start orb.
2. In the Search box, type **reliability**.
3. Click View Reliability History. The Reliability Monitor opens.
4. Select an application failure from the Stability Index.
5. Click the Check for a Solution link. Problem reporting connects with the Windows Error Reporting service to locate and provide a solution.

The Resource Monitor

The Resource Monitor (see Figure 11.4) shows a real-time view of your system's CPU, Memory, Disk and Network usage. As shown in Figure 11.4, you can select items in the CPU group to show those items in the graphs shown to the right. In addition, you can use the Resource Monitor to stop processes, start and stop services, analyze process deadlocks, view thread-wait chains, and identify processes-locking files.

 LET ME TRY IT

Open the Resource Monitor

The following steps show you how to open the Resource Monitor.

1. Click the Start orb.
2. In the Search box, type **resource**.
3. Click Resource Monitor.
4. If a UAC window opens, click Yes. The Resource Monitor opens.

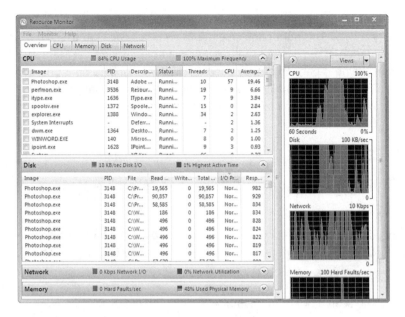

Figure 11.4   *The Resource Monitor.*

When you first look at the Resource Monitor, you might not realize just how much data is available for analysis. There is a lot going on in the various tabs shown:

- **Overview:** This is the default tab shown the first time you start Resource Monitor. (On subsequent starts, Resource Monitor displays the last tab you viewed before closing it.) The center view pane displays four sections: CPU, Disk, Network, and Memory. Click the Down arrow to the right of each section to expand the section and display real-time stats.

- **CPU:** This tab contains four sections related to your processor: Processes, Services, Associated Handles, and Associated Modules.

- **Memory:** This tab shows a graphical display of your memory in use and includes a Processes tab.

- **Disk:** Click this tab to view processes with disk activity, disk activity, and storage sections.

- **Network:** Click this tab to view processes with network activity, network activity, TCP connections, and listening ports.

To the right, a view pane displays a graphical readout of CPU, Disk, Network, and Memory activity. This right pane changes as you click each tab to show a graphical representation of the data for that tab. For example, clicking the Memory tab changes the right pane to display Used Physical Memory, Commit Charge, and Hard Faults/Sec. Additionally, clicking the drop-down arrow at the top of the right pane allows you to customize the size of these graphs.

 LET ME TRY IT

Identifying the Network Address To Which a Process Is Connected

You need a working network connection to complete the following steps, which show you how to find a network address that a process is connected to.

1. Click the Start orb.

2. In the Search box, type **resource**.

3. Click Resource Monitor.

4. If UAC window opens, click Yes.

5. The Resource Monitor opens. Click the Network tab.

6. Find the process for which you want to see the network address it is connected to and select its checkbox. (If you don't recognize a process, select the System process.)

7. Click the TCP Connections title bar.

8. Examine the Remote Address to see which network address the process is connected to.

You might have noticed that when you select the process checkbox, it moves that process to the top of the list. This enables you to focus on this particular process rather than search for it as the list dynamically updates.

Another invaluable use for the Resource Monitor is the ability to view applications that are not responding. You can view the Wait Chain of a process (see Figure 11.5) and end processes that are preventing a program from working properly.

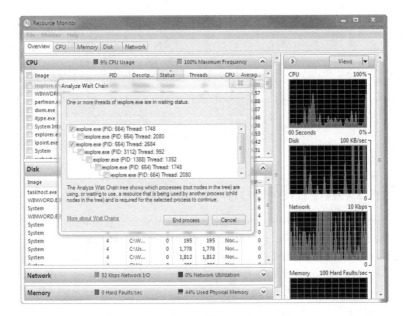

Figure 11.5 *Examining an unresponsive process wait chain.*

 LET ME TRY IT

Troubleshooting an Unresponsive Application Through the Resource Monitor

The following steps show you how to use the Resource Monitor to analyze applications. Before you begin, open a couple applications—such as Notepad and Paint—without saving them. Use these applications for analysis through Resource Monitor.

1. Click the Start orb.

2. In the Search box, type **resource**.

3. Click Resource Monitor.

4. If UAC window opens, click Yes.

5. The Resource Monitor opens. Click the Overview tab.

6. Locate any process that is not responding, as noted by its blue appearance. Right-click the process and choose Analyze Wait Chain. The Analyze Wait Chain dialog box opens with a tree displaying organized by dependency.

7. Select a process and click the End Process button.

8. Repeat Step 8 until the application responds.

Under normal circumstances, if you want to end an unresponsive application, you might use the Task Manager to end a task. Use caution when you use the Resource Monitor to end a task. You should use Resource Monitor to end a process only if you are unable to close the program by normal means. By ending an application process, the application associated with the process will close immediately and you will lose any unsaved data. If you end a system process, it might result in system instability and data loss.

Working with the Performance Monitor

For many years, the Performance Monitor tool stood alone. In Vista, it was combined with the Resource Monitor and the Reliability Monitor. It was also given a new structure for collecting data. The Performance Monitor can show you performance data in either real-time or from a log file. Data Collector Sets can be set to run immediately or on a schedule to collect and analyze specific aspects of your system.

Monitoring Tools, Performance Monitor (see Figure 11.6) displays a visual representation of your system so you can inspect a variety of components, beyond what the Resource Monitor shows you. Initially, you won't see more than the % Process Time. You can add more performance metrics (called *counters*) by hitting the + sign.

When you first see the number of possible counters and instances, the task of choosing which items to monitor can seem overwhelming. There are roughly 100 different Performance objects for any given system (you can monitor the local system or a remote one). Each of those objects contains counters. (There are way too many counters to know them all.) Once you have all your counters set up, you can make changes to the way they are displayed. For example, you can change the line colors for each counter to make it easier to determine which line you are watching. You can change the format of the display to a graph, a histogram, or a report (numeric display).

Data Collector Sets allow you to use System-defined sets (there is one for System Diagnostics and one for System Performance) or User-defined sets (which is empty to start with, you literally have to create your own). You can also look at Event Trace Sessions and Startup Event Trace Sessions.

The goal is to use Data Collector Sets to collect the data and then the Report sections to view the data collected. As shown in Figure 11.6, we ran a System Diagnostics report and then viewed the results in the Reports section.

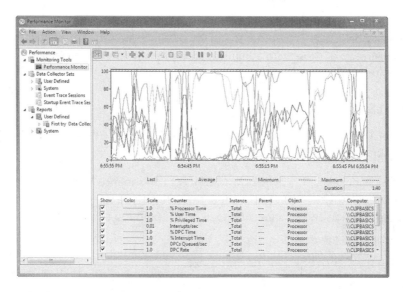

Figure 11.6   *Real-time Performance Monitor.*

 LET ME TRY IT

Configuring the Performance Monitor to Display Results As a Web Page

The following steps show you how to open the Performance Monitor and configure it to save performance results for viewing in a in a web browser.

1. Click the Start orb.

2. In the Search box, type **perfmon.exe**.

3. Click Performance Monitor.

4. If a UAC window opens, click Yes.

5. In the left pane, click Performance Monitor.

6. Right-click in the Performance Monitor display area and click Save Settings As.

7. Choose where you want to save the file.

8. Type a name for HTML file.

9. Click OK.

10. Navigate to the saved HTML file and open it. It will display captured performance information in your browser.

As an admin, you would find it both time-consuming and monotonous to have to physically be at every computer to run Performance Monitor. Fortunately, network administrators or those with administrator rights can now remotely gain access to this feature and connect.

 LET ME TRY IT

Connecting to a Remote Computer with Performance Monitor

The following steps show you how to connect Performance Monitor to another computer on the network. To complete these steps, you will need a working network connection and a connection to another computer on the network.

1. Click the Start orb.
2. In the Search box, type **perfmon.exe**.
3. Click Performance Monitor.
4. If a UAC window opens, click Yes.
5. In the left pane, click Performance Monitor.
6. On the top menu, click Action and then choose Click Connect to Another Computer.
7. If you know the name of the computer you want to monitor, type that name; if you don't know the name, click Browse to locate it.
8. Click OK.

> There are two requirements to viewing performance counters from a remote computer. First, the Performance Logs and Alerts firewall exception must be enabled on the remote computer. Second, users in the Performance Log Users group must also be listed inthe Event Log Readers group on the remote computer.

 LET ME TRY IT

Creating Data Collector Sets from Performance Monitor

The following steps show you how to use Performance Monitor to collect data. You will have the opportunity to configure settings to complete this task.

1. Click the Start orb.
2. In the Search box, type **perfmon.exe**.

3. Click Performance Monitor.

4. If a UAC window opens, click Yes.

5. In the left pane, click Performance Monitor.

6. Click New and then click Data Collector Set. The New Data Collector Set Wizard opens.

7. Type a Name for this data set.

8. Click Next.

9. Select a Root Directory for your saved data. Do not enter a back slash at the end of the directory name.

10. Click Next to define a user for the Data Collector Set to run as, or click Finish to save the current settings and exit.

After you click Finish and return to the Windows Performance Monitor, there are a few things you can do with this saved data (as you will learn in the following section).

 LET ME TRY IT

Editing the Properties of a Created Data Collector Set

The following steps build on the previous steps and show you how to modify the properties of a Data Collector Set.

1. Click the Start orb.

2. In the Search box, type **perfmon.exe**.

3. Click Performance Monitor.

4. If a UAC window opens, click Yes.

5. In the left pane, click User Defined to expand it.

6. Click User Defined.

7. Right-click the data collection set for which you would like to modify the properties and choose Properties.

8. After completing your modifications, click OK.

To start the Data Collector Set immediately, right-click it and choose Start.

After you have set up your data collectors, you can save the data in the form of logs that you can review later.

Not all log files are created equal. If you create a log file in Windows 7, it is not backward compatibility with earlier versions of Windows. However, log files created in earlier versions are viewable in Windows 7.

 **LET ME TRY IT**

Setting Up a Log Schedule for a Data Collector Set

The following steps show you how to create a log schedule for a Data Collector set.

1. Click the Start orb.

2. In the Search box, type **perfmon.exe**.

3. Click Performance Monitor.

4. If a UAC window opens, click Yes.

5. Click Data Collector Sets.

6. Double-click User Defined.

7. In the console pane, right-click the name of the Data Collector Set that you want to schedule and choose Properties.

8. Click the Schedule tab and click Add.

9. Using the drop-down arrows, configure the Beginning Date, Expiration Date, and the Start Time (under Launch).

10. Click OK.

11. Click the Stop Condition tab.

12. Select the Overall Duration checkbox.

13. Select the Stop When All Data Collectors Have Finished checkbox. (This permits the data collector to complete recording the most recent values before the Data Collector Set is stopped.)

14. Click OK.

You can also configure how your data is archived. If you log reports on a daily basis, log files will generate automatically and start to consume disk space. You can define preset limits and actions to take with these files.

 **LET ME TRY IT**

Configuring Data Collector Sets to Delete the Oldest Log File When Starting Data Collection

The following steps show you how to configure Data Collector Sets to delete the oldest log file when starting data collection.

1. Click the Start orb.

2. In the Search box, type **perfmon.exe**.

3. Click Performance Monitor.

4. If a UAC window opens, click Yes.

5. Click Data Collector Sets.

6. Double-click User Defined.

7. In the console pane, right-click the name of the Data Collector Set that you want to schedule and choose Data Manager.

8. Select the Maximum Folders checkbox.

9. In the drop down below, choose 5.

10. Change the Resource policy to Delete Oldest.

11. Select the Apply Policy Before the Data Collector Set Starts checkbox.

12. Click Apply.

13. Click OK.

In the previous example, with the Maximum Folders checkbox selected, previous data will be deleted when the limit is reached. And since the Apply Policy Before the Data Collector Set Starts checkbox was chosen as well, previous data will be deleted before the Data Collector Set creates its next log file.

It's a good idea to know your Resource policy (Delete Oldest or Delete Largest) before making other data choices on the Data Manager tab. Minimum Free Disk Space, Maximum Folders, and Maximum Root Path all revolve around your policy. Here are some other points to understand when working with these features:

- **Minimum Free Disk:** This is the disk space that needs to be available on the drive where you store the log data. When you choose this, previous data will be deleted when the limit is reached.

- **Maximum Folders:** This is the maximum total of subfolders that can be in the Data Collector Set data directory. Like the Minimum Free Disk Space option, previous data will be deleted when the limit is reached.

- **Maximum Root Path Size:** This represents the total size (including subfolders) of the data directory for the Data Collector Set. Be advised that choosing this option causes your Minimum free disk and Maximum Folders limits to be overridden and previous data will be deleted when the limit is reached.

Unless you have a trained eye or have spent some time reading reports, you might not understand the results of the data you have collected. To help with this, Windows Performance Monitor provides assistance diagnosing your reports. These reports are easy to understand and contain a wealth of data that helps you pinpoint potential problems (see Figure 11.7).

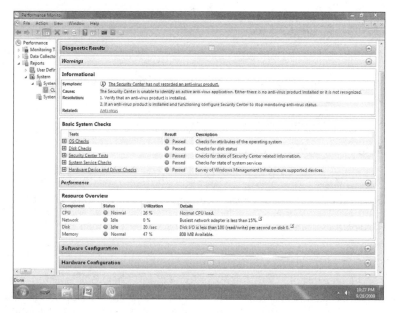

Figure 11.7   *Viewing a System Diagnostics report in Performance Monitor.*

SHOW ME   Media 11.2—Performance Monitor Data Collector Sets
Access this video file through your registered Web Edition at my.safaribooksonline.com/9780768695212/media

 **LET ME TRY IT**

Enabling and Viewing a System Diagnostics Report on a Data Collection Log

The following steps show you how to enable and view a System Diagnostics report on a data collection log. The steps below show you exactly how this is accomplished.

1. Click the Start orb.

2. In the Search box, type **perfmon.exe**.

3. Click Performance Monitor.

4. If a UAC window opens, click Yes.

5. Click Data Collector Sets.

6. Double-click System.

7. Right-click System Diagnostics and choose Start.

8. The next time your data collection starts and finishes, a diagnostic report is available. View it by double-clicking Reports.

9. In the left pane, double-click System.

10. Click System Diagnostics.

11. Reports will show up in the view pane. Identify the report you would like to view and double-click it. A System Diagnostic report opens.

12. To view details on items, click the Down arrows to access the data collected and reported on.

One simple method to run the diagnostic test is to open a command prompt (elevated or non-elevated—if it is non-elevated, it will ask you for permission to proceed) and then type **perfmon /report**. If you wanted to run a different Data Collector Set, you could type **perfmon /report** *"Name of Data Collector Set"* to start it.

Task Manager

Task Manager, for many of us, is our "go-to" tool for solving problems. You have a problem, you go to Task Manager—it's almost ingrained in us. You'll see immediate information about your processes, CPU usage, memory, network, and so forth.

For one thing, the first time you start Task Manager, you'll notice that you can now choose to see processes from all the users of the system. One thing you'll notice right away is the Description aspect to the Processes tab and the Services tab (see Figure 11.8). This was added in Vista.

One of the new features of Task Manager is the ability to create a mini-dump file of an application that is running. You can right-click an application or process that is running and choose Create Dump File, which displays a dialog box that shows you where that file has been written. You can use this feature to discover why a particular application might be crashing so often. Or if a process has already crashed and is no longer responding, you can try to discover the cause.

Figure 11.8 *Task Manager showing the descriptions and options for Services.*

Task Manager has six tabs:

- Applications
- Processes
- Services
- Performance
- Networking
- Users

In addition to the tabs, there is a menu at the top that serves up even more options that we'll also cover in the following section. Let's start by looking at the Applications tab.

Applications

This is the starting point for Windows Task Manager and there is more here than meets the eye. The Task column displays a list of open applications. This is a live look at your system. If you close one of the applications, it removes itself from this list.

The Status column shows whether the application is Running or Not Responding. This simple layout allows you to quickly see what application is acting up. At the bottom are three buttons:

- **End Task:** Closes an application or process.

- **Switch To:** Switches between applications or processes.

- **New Task:** Starts an application from the dialog box that opens when you click this button.

Below these buttons are real-time information regarding Processes, CPU Usage, and the amount of used Physical Memory. At a glance, you can see what resource is affected by this view in the Task Manager.

 LET ME TRY IT

Using Task Manager to End an Application

The following steps show you how to use Task Manager to end an application.

1. Press Ctrl+Alt+Del.

2. Click Start Task Manager.

3. In the Task area, locate an application that is running and click it.

4. Click the End Task button.

With this simple process, you see how easy it is to close an application. Of course, the purpose of Task Manager is to help you troubleshoot and cope with crashed applications, not ones that are working fine. So the next time an application hangs too long, follow the above steps again. When an application hangs too long, the Status column shows Not Responding. Clicking End Task should close the application.

On rare occasion, an application might stubbornly stay open despite your attempts to end it. In this situation, press Ctrl+Alt+Del again and repeat the steps to close it.

LET ME TRY IT

Using Task Manager to Start an Application

The following steps show you how to use Task Manager to start an application. In this example, you learn to end explorer.exe and restart it through Task Manager.

1. Press Ctrl+Alt+Del.

2. Click Start Task Manager.

3. Click the Processes tab.

4. In the Image Name column, locate explorer.exe.

5. Click the End Process button. Windows Explorer closes but all other applications, including Task Manager, remain open.

6. Click the Applications tab.

7. Click the New Task button. The Create New Task dialog box opens.

8. In the Open text box, type **explorer**.

9. Click OK. Windows Explorer opens.

The Create New Task button comes in handy in situations that call for you to reopen an application. If you know the path to the application, you can enter it; otherwise, you can click the Browse button to navigate to the application name.

One other option to mention on the Applications tab appears when you right-click any application. You will find Create Dump File. Dump files capture data from the application that you can share with software developers and programmers who are trying to determine why an application crashes or has other faults. The dump file is saved locally and is a copy of what the application looks like in memory. You can send it to your help and support department, which can analyze its contents.

Processes

This tab gives you a bird's-eye view of all your processes, including a button to Show Processes from all Users and the aforementioned End Process button. The Process tab is invaluable if your computer is running slow for an undetermined reason. By viewing the Image Name, CPU, Memory, and Description columns, you can focus on the precise area causing trouble.

Using Task Manager to Monitor an Application's CPU and Memory Usage

The following steps show you how to monitor an application's CPU and memory usage. In this example, you monitor Windows Media Player.

1. Press Ctrl+Alt+Del.
2. Click Start Task Manager.
3. Click the Processes tab.
4. While still keeping the Task Manager in view on-screen, open Windows Media Player. As the application opens, watch the CPU and Memory columns for the information it displays for Windows Media Player. (You may need to resize the column to see the heading names.)
5. Close Windows Media Player.
6. Open other applications and monitor their resource usage through the processes tab.

By viewing your process resource usage, it becomes evident very quickly which process is causing the problem. If you are looking for a specific process and you have several open, click Image Name to sort the column.

If a process is causing problem, it can be stopped by using the Processes tab—as you learn in the following section.

 LET ME TRY IT

Using Task Manager to End a Process

This short exercise teaches you how to end a process through Task Manager. Use caution when doing this on applications not discussed in this exercise. Not ending a process safely can result in data loss or in rare cases, system instability.

1. Press Ctrl+Alt+Del.
2. Click Start Task Manager.
3. Click the Processes tab.
4. Look at the Description column and select a process that you know (for example, select Windows Task Manager).
5. Click the End Process button. You are asked to confirm this.
6. Click End Process again. The process ends.

A quick way to find a process associated with an application is to first locate the app on the Applications tab, right-click it, and then choose Go To Process. This takes you to the Processes tab with the associated process highlighted.

If more than one user is logged-on to your machine when you run Task Manager and you are unable to see the process you are looking for, the Processes tab includes a Show Processes From All Users button that you can click to see any processes in use by other users logged on.

You can also right-click an application and choose Properties to access the properties of that particular executable. For example, you can change compatibility options, permissions, as well as other aspects of the program.

Services

This tab shows you your services, some descriptive information regarding them (Description and Group information), and if they are running or not. You can use this tab to stop or start services.

 LET ME TRY IT

Using Task Manager to Stop and Restart a Service

The following steps show you how to stop and restart a service through Task Manager.

1. Press Ctrl+Alt+Del.

2. Click Start Task Manager.

3. Click the Services tab.

4. n the Description column, scroll down to Print Spooler, right-click it, and choose Stop Service.

5. Depending on your security configuration, you might receive an access-denied message. If this is the case, click Print Spooler again.

6. Click the Services button in the lower right.

7. If a UAC window opens, click Yes.

8. In the main pane, scroll down to Print Spooler, right-click it, and choose Stop.

9. To restart the service, follow these same steps, but when you right-click Print Spooler, and choose Start instead.

Performance

This tab includes a feature that is new to Windows 7 (although you might not notice it). Under Physical Memory (MB) group, Vista features Total, Cached, and Free. Windows 7 has added Available to that group.

- **Total:** The amount of RAM installed on the system in MB.

- **Cached:** The amount of physical RAM used for system resources.

- **Available:** The total of standby and free memory for programs.

- **Free:** The amount of memory that is currently unused or doesn't contain useful information.

The Performance tab also includes the Resource Monitor button. This is a logical location since you might be coming to the Performance tab to troubleshoot a problem. You can usually find what you are looking for in the CPU and Memory Usage graphs (see Figure 11.9). If you can't find it there, click the Resource Monitor button to access a plethora of monitoring tools.

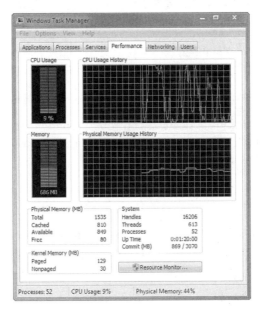

Figure 11.9   *Get real-time stats in the Performance tab.*

Networking

The Networking tab shows a graph of your active network connection, where you can view the network utilization of your connections. The bottom of this tab also includes columns showing the Link Speed and the connection State.

Users

This tab shows you the users who are logged on now. By right-clicking a user, you can Disconnect a user who is remotely connected to your computer or Log Off a local user.

 LET ME TRY IT

Using Task Manager to Log-Off a Local User

The following steps show you how to log-off a local user through Task Manager. To complete this exercise, you will need multiple users logged-on at once.

1. Press Ctrl+Alt+Del.

2. Click Start Task Manager.

3. Click the Users tab.

4. Right-click the User you would like to log off and choose Log Off.

5. A warning message appears, asking you to confirm that you want to log off this user (because the user's unsaved data might be lost). Click Log Off User and the user is logged off.

Menu Items

There are a few notable selections available on the Task Manager menu:

- On the File menu, you can select New Task to open a program (just as you can by using the Applications tab).

- On the View menu, you can adjust the refresh speed of the monitoring of your incoming resources. To see faster refreshes on your incoming data for CPU and Memory, go to View, click Update Speed, and then choose High.

System Properties

The System Properties dialog box has been a cornerstone of configuring advanced Windows options. In Vista, the location for this was moved to Advanced System Settings. Windows 7 retains this location for System Properties. This link can be found on the System page in the Control Panel.

The System Properties dialog box might not look like much, but it controls some very powerful configuration options. Don't worry, all the functions that existed in previous versions of Windows are still available; they are just accessed from different areas now (mostly from the Control Panel). This section examines the five tabs that are still present along with some new features:

- Computer Name
- Hardware
- Advanced
- System Protection
- Remote

Computer Name

This tab is essential for joining a domain or workgroup. A step-by-step walk through of how to accomplish this was discussed in Chapter 9. The Change button here allows you to change your computer name. If you are working on a stand-alone machine, this may not be critical. But if you join a network or workgroup with several other computers, all of a sudden the computer name Computer-jd2d332 (or any other meaningless default name) will not distinguish your machine as yours. In that case, you need to change the computer name.

 **LET ME TRY IT**

Using System Properties to Change Your Computer Name

The following steps show you how to change your computer name using the System Properties dialog box (see Figure 11.10). During this exercise, a reboot of your sytem is required before you can see the final result.

1. Click the Start orb.

2. Click Control Panel.

3. Click System and Security.

4. Click System.

5. In the left pane, click Advanced System Settings.

6. If a UAC window opens, click Yes.

7. The System Properties dialog box opens. Click the Computer Name tab.

8. Click the Change button. In the Computer Name box, type a new name and click OK.

9. A message appears, stating you need to restart your computer for changes to take effect. Click Close.

10. A dialog box displays, asking if you want to restart now or later. Select either option.

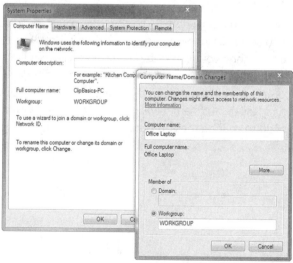

Figure 11.10 *Changing the computer name to identify a specific machine.*

After you restart your computer, verify your name change by following these steps:

11. Click the Start orb.

12. Click Control Panel.

13. Click System and Security.

14. Click System.

15. In the main pane, you will see your updated name in the Computer Name, Domain, and Workgroup Settings group.

Hardware

The Hardware tab provides access to the Device Manager button and the Device Installation Settings button. Device Manager should be a crucial part of your hardware troubleshooting routine. If a device is having problems, look here first.

Device Installation Settings includes an option to Replace Generic Device Icons With Enhanced Icons (see Figure 11.11). The new Device Stage feature of Windows 7 (discussed in chapter 10) uses these high-resolution icons to enhance your device experience. Seeing the icons of two mobile phones or two external hard drives connected to your computer helps you quickly distinguish one from the other.

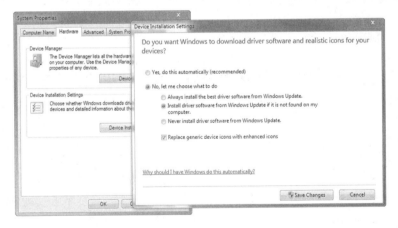

Figure 11.11 *Windows can automatically locate high-resolution icons for your devices.*

Advanced

The Advanced tab requires administrator privileges to make most of the changes on this tab. Three buttons are here-Performance, User Profiles, Startup and Recovery and Environment Variables. For the most part, these settings should be left to Windows for automatic configuration. Still, there are times when you will need to make a change. For example, if you are dual-booting Windows 7 and another OS, you might want to make changes to the dual-boot menu (see Figure 11.12).

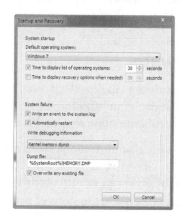

Figure 11.12   *Setting up the dual-boot startup menu from Windows 7.*

 LET ME TRY IT

Using System Properties to Configure Dual-Boot Settings

The following steps show you how to configure dual-boot settings from the System Properties dialog box.

1. Click the Start orb.

2. Click Control Panel.

3. Click System and Security.

4. Click System.

5. In the left pane, click Advanced System Settings.

6. If a UAC window opens, click Yes.

7. The System Properties dialog box opens.

8. Click the Advanced tab.

9. In the Startup and Recovery group, click the Settings button. The Startup and Recovery dialog box appears.

10. In the Default Operating System group, click the drop-down arrow to select the OS you want to boot first.

11. In the Time to Display List of Operating Systems section, select 15 seconds.

If the system stops booting unexpectedly for no apparent reason, you might want to view a memory dump to isolate the issue. The Startup and Recovery dialog box includes a Write Debugging Information group; click the drop-down arrow to configure the size of the memory dump—ranging from None through Complete Memory Dump.

System Protection

This tab manages the advanced features for System Protection. This forms the backbone for System Restore. System Protection serves you in two ways:

1. If your machine is experiencing trouble (such as a malfunctioning driver or an application install gone awry) and you are unable to resolve it, you can restore your computer to a previous good working state. System Protection automatically creates restore points every seven days or just before a significant system event, such as a software installation.

2. System Protection records changes in previous files or folders, allowing you to restore them from earlier saved copies. By clicking the Configure button on the System Protection tab, you can configure the settings and disk space (see Figure 11.13).

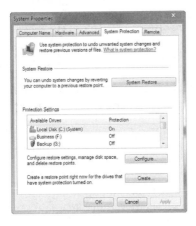

Figure 11.13 *Advanced System Protection settings.*

Remote

The Remote tab enables you to allow connections for both the Remote Assistance application and the Remote Desktop Connection application. For example, you might want to allow a user to connect to your system who has a previous version of Remote Desktop (see Figure 11.14). To do this, select the Allow Connections From Computers Running Any Version of Remote Desktop radio button.

Figure 11.14   *Allow users with previous versions of Remote Desktop to assist you.*

System Information

System Information contains extensive details about your computer system (see Figure 11.15). There are four components in the left pane which, when expanded, reveal myriad specifics:

- **System Summary:** Provides general computer information, including Bios settings and System Manufacturer.

- **Hardware Resources:** Provides hardware information, includingConflicts/Sharing, DMA, Forced Hardware, I/O, IRQs and Memory.

- **Components:** Provides component information, including Multimedia, CD-ROM, Sound Device, Display, Infrared, Input, Modem, Network, Ports, Storage, Printing, Problem Devices, and USB.

- **Software Environment:** Provides software information, including System Drivers, Print Jobs, Running Tasks, Program Groups and more.

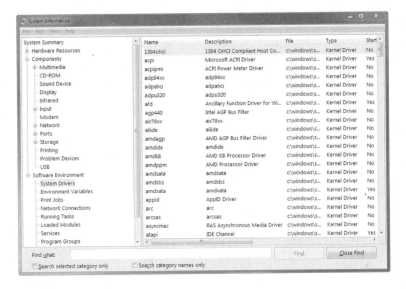

Figure 11.15   *Get the facts with System Information.*

 **LET ME TRY IT**

Accessing System Information

The following steps show you how to access System Information.

1. Click the Start orb.

2. In the search field, type **system**.

3. Click System Information. The System Information application opens.

At the bottom of the application is a Find What search feature where you can type your search parameter and click Find to search for it in System Information. To look in a specific subcategory, use the checkbox in the lower left.

TELL ME MORE   Media 11.4—A Discussion of the New Monitoring Features in Windows 7
Access this audio recording through your registered Web Edition at
my.safaribooksonline.com/9780768695212/media.

This final chapter considers a variety of administrative tools and how to use them.

12

Working with Administrative Tools

Using Administrative Tools

Once you go though Control Panel (assuming you haven't pinned these to your Start menu yet), you can see a shortcut to Administrative Tools located in the System and Security group that takes you to the list of shortcuts (see Figure 12.1).

Some of the tools you see in the Administrative Tools section have been covered already in other sections of the book. For example, Performance Monitor was covered in Chapter 11.

For those of you who would like to access these tools with one click from the Start menu, here is a quick way to do just that.

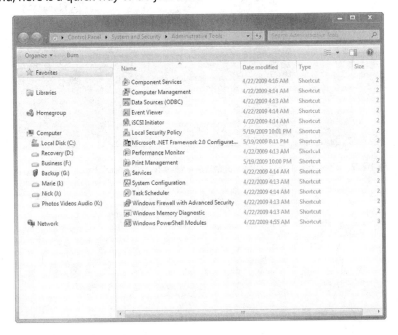

Figure 12.1 *The Administrative Tools section.*

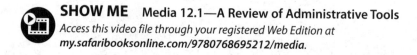

SHOW ME   Media 12.1—A Review of Administrative Tools
Access this video file through your registered Web Edition at
my.safaribooksonline.com/9780768695212/media.

LET ME TRY IT

Creating a Link to the Administrative Tools Section from the Start Menu

The following steps show you how to create a shortcut to the Administrative Tools section on the Start menu (see Figure 12.2).

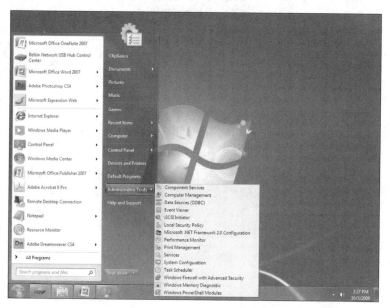

Figure 12.2   *Creating a shortcut for Administrative Tools on the Start menu.*

1. Right-click an empty area of the Taskbar and select Properties. The Taskbar and Start Menu Properties dialog box opens.

2. Click the Start Menu tab.

3. Click the Customize button. The Customize Start Menu dialog box opens.

4. Scroll down to System Administrative Tools and choose Display on the All Programs Menu and the Start Menu.

5. Click OK twice.

Now you have access to these tools right from the Start menu. (There are still other ways to access these tools, and these will be shown in the exercises to follow later in the chapter.)

Tools You Might Never Use

There are some tools you might never have a need to work with. Others will be your best friend when it comes to administering your system. Let's first take a look at some of the more obscure tools.

Component Services

This is not a new feature in Windows 7. In fact, it has existed for some time. However, typical users will never (never ever) need to use this feature. It is used to configure and administer your COM (Component Object Model) applications.

Data Sources (ODBC)

This allows you to add, delete, or configure data sources with DSNs (Data Source Names) for the current system and user. Again, not something the everyday user (or even administrator) might ever work with.

iSCSI Initiator

This was an applet in Control Panel in Windows Vista, but it was appropriately moved in Windows 7 to the Administrative Tools section. Internet Small Computer System Interface (iSCSI) uses TCP/IP for its data transfer over a common Ethernet network. But you need iSCSI devices to make it work and the OS needs an initiator to communicate with the iSCSI devices. iSCSI devices are disks, tape drives, CDs and other storage devices that you can connect to. In the relationship with the other device, your computer is the initiator and the device is the target.

In Windows 7 (as in Vista), the initiator is included. However, you can download the initiator from Microsoft for 2000 (SP3), XP, or Server 2003. The shortcut under Administrative Tools lets you configure and control the interaction between your system and the device.

Local Security Policy

Although typically a security policy is something you configure on a network domain, there are times when you might want to create password policies, account lockout policies, and so forth on your Windows 7 standalone systems. This is the place to do that. You might be deploying Windows 7 in a school, a library, or as a kiosk system (or even at home); you can adjust these security settings to ensure they are enforced.

Print Management

Although you might not think of using your computer as a print server, it is a possibility. If you have multiple print devices connected to your Windows 7 machine and you have users in the office printing through that system to your print devices, you might want to work with the Print Management tools to help you to see your printers, printers with jobs, and so forth. You can view how the printers are doing and manage those printers from this console.

Windows PowerShell Modules

Using this shortcut is one of the ways you can open up a PowerShell window that includes all of the available commands from optional modules and snap-ins, including those that aren't added by default. The modules run in a separate session to avoid name conflicts and these modules allow you to organize your scripts and functions independently of one another. The modules also run under the administrator's account.

Another way to open PowerShell with all modules is to right-click the PowerShell icon from the Taskbar (if PowerShell is pinned to the Taskbar) and click Import System Modules.

Working with Computer Management

This is one-stop spot for multiple tools. The shell of Computer Management is the Microsoft Management Console (MMC). This is a highly customizable interface that lets you load and unload specific mini-applications (called snap-ins) that help you manage your computer. It's a super console of sorts (see Figure 12.3) where users might find everything they need to monitor system events, manage shared folders, view services, view storage devices and settings, and much more.

Many of the individual components of Computer Management will be discussed later on in the chapter. One feature that is key to Computer Management is Disk Management (see Figure 12.4). With Disk Management you can manage hard disks and their volumes and partitions. There are a wide variety of options at your disposal. For example, you can initialize disks, create volumes, and format volumes with the FAT, FAT32, or NTFS file systems.

Since most configuration changes in Disk Management take place immediately, you can accomplish most disk-related tasks without restarting your computer. One of the most common tasks performed in Disk Management is to create a partition (volume) on a hard disk. In order to accomplish this, you need to be logged in as an administrator and there has to be either unallocated disk space or free space within an extended partition on the hard disk.

If you find that you don't have any unallocated disk space, you can create some in various ways. You can shrink an existing partition, delete a partition, or add an extra hard drive to the system.

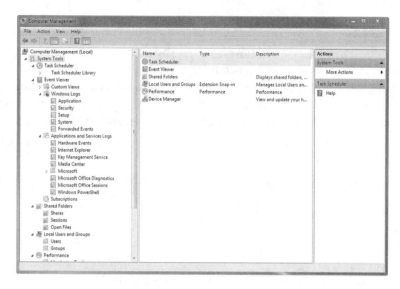

Figure 12.3   *Computer Management.*

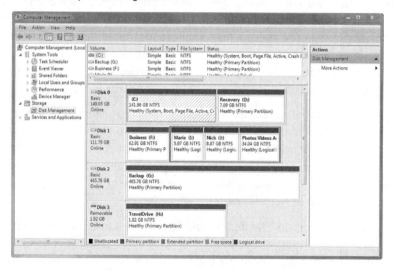

Figure 12.4   *Disk Management lets you configure all your disks from one spot.*

 **LET ME TRY IT**

Creating and Formatting a New Partition

The following steps show you how to create and format a new partition. In this example, you create a new drive letter for you to access.

1. Click the Start orb.

2. In the search field, type **manage**.

3. Select Computer Management.

4. If a UAC window appears, click Yes.

5. In the left pane, under Storage, click Disk Management.

6. In the main pane, locate the hard disk you would like to create the partition on. Right-click an unallocated region of it and select New Simple Volume. This opens the New Simple Volume Wizard.

7. Click Next.

8. Accept the maximum default size and click Next.

9. A default drive letter is provided for you. Accept this and then click Next. This opens the Format Partition dialog box.

10. Verify that you accept the default settings and click Next.

11. After reviewing your choices, click Finish.

The first three partitions on a basic disk that is newly created will be formatted as primary partitions. Starting with the fourth, each partition (on the same disk) will be configured as a logical drive within an extended partition. Remember, formatting deletes any data you have on the drive, so make sure it is backed up if need be. Many times an error as simple as selecting the wrong drive for formatting can quickly erase years of data.

One main reason for creating a partition and formatting a drive is to prepare it for an operating system. If you are planning on creating a multi-boot setup, there are a couple of things to be aware of.

For one, you need to install the oldest operating system before installing the newer operating system. If, for example, you install Vista on a computer already running Windows 7, you can render your system inoperable; earlier versions of Windows don't recognize the startup files used in more recent versions of Windows and can overwrite them.

Another aspect to consider is making certain to use the NTFS file system of the partition or disk where you plan to install a new version of Windows. While you have the option within Disk Management to select FAT or FAT32 when formatting a drive, these older files systems cannot utilize all the features in Windows 7 and they are not as efficient as NTFS. Unless you have a special requirement, stick with the NTFS file system.

Changing the drive letter has become a simple task, thanks to Computer Management. Right-click your drive of choice and select Change Drive Letter or Path. A drop-down menu provides you with available options for your new drive letter (see Figure 12.5).

Computer Management also supports the Virtual Hard Disk (VHD) format. This style of file system can be used in conjunction with virtualization software such as the Hyper-V feature of Windows Server 2008 R2, Microsoft Virtual PC/Virtual Server or VmWare. From Disk Management you can create, attach, and detach virtual hard disks.

You will find that VHDs look just like physical disks in Disk Management. When a VHD has been attached, it appears blue. If the disk is detached, its icon reverts back to gray.

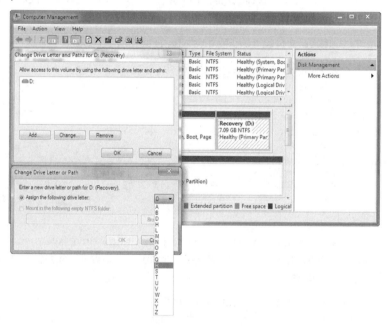

Figure 12.5   *Choose your new drive letter from the drop-down menu.*

 **LET ME TRY IT**

Using Disk Management to Create a VHD

Sometimes you want to work with virtual drives rather than physical hard drives within your system. The following steps show you how to do this by creating a VHD through Disk Manager.

1. Click the Start orb.

2. In the search field, type **manage**.

3. Select Computer Management.

4. If a UAC window appears, click Yes.

5. In the left pane, under Storage, click Disk Management.

6. Click the Action menu and then click Create VHD. This opens the Create and Attach Virtual Hard Disk dialog box.

7. In the Location text box, click Browse to choose the location where you want the VHD file to be stored.

8. In the Virtual Hard Disk Size text box, select the size of the VHD.

9. In the Virtual Hard Disk Format section, accept the default and click OK. You are returned to Computer Management, where your VHD is created. Follow its initializing progress in the lower right.

10. On successful completion, click the VHD in the main pane.

11. Click the Action menu and then click Attach VHD.

12. In the Location text box, click Browse to choose the location.

13. Click OK.

If you are having an issue creating a VHD, it might be due to the fact you're not meeting these requirements:

- The minimum size for a VHD is 3MB.
- The path specifying the location for the VHD needs to be fully qualified and can't be located in the \Windows directory.
- A VHD can be only a basic disk.
- A VHD is initialized when it is created. If you are creating a large, fixed-size VHD, it's going to take a while to finish creation.

Event Viewer

Event Viewer has been around for a while but it received a face-lift in Vista and had some tremendous improvements added in. In Windows 7, it has become a real troubleshooting tool (as opposed to simply being an informational go-to utility on what might be wrong with your system).

Often times you might have an error occur that might even crash your system or simply crash the application you are working with. Typically, if this happens once or twice, you might not think anything of it. But if it happens repeatedly, you might become concerned that there is a real problem you need to fix. The Event Viewer is an invaluable tool in this regard because it can show you the incident in question and might even be able to determine the cause of the failure.

The Event Viewer (see Figure 12.6) allows you to see more than the standard Windows logs (Application, System and Security logs). There are Applications and Services Logs, which include diagnostic logs, logs for specific applications within Windows 7 like your IE logs. In the past, you had to go hunting to find logs for certain applications, but Microsoft has tried to bring them all together here.

In addition to the design enhancements, there were features added that can really assist in locating and eliminating system issues. One is the ability to create custom views.

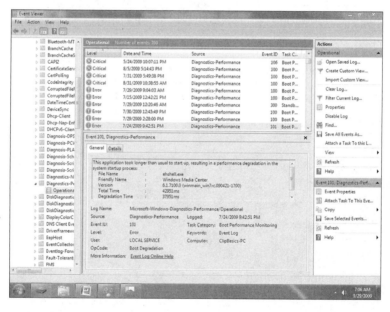

Figure 12.6   *Event Viewer is more robust, offering enterprise monitoring functionality.*

So many events come into the Event Viewer that it's almost impossible to track down the problem you are investigating without some form of filter. Views allow you to create filters that not only filter the events of one log, they allow you to select multiple logs to view. To create a custom view, select a log, click the Action menu, and then choose Create Custom View or Import Custom View. Keep in mind that you can still use filters, but custom views can be retained and quickly selected from the navigation section.

You might have noticed that there are different levels of events alerting you to possible issues. They are:

- **Information:** This message occurs when there has been a change in an application or component. For example, a service started/re-started or an operation has successfully completed.

- **Warning:** When this message appears, an issue has happened that can impact a service or produce a bigger problem if action is not taken.

- **Error:** This message indicates that a problem has taken place that might impact functionality and is outside the application or component that triggered the error message.

- **Critical:** Usually the most serious event, a Critical event means that a failure has occurred where the application or component that triggered the event can't automatically recover.

 LET ME TRY IT

Opening Event Viewer and Viewing all Error Events Recorded

The following steps show you how to open Event Viewer and view all error events recorded.

1. Click the Start orb.

2. In the search field, type **event**.

3. Select Event Viewer.

4. If a UAC window opens, select Yes.

5. After Event Viewer opens, in the left pane, double-click Custom Views.

6. Click Administrative Events.

7. In the main Operational pane, click Level to sort your events by type.

8. Using the scroll bar, scroll through any Error events recorded.

9. Click any Error event. In the General tab near the bottom of the pane, view more information about the event.

Another nice feature in Event Viewer is the ability to attach a task to an event. This feature works with Task Scheduler in assigning events as triggers that require actions.

 **LET ME TRY IT**

 **SHOW ME**   **Media 12.2—Using the Event Viewer**
Access this video file through your registered Web Edition at
my.safaribooksonline.com/9780768695212/media.

Scheduling an Email to be Sent to You in Response to an Event

This exercise builds off the previous one. After opening Event Viewer, you will schedule an email sent to you in response to an event. Complete the steps below to accomplish this.

1. Click the Start orb.

2. In the search field, type **event**.

3. Select Event Viewer.

4. If a UAC window opens, select Yes.

5. Locate an event that you would like to be emailed about and right-click it.

6. Select Attach Task to this Event. This opens the Create Basic Task Wizard.

7. Create a description for this event.

8. Click Next.

9. Click Next again.

10. Choose Send a E-mail.

11. Click Next.

12. Fill out the email fields (From, To, Subject and Text) and the SMTP Server field.

13. Click Next and then Finish. This creates the task and adds it to your Windows task schedule.

Services

Services are the underlying core features that handle any number of things on your system—from web service to print services and more. You've probably seen the services console before in XP or Vista.

The Services structure hasn't changed much in Windows 7 (see Figure 12.7). You might notice a few more services in Windows 7 depending on which older version of Windows you are comparing it to (from XP to Windows 7 there are new services to note). You will quickly notice some new services in Windows 7, such as the new BranchCache service.

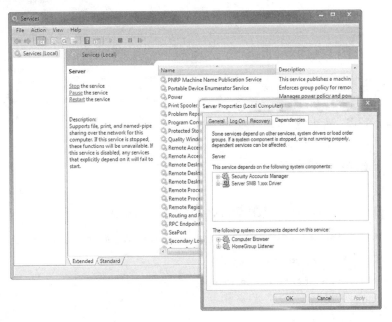

Figure 12.7   *Start, stop and restart local services.*

One reason to open Services is when a service is not responding correctly. For example, you might send a print job to a printer that appears as if it went through correctly. However, there is nothing on the printer. If the hardware is on and working correctly, it's time to look at the software end of things. One possible solution would be to stop and restart the Print Spooler service (see Figure 12.8).

Someone might suggest that you just reboot the machine to fix it; that might work because it stops and starts all services. However, instead of stopping and starting all the services, why not just stop and restart the one causing the problem?

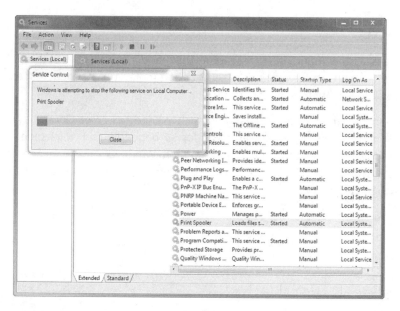

Figure 12.8 *Stopping the Print Spooler service.*

 **LET ME TRY IT**

Stopping and Restarting the Print Spooler Service

The following steps show you how to stop and restart the Print Spooler service.

1. Click the Start orb.

2. In the search field, type **services**.

3. Select Services.

4. If a UAC window opens, select Yes.

5. Scroll through the Services names until you locate Print Spooler. Double-click it. This opens the Print Spooler Properties dialog box.

6. Under the lower section on the first tab called Service Status, click Stop.

7. A window opens, indicating Windows is stopping the service. Verify it is stopped by reviewing its service status. When it has stopped successfully, under Service Status, click Start.

8. A window opens, indicating Windows is starting the service. Verify it is started by reviewing its service status. When it has started successfully, click OK.

From within Services you can do the following:

- Stop, start, pause, resume, or disable a service. You can also see the description of what each service does and what other services rely on it to work.

- Configure recovery actions in the event of a service failure (like restarting the service).

- Configure a service to run under the security context of a user account that is different from the logged-on user or the computer account.

- Configure hardware profiles that use different services enabled or disabled.

- Export your services information to a .txt or .csv file.

- Monitor the status of each service.

If you have an issue where a service regularly fails and you are trying to troubleshoot it, the General tab in the Server Properties dialog box might have just what you need. On this tab, you can select the computer's response if a service fails. For example, the first time it fails, you might want to restart the service. If it fails again, you might want to automatically run an application in response to this failure. If it fails again, you might have the machine reboot to reset all services. For example, if you had multiple failures using Internet Connection Sharing and discovered a problem with the Network Connections service, you might want to start the Resource Monitor to see which processes are utilizing the network.

 LET ME TRY IT

Setting Up Recovery Actions to Take Place When a Service Fails

The following steps show you how to set up recovery actions when a service fails. In this example, a command is provided to start Perfomance Monitor when the Network Connections service fails.

1. Click the Start orb.

2. In the search field, type **services**.

3. Select Services.

4. If a UAC window opens, select Yes.

5. Scroll through the Services names until you locate Network Connections. Double click-it.

6. Click the Recovery tab.

7. From the Second Failure drop down, select Run a Program.

8. In the Run Program area at the lower part of the tab, in the Program box, type **%windir%\system32\perfmon.exe /res**.

9. Click Apply.

10. Click OK.

> When you click Run a Program, under Run program, you need to type the full
> path for the specified computer. UNC names are not supported.
>
> For example, type **C:\system32\dfrgui.exe** rather than **\\\computername\c$\
> system32\dfrgui.exe**.

It's not always clear which system drivers or applications depend on a service in
order to function correctly. In narrowing it down, take advantage of the Dependen-
cies tab on any service properties box. This tab reveals any services or drivers that
depend on that service in order to run.

System Configuration As a Troubleshooting Tool

Often overlooked, System Configuration is a troubleshooting tool that helps identify issues that might prevent Windows from starting correctly or quickly. You can
access the System Configuration tool either through your Administrative Tools or
by clicking your Start orb, typing **configuration** in the search field, and then hitting Enter.

Through System Configuration (see Figure 12.9), you have the ability to start Windows with common services and startup programs disabled and then turn them
back on, one by one. This makes for easy troubleshooting: If a problem doesn't
happen with a service disabled, but does happen when that service is enabled,
then the service could be the source of the issue.

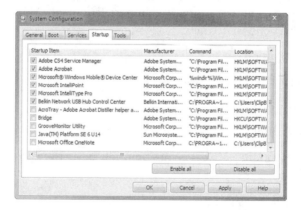

Figure 12.9   *Troubleshooting startup issues from System Configuration.*

Another use of System Configuration is to monitor and adjust your startup services to accelerate your initial boot-up time. For example, you might have software applications that look to the Internet for updates each time you start your computer. While helpful, this can compete with several other startup services and actually slow your boot-up. In System Configuration, you can manually remove services from startup while not uninstalling them completely. Thus, instead of an application checking for the latest updates each time you boot and hogging your startup resources, you can elect to do that manually at a time when the system isn't being taxed as much.

 LET ME TRY IT

Speed Up Windows Startup by Removing Startup Items

The following steps show you how to use System Configuration to speed up Windows 7 startup by removing startup items.

1. Click the Start orb.

2. Click Control Panel.

3. Click the System and Security group.

4. At the bottom of the page, click Administrative Tools.

5. Double-click System Configuration.

6. If a UAC window appears, click Yes.

7. Click the Services tab.

8. In the lower-left, select Hide all Microsoft Services.

9. Uncheck any services here not critical to startup.

10. Click the Startup tab.

11. Uncheck any Startup Items not critical to startup.

12. Click Apply.

13. Click OK.

Once within System Configuration, you will see the five tabs covered in the following section.

General

This tab provides three choices for system startup and configuration modes:

- **Normal Startup:** This starts Windows in the standard configuration. Once you have finished using the other two modes to troubleshoot the problem, choose this mode to start Windows 7 normally.

- **Diagnostic Startup:** This starts Windows with minimal services and drivers. The purpose of this mode is to help you rule out basic Windows files as the source of the issue.

- **Selective Startup:** This mode allows you to select which services and startup items open on boot-up.

Boot

This tab shows boot options for the operating system and advanced options to assist in debugging, including:

- **Safe Boot—Minimal:** This will default your startup to open Windows Explorer in safe mode. This mode runs only a basic set of critical system services. Also, networking is disabled with this selection.

- **Safe Boot—Alternate Shell:** This opens on startup the Windows command prompt in safe mode and runs only critical system services. Both networking and the GUI are disabled.

- **Safe Boot—Active Directory Repair:** This opens on startup the Windows command prompt in safe mode and runs only critical system services and Active Directory.

- **Safe Boot—Network:** This opens on startup the Windows command prompt in safe mode and runs only critical system services and networking.

Services

This tab displays all the services that start with the computer when it boots. You can see the current status of these services and enable or disable them from here. As shown in the previous exercise, you can also deselect a checkbox to prevent that particular service from starting up the next time you boot the system. Selecting the Hide all Microsoft Services checkbox shows you only the services from third parties.

Do not just stop services indiscriminately. Stopping services that normally run at startup might cause some programs to crash or might result in system instability. Also, clicking the Disable All button does not disable some secure Microsoft services required for the operating system to start correctly. The following Microsoft services can be stopped without jeopardizing system stability:

- Application Experience
- Computer Browser
- Desktop Window Manager Session Manager
- Diagnostic Policy Service
- Distributed Link Tracking Client
- IP Helper
- Offline Files
- Portable Device Enumerator Service
- Print Spooler
- Protected Storage
- Remote Registry
- Secondary Logon
- Tablet PC Input Service
- TCP/IP NetBIOS Helper
- Themes
- Windows Error Reporting Service
- Windows Media Center Receiver Service
- Windows Media Center Scheduler Service
- Windows Search
- Windows Time

Startup

This tab provides you with a list of applications that start on boot-up, including the name of the application, the manufacturer, the location of the executable, and the registry key for the startup application. Another thing you can see is a date when you disabled an application. An option you have here you is to deselect the checkbox to stop the application from running on the next start up. If you feel there is an issue with a particular application, you can also verify the location of the application.

Tools

This tab shows a list of different diagnostic and informational tools and shows the location of these tools. From within this tab you can easily launch an application.

 LET ME TRY IT

Starting Even Viewer from Within System Configuration

The following steps show you how to start Event Viewer from within System Configuration.

1. Click the Start orb.
2. Click Control Panel.
3. Click the System and Security group.
4. At the bottom of the page, click Administrative Tools.
5. Double-click System Configuration.
6. If a UAC window appears, click Yes.
7. Click the Tools tab.
8. Locate and click Event Viewer.
9. Click Launch and Event Viewer opens.

> Between Vista and Windows 7, the System Configuration tool has remained somewhat the same. The only noticeable change is the removal of the Tools option to Enable or Disable UAC. With Windows 7, this tool is no longer necessary because we can now use the slider to accomplish this (and it doesn't require a reboot like it did in Vista).

Task Scheduler

Task Scheduler is not a new sfeature to the Windows OS but the enhancements introduced with Vista and carried into Windows 7 sure make this a tool to reconsider. Under previous versions of Windows, you could use Task Scheduler to launch tasks at a specific times or in response to minimal sets of conditions that might occur with the system. There was no way to maintain a task history or configure multiple actions to occur. It was still a great tool, but it was limited—thus forcing admins to find other software to fulfill their needs.

Within Windows 7, you can configure the Task Scheduler to perform tasks on a timed basis, but it can also respond to situations that occur on a variety of levels. The response system can even restart a service that has failed or send an email to the admin when a certain event has occurred.

In addition, there is an entire Task Scheduler Library that has preconfigured tasks for you to work with (see Figure 12.10).

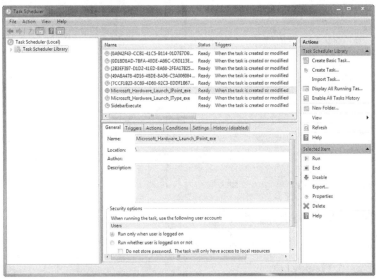

Figure 12.10　*The Task Scheduler with the Library of tasks to choose from.*

One practical feature of Task Scheduler is its ability to open applications automatically for you at intervals you specify. For example, you might have Windows Backup and Restore configured to run over the weekend while you are away from your machine. As a reminder, you could set Task Scheduler to open Backup and Restore for you every Monday so you could verify the backup.

 LET ME TRY IT

Scheduling Backup and Restore to Launch Every Monday

The following steps show you how to schedule Backup and Restore to launch every Monday and perform a backup.

1. Open Task Scheduler.

2. In the right pane, click Create Basic Task. This opens the Create Basic Task Wizard (see Figure 12.11).

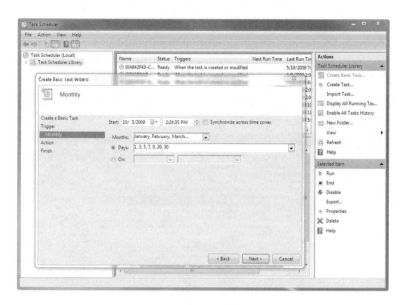

Figure 12.11   *Easily configure a task from the Create Basic Task Wizard.*

3. Type a Name and Description for this event.

4. Click Next.

5. Choose Weekly.

6. Click Next.

7. Select the Monday checkbox.

8. Click Next.

9. Make sure Start a Program is selected and then click Next.

10. In the Program/Script text box type **%SystemRoot%\System32\control.exe**.

11. In the Add Arguments text box, type **/name Microsoft.BackupAndRestore**.

12. Click Next.

13. Click Finish.

The Task Scheduler is integrated with Event Viewer now so that it can react to situations based upon events that occur. There is also a way to view the task history. You can see which tasks are running, have run, or are scheduled to run.

A Trigger is what causes the task to run, and an Action is what you have configured to occur in the event the trigger goes off. Some triggers are schedules that you put into effect. For example, if want a specific action to occur each day at 1 p.m., then the Trigger is the scheduled time. But a Trigger can also be when a user logs in, when the system starts up, when a specific event occurs, and so forth. An action can include running a program, sending an email, or even displaying a preconfig- ured message. The Wizard provides a list of possible actions to take, including run- ning scripts with the cscript.exe application, copying a file with robocopy, starting and stopping services, shutting down the system, and a host of others.

You can do this in several different ways. First off, from the Task Scheduler console, in the Actions pane, you can click Create Basic Task. The Create Basic Task Wizard walks you through the following options:

1. **Create a Basic Task**: Start with a Name and Description.

2. **Trigger**: You can work from a schedule (Daily, Weekly, Monthly, One Time) where you set time parameters for the triggered event. Or you can select When the Computer Starts, When I Log On, or When a Specific Event is Logged. With that last one you can choose the Log, the Source, and even the Event ID that triggers the next step.

3. **Action**: You can start a program (and choose which program that is), send an email (with the information for the email), or display a message (and write the message you want displayed).

4. **Finish**: You can review your new task and tell it to open the properties of the task. When this happens, you can see a much more complicated tabbed view of a task. These options help you go beyond the basic task. You can create and manage your tasks in this way, or you can create a task from the more complicated tabs to start with.

The capability to create tasks is not limited to the local computer you are working on. Task Scheduler gives you the opportunity to connect to another computer on your network and configure a task for it. You can connect to remote computers running Windows Server 2008, Vista, Windows Server 2003, XP, or Windows 2000.

There are a couple things to have in place before connecting, depending on the OS you are connecting to. Here are some reminders from Windows 7 Help and Support:

If you are connecting to a remote computer running Vista or Windows Server 2008 from a computer running Vista or Windows Server 2008, you need to enable the Remote Scheduled Tasks Management firewall exception on the remote computer. To allow this exception, click Start, Control Panel, System and Security, Allow a Program Through Windows Firewall and then select the Remote Scheduled Tasks Management checkbox. Then click the OK button in the Windows Firewall Settings dialog box.

If you are connecting to a remote computer running XP or Windows Server 2003 from a computer running Vista or Windows Server 2008, you need to allow the File and Printer Sharing firewall exception on the remote computer. To allow this exception, click Start, Control Panel, double-click Windows Firewall, select the Exceptions tab, and then select the File and Printer Sharing firewall exception. Then click the OK button in the Windows Firewall dialog box.

 LET ME TRY IT

Connecting to a Remote Computer to Create a Task

The following steps show you how to use Task Scheduler to create a task on a remote computer. This exercise requires you to be connected on a network to another computer.

1. Open Task Scheduler.

2. In the left pane, click Task Scheduler.

3. In the Actions pane, click Connect to Another Computer. This opens the Select Computer dialog box.

4. Select the Another Computer radio button.

5. In the Another Computer text box, type the name or IP address of the remote computer or click the Browse button to browse for a remote computer.

6. Once you have selected a remote computer, click OK.

7. You can now create a task on the remote computer.

To create a more advanced task, click the Create Task option in the Action pane. The Create Task dialog box offers the following five tabs to configure your tasks:

- **General:** Allows you to configure the name and description, which user account it should run under, and if it should run only when that user is logged in or not.

- **Triggers:** Allows you to schedule an extensive list of triggers, starting with the time triggers you can set up. If you change the Begin the Task options, the settings will change. The most complex of the triggers involves Events.

- **Actions:** These actions are the same as the actions listed in the basic settings. Allows you to configure a program to run, send an email, display a message—or you can do all three if you like. That is the benefit to using the advanced tabbed task creator. You can configure different actions to occur from here.

- **Conditions:** Allows you to specify conditions to your task. For example, you might want certain tasks to run only if the system is idle. Depending on if the computer is running on AC power or battery, you might not want the task to run (or you might not want it to run if it isn't connected to a certain network).

- **Settings:** Allows you to determine if you can start the task manually, what to do if your task couldn't run on schedule, and what to do in the event a task is running too long.

Every once in a while, a task that you have scheduled to start will not run as planned. When troubleshooting the cause of a failed task, keep the following in mind:

- Task Schedule will not run while the computer is in Safe Mode.
- Verify the triggers for the task have been set correctly.
- Check the task history, making sure it ran correctly on previous occasions and there were no errors.
- A task will run only if all its conditions are met.
- Make sure the user who is logged on when the task is scheduled to run has the correct security level to run the task.

Windows Memory Diagnostic

Windows Memory Diagnostic (see Figure 12.12) is a feature that runs in the background of Windows 7. If it discovers a problem, it runs diagnostic tests, which are then added to the event logs. However, you can also kick-start it if you think you are having memory issues. You can run the tool from the Administrative tools or by typing **mdsched.exe** in the command prompt.

You will be asked if you want to run the tool now or to run the tool the next time you start your computer. You'll have to restart the computer for the test to be run, so make sure you save your work before you run the test. —

If you decide to restart your computer and run the tool immediately, make sure you save your work and close all of your running programs. The Memory Diagnostic tool runs automatically when Windows restarts. In order to thoroughly check your computer's memory, it might take several minutes for the tool to complete. Once the test is finished, Windows restarts automatically. If the tool does find problems, it's likely the issue is a malfunction with your hardware memory chip aboard your computer. Consider replacing it yourself or contacting your computer manufacturer for information about replacement.

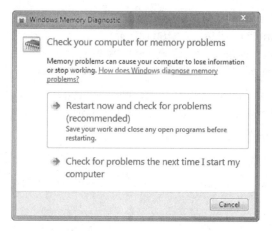

Figure 12.12 *Track down memory issues with Windows Memory Diagnostic.*

SHOW ME Media 12.3—Using Memory Diagnostics
Access this video file through your registered Web Edition at
my.safaribooksonline.com/9780768695212/media.

LET ME TRY IT

Starting the Memory Diagnostic Tool with Advanced Options

The following steps show you how to start the Memory Diagnostic tool with advanced options. During the exercise your computer will reboot.

1. Click the Start orb.

2. In the search field, type **memory**.

3. Click Windows Memory Diagnostic.

4. If a UAC window appears, click Yes.

5. This opens the Windows Memory Diagnostic dialog box.

6. Close any applications you have open.

7. Click Restart Now and Check for Problems. Windows reboots and starts the Memory Diagnostic tool.

8. As the tool begins, press F1. This opens the advanced options screen.

9. Select from Test Mix, Cache or Pass Count. (A description of each follows these steps.)

10. Complete running the test by pressing F10.

If you you're wondering what these advanced options are, here's a quick explanation:

- **Test mix:** Select from Basic, Standard, or Extended. Details regarding each choice is described in the tool.

- **Cache:** Select the cache setting you want for each test: Default, On, or Off.

- **Pass Count:** Select the number of times you want to repeat the test.

 TELL ME MORE   Media 12.4—A Discussion of Administrative Tools

Access this audio recording through your registered Web Edition at my.safaribooksonline.com/9780768695212/media.

index

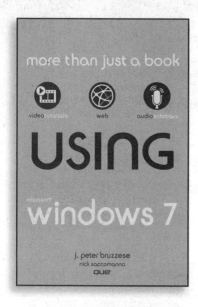

FREE Online
Edition

Your purchase of **Using Microsoft Windows 7** includes access to a free online edition for 45 days through the Safari Books Online subscription service. Nearly every Que book is available online through Safari Books Online, along with more than 5,000 other technical books and videos from publishers such as Addison-Wesley Professional, Cisco Press, Exam Cram, IBM Press, O'Reilly, Prentice Hall, and Sams.

SAFARI BOOKS ONLINE allows you to search for a specific answer, cut and paste code, download chapters, and stay current with emerging technologies.

Activate your FREE Online Edition at
www.informit.com/safarifree

> **STEP 1:** Enter the coupon code: HYSFQGA.

> **STEP 2:** New Safari users, complete the brief registration form.
>   Safari subscribers, just log in.

If you have difficulty registering on Safari or accessing the online edition, please e-mail customer-service@safaribooksonline.com

Addison Wesley   AdobePress   ALPHA   Cisco Press   FT Press   IBM Press   lynda.com   Microsoft Press   New Riders

O'REILLY   Peachpit Press   PRENTICE HALL   QUE   Redbooks   SAMS   SAS   Sun microsystems   WILEY